Christmas Play Favorites *for* Young People

Edited by

Sylvia E. Kamerman

Publishers   PLAYS, INC.   *Boston*

Copyright © 1982 by PLAYS, INC.

Reprinted 1983
Reprinted 1987

CAUTION

Library of Congress Cataloging in Publication Data

Christmas play favorites for young people.

   Summary: Seventeen plays including adaptations of the classics, "A Christmas Carol," "Little Women," "Christmas Every Day," and "The Birds' Christmas Carol."
   1. Christmas — Juvenile drama. 2. Children's plays, American. 3. One-act plays, American. [1. Christmas — Drama. 2. Plays] I. Kamerman, Sylvia E. II. Plays (Boston, Mass.)

PS627.C57C47   1982   812'.041'0833   82-13348
ISBN 0-8238-0257-4 (pbk.)

Printed in the United States of America.

CONTENTS

Junior/Senior High

Middle/Lower Grades

iii

Creative Dramatics

Christmas Classics

Christmas Spirit

by Earl J. Dias

Characters

SALLY GILLUM, *seventeen*
MRS. GILLUM
MR. GILLUM
TOM GILLUM, *eighteen*
BOB ABBOTT, *Tom's friend*
MR. GRIGGS, *a Laneville selectman*
MISS PENNYPACKER, *librarian*
MRS. GRAY

TIME: *About 8:30 on Christmas Eve.*
SETTING: *The living room of the Gillum home, located in a New England village.*
AT RISE: SALLY *is inspecting the Christmas tree.* MRS. GILLUM *sits on the sofa, her hand on her forehead.*

MRS. GILLUM: Goodness, I have a headache that seems to go right down to the tips of my toes.
SALLY (*Standing back to admire tree*): It's all this Christmas rush, Mother. You've been on the go for over a week now. And, golly, we have so many cousins and uncles and aunts to buy presents for. It's a wonder that you're still up and around.
MRS. GILLUM: Oh, I don't mind Christmas shopping, Sally. It's rather fun to buy gifts for people, anyway. I

1

really enjoy trying to decide what particular present will please each person.

SALLY: Well, I don't.

MRS. GILLUM: You mean you don't like shopping?

SALLY: It's bedlam! And the stores are so crowded—even in a one-horse town like ours.

MRS. GILLUM: One-horse town? You'd better not let your father hear you talk that way about Laneville.

SALLY (*Picking up one of presents and moving it to another place under the tree*): Oh, it's fine for him. He can get his writing done here easily enough. Heaven knows there's plenty of peace and quiet. In fact, the place is a morgue.

MRS. GILLUM: But that's what is so pleasant about it, Sally. After the hustle and bustle of New York, Laneville is positively heavenly. And your father has really made progress here on his new novel.

SALLY: That's something, I suppose. Personally, though, I think the place is full of hicks. You can almost see the hay in their hair.

MRS. GILLUM: That isn't a very nice thing to say. I think the people here are very pleasant and friendly.

SALLY (*Crossing and sitting in chair at left of table*): Friendly? They're a lot of cold fish, if you ask me. I've heard of New Englanders and how they're supposed to be reserved and rather distant. Well, I've found out.

MRS. GILLUM (*Sighing*): You don't seem to have much Christmas spirit, Sally.

SALLY: Christmas spirit? That's a joke, Mother. Christmas is nothing but a commercialized affair, anyway. The only ones it benefits are the merchants. They're making money hand over fist, just as they do on Mother's Day and Father's Day and all those other so-called sentimental occasions whose whole purpose is to make everyone spend as much money as possible.

MRS. GILLUM: Goodness, you're getting cynical!

SALLY: I just see things as they are. And honestly, Mother, if I have to spend much more time in this ghost town, I'll lose my mind. I dread going back to Laneville High after Christmas vacation.

MRS. GILLUM (*Dryly*): Your father and I have noticed that you don't seem to be very happy there.

SALLY: Happy! The place gives me the creeps. A lot of kid stuff about Saturday night dances and silly basketball games. At Miss Fenwick's School in New York, we concerned ourselves with important things.

MRS. GILLUM: Such as?

SALLY: The latest books and plays and concerts—you know, things that really matter.

MRS. GILLUM: Your father and I have thought of sending you back to Miss Fenwick's for the last half of the school year.

SALLY (*Rises and goes over to hug her mother*): Oh, Mother, have you really? That would be just wonderful! (*She stretches happily*) Back to civilization once more. (MR. GILLUM *enters from right.*)

MRS. GILLUM: Well, John. You've worked late tonight.

MR. GILLUM (*Sighing wearily and sitting in chair at right of table*): Yes, the writing was going well, and I didn't want to leave it. One of my characters has me on the run, though. She's a woman—one of those slinky, attractive creatures—and she seems to keep popping into the book when I least expect her.

SALLY (*Laughing*): Why, Dad! I didn't know you were interested in such types.

MR. GILLUM: I'm interested in them only as characters in a novel.

MRS. GILLUM: I should hope so!

SALLY: Do you remember last Christmas Eve? We all went to Mr. Hammond's wonderful party, and then on

Christmas Day we went to the theatre. Oh, New York is the place to be on holidays—or any other day.

MRS. GILLUM: That's all I've had from her for the last hour, John.

MR. GILLUM: I take it Laneville doesn't agree with you, Sally.

SALLY: Or I don't agree with it.

MR. GILLUM: Strange, because your brother likes it here very much.

SALLY: Of course he does. Tom's a hero at school—football and basketball and all that sort of adolescent drivel. Besides, he's very fond of Sue Benson, too—and she's enough all by herself to make him think Laneville's wonderful.

MR. GILLUM: At least he's entered into the spirit of things. You, on the other hand, have been rather aloof. Why haven't you taken part in more school activities and learned to know some of the local young people better?

MRS. GILLUM: Don't you know, John? Your daughter thinks the entire population of Laneville is composed of hicks.

MR. GILLUM: Indeed?

SALLY: They don't have any sophistication whatsoever.

MR. GILLUM: I've found them to be intelligent and well-informed.

SALLY (*Laughing*): I gathered that from your short story.

MR. GILLUM: You mean "A Village Incident"?

SALLY: Yes, the one that came out in the *Saturday Evening Post*. You made that small town sound like paradise. (*Shakes her head*) Laneville is a far cry from paradise, as far as I'm concerned.

MR. GILLUM: It's a very pleasant place. And you'd be surprised how many townspeople have spoken to me about the story. They're delighted that I used Laneville as a setting.

SALLY: It's probably the first publicity the town has received since the Revolutionary War.

MRS. GILLUM: I've told Sally she can probably go back to Miss Fenwick's for the last half of the school year.

MR. GILLUM: Yes, she can—if she wants to.

SALLY: I do want to, Dad, very much.

MR. GILLUM (*Sighing*): I'll miss you, Sally, but if it's what you really want, I'll get a letter off to Miss Fenwick's tonight before I go to bed.

SALLY (*Jumping up and going over to kiss her father on the forehead*): Thank you, Dad. You're a darling.

MR. GILLUM (*Looking at watch*): Hmm—nine o'clock. Where's Tom tonight?

SALLY: My glorious-voiced brother is out singing Christmas carols with some of his pals.

MRS. GILLUM: Why didn't you go with them, Sally?

SALLY (*Contemptuously*): Kid stuff.

MRS. GILLUM: I think it's a very charming custom. You don't seem to have any Christmas spirit at all.

SALLY: Christmas is commercialized just like—

MRS. GILLUM: Please, Sally, spare us the sermon. We've been all over that once before. (*Voices are heard outside singing "Silent Night." MRS. GILLUM picks up her knitting, SALLY re-arranges decorations on Christmas tree, and MR. GILLUM picks up some typewritten pages from table and reads them over, correcting them occasionally with a pencil. When the song is over, MR. GILLUM smiles.*)

MR. GILLUM: Very well done. I couldn't even hear Tom's monotone.

MRS. GILLUM (*Pretending to be angry*): Tom is *not* a monotone! Besides, anyone sounds wonderful when he's singing Christmas carols. (*The carolers now sing "Adeste Fidelis." When the singing is completed, there are cries of "Good night," "See you tomorrow," and*

"Merry Christmas." Then TOM GILLUM *enters at up-stage center, followed by* BOB ABBOTT.)

TOM: Hi, folks—and Merry Christmas!

BOB: Merry Christmas, everybody!

TOM: I've brought Bob back for a soda. After all that singing, we need to wet our whistles.

MRS. GILLUM: There's plenty in the refrigerator.

MR. GILLUM: Your caroling was excellent.

TOM: You bet. We're full of the good old Christmas spirit. Come on to the kitchen, Bob.

BOB: Want to join us, Sally?

MRS. GILLUM: Yes, Sally, why don't you have a cold drink with the boys?

SALLY: No, thank you. I'm too comfortable right here.

BOB (*Disappointed*): O.K.

TOM: My sister is Little Miss Comfort herself, Bob.

SALLY: Ha! Ha! Very funny. (TOM *and* BOB *exit right, with* BOB *casting a last look at* SALLY, *who ignores him.*)

MRS. GILLUM: I think you might have been a little more hospitable, Sally.

SALLY: Tom is hospitality personified. He doesn't need any help.

MR. GILLUM: That Bob Abbott seems to be a very fine boy.

SALLY: He's all right, I guess.

MR. GILLUM: You don't sound too enthusiastic.

SALLY: He's so much like Tom—crazy about sports and dances and that sort of thing.

MR. GILLUM: Aren't those natural interests for young people?

SALLY: There are other things in life. Besides, Bob is like all New Englanders. Why, I don't think he ever spoke ten words to me before tonight.

MRS. GILLUM: And how many words have you spoken to him?

SALLY: It's certainly not *my* place to make advances to the male population of Laneville. (*Doorbell rings.*)

MR. GILLUM (*Rising*): I'll get it. (*He goes to door and opens it, ushering in three visitors.*) Well, this is a surprise. Merry Christmas to you all! Let me take your coats. (*The three enter, give him their wraps, and then go to greet* MRS. GILLUM. MISS PENNYPACKER *is a tall, lean woman of indeterminate age. She is carrying a long, narrow, attractively-wrapped package.* MRS. GRAY *is stout and jolly-looking.* MR. GRIGGS *is about* MR. GILLUM's *age. He carries a scroll.* MR. GILLUM *takes the wraps and exits with them at right, returning a moment later.*)

MRS. GILLUM (*Rising and coming forward to greet the guests*): How are you, Miss Pennypacker? How nice to see you, Mrs. Gray. And you too, Mr. Griggs. Merry Christmas. (*The three smile and respond "Merry Christmas."*)

MR. GRIGGS: I suppose you're wondering just what the three of us are doing here. Well, we're not trying to imitate the Three Wise Men of old, but we do come, like them, bearing gifts.

MISS PENNYPACKER (*Holding up her parcel*): Indeed we do.

MRS. GRAY: And happy to do it!

MRS. GILLUM: Gifts? Why, how lovely! But what have we done to deserve such kindness?

MR. GRIGGS: Well, as Laneville's selectman, I suppose I had better act as spokesman.

MISS PENNYPACKER: Please do, Mr. Griggs.

MR. GRIGGS: Thank you, Miss Pennypacker.

MRS. GRAY: I can't think of anyone who could do the job more nicely.

MR. GRIGGS: And thank you, Mrs. Gray.

MISS PENNYPACKER: I always love to hear Mr. Griggs speak

at our town meetings. He always says just the right thing in just the right words.

MRS. GRAY: Indeed he does.

MR. GRIGGS: Please, ladies, spare my blushes. Anyway, Mr. and Mrs. Gillum, although my companions, I assure you, are overestimating my poor talents, I do have something to say—if you'll bear with me.

MR. GILLUM: Of course. (*Smiling*) I'm on tenterhooks.

MR. GRIGGS: Not to keep you in suspense any longer, I'll get down to business. You see, Mr. Gillum, we citizens of Laneville are extremely grateful to you.

MISS PENNYPACKER (*Nodding vigorously*): Yes, indeed.

MRS. GRAY: We're more than grateful.

MR. GRIGGS: And a group of us, at a meeting the other night, decided we ought to show some concrete evidence of our gratitude.

MR. GILLUM: All this is very flattering—but grateful for what, may I ask?

MR. GRIGGS: For several things. First of all, we like the way in which you have, in a short time, adjusted yourself to our Laneville way of life. Second, your presence in our community has brought us honor and some degree of fame.

MRS. GRAY: It was your story that did it, Mr. Gillum.

MISS PENNYPACKER: Such a lovely piece of writing—and how admirably you captured the spirit and the essence of Laneville in it.

MRS. GRAY: We mean, of course, "A Village Incident."

MR. GRIGGS: You see, Mr. Gillum, all of us thought it remarkable that an outsider such as yourself could get to the very heart of what we stand for here and what our mode of living means to us.

MISS PENNYPACKER: And we want you to know how much we appreciate and admire what you've done.

MR. GRIGGS: I haven't much more to say. But, as select-man, I have been authorized to have this scroll pre-pared. (*He gives it to* MR. GILLUM) It's not much, perhaps, but please believe that what it says is sincerely meant and that it reflects accurately the sentiments of Laneville's citizens.

MR. GILLUM: Why, thank you. I—I just don't know what to say.

MRS. GRAY: Please read it aloud, Mr. Gillum.

MR. GILLUM (*Opening the scroll*): "To our friend and neighbor, John Gillum, the affection and respect of his Laneville neighbors is evidenced in this scroll. For his ability as a writer who understands the human heart and for his understanding of our community, we offer him our friendship and admiration. And to a new but already well-loved citizen of our town, we extend the hand of neighborliness."

MRS. GILLUM: Why, John—that is wonderful!

MISS PENNYPACKER (*Coughing slightly*): Ahem!

MR. GRIGGS: Oh, yes, Miss Pennypacker also has some-thing for you that we hope you'll like.

MR. GILLUM: Well, this really *is* Christmas for me!

MISS PENNYPACKER (*Handing package to* MR. GILLUM): Because I am the librarian in Laneville, our committee thought I was the logical person to present this to you. We have had your story bound in leather for you. We all thought it would be most appropriate.

MR. GILLUM: I can't think of anything that would have pleased me more.

MRS. GRAY (*Smiling*): It's my turn now, I think.

MR. GILLUM: You mean there is more?

MRS. GRAY: Really, it isn't much, but we hope you'll like it. As president of the Laneville Historical Society, I've been instructed by our members to present you and your entire family with a life membership in the Society. (*She hands him a certificate*) This includes you, Mrs. Gillum, and your son and daughter.

MRS. GILLUM: Thank you very much.

SALLY: It's very thoughtful of you.

MR. GILLUM: I hardly know what to say, although, (*Grinning*) I'm supposed to be a man of words. But I want all of you to know how much I appreciate your kindness. You merely illustrate what I've known all along—that Laneville is a neighborly place.

MR. GRIGGS (*Begins to applaud and is joined by* MISS PENNYPACKER *and* MRS. GRAY): Bravo!

MRS. GILLUM: Won't all of you please have some refreshment with us? John, let's go into the dining room for a snack.

MR. GILLUM: Wonderful idea.

MRS. GRAY: Thank you. I'm supposed to be on a diet—but certainly one ought to be able to cheat a little on Christmas Eve.

MRS. GILLUM (*Laughing*): Indeed one should. (*She leads way to door right and all but* SALLY *exit.* MRS. GILLUM *stops at door*) Coming, Sally?

SALLY: I'm not hungry, Mother—thanks. (SALLY *rises and goes to table at center. She takes up scroll, which* MR. GILLUM *has left on table, and reads it aloud. Then she sets scroll down on table once more, goes to sofa, sits down, and seems to be very thoughtful. After a moment or two,* BOB *enters from right.*)

BOB: Hi.

SALLY: Hello, Bob. Where's Tom?

BOB: He's helping your mother with the refreshments. Say, isn't it wonderful about your father? The old town has really gone all-out for him.

SALLY: It's very nice.

BOB: That story of his was good.

SALLY: I didn't know you'd read it.

BOB: Sure. I've been wanting to tell your father how much I liked it—but, well, you know—it's kind of hard to tell the author exactly how you feel about his story.

SALLY: And you New Englanders have never been famous for talking a lot.

BOB (*Smiling*): I guess that's right. (*Seriously*) You know, parts of your father's story reminded me of Thoreau. It has the same viewpoint that *Walden* does.

SALLY: Dad would be flattered to hear you compare him to Thoreau. I had no idea *you* were a Thoreau fan.

BOB: Gosh, yes. His writing is always meaty—something you can sink your teeth into. Emerson is the same way, too. You really have to think when you read him. Last summer I read Emerson's essay on "Self-Reliance" a dozen times or more—and I found something new in it each time.

SALLY (*Enthusiastically*): I've read it several times, too. When I was to Miss Fenwick's in New York, I thought it was wonderful. (*Slowly*) But I didn't expect you to feel that way.

BOB: What do you mean, Sally?

SALLY: I've always thought that about all you were interested in was football and baseball.

BOB: There's nothing wrong with football and baseball— but for Pete's sake, I know there are other things in life.

SALLY: It just seems strange to hear you talking about Thoreau and Emerson. I never realized—

BOB (*Grinning*): In other words, you thought I had a pointed head or something.

SALLY (*Upset*): Oh, no—it was just that I never thought of you as liking books.

BOB: Well, after all, how would you know I liked to read? You hardly speak to me at school. In fact, you just brush by me in the corridor with your head way up in the air.

SALLY (*Heatedly*): That's not true. It's just that everyone at Laneville High seems so reserved. They hide in their shells like turtles all the time.

BOB: You just don't understand. Some of the kids are shy, and they don't want to impose themselves on anyone. But you should have heard what the boys said when you first came.

SALLY: What do you mean?

BOB: They were all talking about how pretty you were— and what an addition you made to the school.

SALLY: Not one of them has even hinted he was glad to see me around.

BOB: They were all afraid to talk to you. Some of the fellows began to think you were conceited, and that you looked down on them because you came from New York. I remember back in October, some of the kids wanted to ask you to be a cheerleader—but they didn't dare. They thought you'd laugh right in their faces.

SALLY: But I would have loved being a cheerleader!

BOB: I'm sure you could be one next year. I'll be glad to tell them if you want me to.

SALLY (*Thoughtfully*): No—I think it might be nice if I told them myself.

BOB: Great! Wish I were going to be around to see you in action.

SALLY: But where are you going?

BOB: To Harvard—I hope.

SALLY (*Impressed*): Harvard!

BOB: Sure. My father went there and my grandfather and my great-grandfather.

SALLY: Golly!

BOB: Sally, there's been something I've wanted to ask you —but I've been afraid you'd give me the cold shoulder.

SALLY: Go ahead, Bob.

BOB (*Squaring his shoulders*): Well, here goes. You probably know that during Christmas week there's always a big dance in Laneville. We have it to celebrate the anniversary of the Battle of Laneville—that was back in the Revolution when a band of Laneville volunteers foiled a British raid on the town.

SALLY: I've heard of it.

BOB: The dance is a costume affair; everyone goes dressed in clothes of the Revolutionary period. You probably think that's silly, though.

SALLY: I think it sounds like a lot of fun!

BOB: You really mean that?

SALLY: Of course I do.

BOB (*Grinning*): Well, then, I guess it's safe to ask you. (*Gulping*) Will you go with me?

SALLY: I'd love to.

BOB: Swell! That makes this a really merry Christmas for me.

SALLY (*Thoughtfully*): For me, too. (MR. *and* MRS. GILLUM, TOM, MISS PENNYPACKER, MRS. GRAY *and* MR. GRIGGS *enter from right. The guests have their wraps on. They move toward upstage door.*)

MRS. GILLUM: And thank you again for coming. You've been very kind.

MR. GILLUM: I never shall forget this night.

MR. GRIGGS: Nor shall we.

MISS PENNYPACKER: It's so wonderful to have a really distinguished writer in our midst.

MRS. GRAY: And I do hope, Mr. Gillum, that you'll be with us a long time.

MR. GILLUM: I assure you I haven't any intention of leaving Laneville.

MRS. GILLUM: It's too nice a place to leave.

TOM: I second the statement!

MR. GRIGGS: Good for you, Tom. And now, ladies, we had best be going. Merry Christmas, everyone. (*All those*

on stage now shout "Merry Christmas!" MISS PENNY-
PACKER, MRS. GRAY, *and* MR. GRIGGS *exit.*)

MR. GILLUM: Now, wasn't that a wonderful gesture on
their part? I don't know when I've encountered such
friendly people.

TOM: You ought to run for selectman yourself, Dad.
You'd be a cinch to win.

MR. GILLUM (*Laughing*): No, thanks. I'll keep out of
politics and stick to my typewriter.

BOB: I have to be going; it's getting late. Thanks for the
soda—and thank you, Sally.

SALLY: Thank *you.*

TOM: Say, what's going on here?

BOB (*Banteringly*): Nothing that concerns you, old boy.

TOM: Hmmm.

BOB: Good-night, everybody—and Merry Christmas.

ALL: Merry Christmas. (*After a final smile in* SALLY's
direction, BOB *exits upstage center.*)

TOM: My, my! Looks serious.

SALLY: What are you talking about?

TOM: That smile Bob just gave you.

SALLY: There was nothing wrong with the smile.

TOM (*Whistling*): I'll say there wasn't! Say, Mom, are we
going to open our presents at midnight as usual?

MRS. GILLUM: Indeed we are.

TOM: I think I'll take a little nap until then. You'll call
me when it's time, won't you?

MRS. GILLUM: Of course.

TOM: Good. See you later. (*He goes to door right and
pauses there*) Boy, what a smile that was! (TOM *exits
right.* MRS. GILLUM *goes over to Christmas tree and
begins to rearrange some of the gifts.*)

MR. GILLUM: I suppose this is as good a time as any for
me to write that letter to Miss Fenwick's. If you're

going to go there next month, we'd better make arrangements as soon as possible.

MRS. GILLUM: That's a good idea, John.

SALLY (*Joining mother at tree*): Dad, I—I don't think you need to write that letter.

MR. GILLUM: Not write it?

SALLY: No, I've changed my mind.

MR. GILLUM (*Smiling*): That's a woman's privilege.

MRS. GILLUM: That's wonderful, Sally. I'd so much rather have you here with us.

SALLY: And I'd rather be here.

MR. GILLUM (*Comes to tree and puts arm about* SALLY'S *shoulders*): Changed your mind about Laneville?

SALLY: Yes, Dad, I have. It's hard to explain and I don't suppose I can put it into words the way you could, but I think I've been a bit hard on Laneville.

MR. GILLUM (*Going to table and picking up the scroll*): Did this have anything to do with your change of heart?

SALLY: Yes, that—and a lot of other things I didn't understand before tonight. I guess I never understood that you have to give in order to get—that in order to have friends you have to be friendly. Maybe it's something like Christmas. It's really more fun when you give presents as well as get them.

MRS. GILLUM: I'm glad to hear you say that, dear.

SALLY: I just wish I'd realized a lot sooner how stand-offish I was being.

MR. GILLUM: Maybe such things take time, Sally.

SALLY: Anyhow, I don't need to make a New Year's resolution to like Laneville. I *know* I'm going to like it.

MR. GILLUM (*Teasingly*): Any particular person in Laneville you know you're going to like especially?

SALLY: Oh, Dad! Bob's a nice boy, and I do like him very much—but I'm thinking of other things besides Bob. I could have joined some of the school clubs, I could have tried out for a part in the school play, I could have done so many things. I'm just lucky I have a second chance to prove myself. Did you know they wanted me to be a cheerleader, and they were afraid to ask me?

MR. GILLUM: You'd make a mighty pretty cheerleader.

SALLY: I'm going to ask if I can be one next year.

MR. GILLUM: Good girl!

SALLY: I think Tom's idea about a nap until midnight is a good one. I'll go to sleep now—but remember to wake me for the festivities! (*She waves at her parents, calls "Merry Christmas" as she reaches the door, and then exits as her parents say "Merry Christmas."*)

MR. GILLUM: Now that's the best Christmas gift of all. Good will toward men. I think Sally's found the meaning of those words.

MRS. GILLUM: Yes, she's grown up a bit tonight, John.

MR. GILLUM: And now, how would you like me to read you what I've written today?

MRS. GILLUM: You mean about that slinky, attractive woman that keeps popping into the book?

MR. GILLUM: Well, she does make an appearance.

MRS. GILLUM: Just to show that I'm full of the Christmas spirit, too, I'll come along with you, John. As you've said, good will toward men—and women, too, slinky or otherwise. (*They exit arm in arm, chuckling, as the curtains close.*)

THE END

Star of Bethlehem

by Anne Coulter Martens

Characters

MARGO, *a busy girl*
BETSY, *a friend*
RICK
JIM
CHARLIE
EMILY, *a worried girl*
MARY SUE, *her little sister, 9*
MISS WAYNE, *a teacher*
MRS. CAREY, *a hospital volunteer*
OTHER CHILDREN, *patients at hospital*
ALICE (EUDORA *in pageant*)
ENID (JUSTINA *in pageant*)
MAC (JARIUS *in pageant*)

FIDELIA
MALCOLM
CRISPIN
CELESTA
AURELIA
SERAPHINA
MRS. TILLSTROM
REPORTER
NETTA NOBLE
ANNOUNCER
MRS. CRANFORD
DONNY
JEAN
ANGELS

} *other characters in pageant*

SCENE 1

TIME: *The afternoon of the day before Christmas.*
SETTING: *The stage of the high school auditorium.*
AT RISE: JIM *stands near center stage, holding clipboard and pencil.* RICK *enters carrying a straight chair and a desk lamp. He walks to desk, upstage left, and* CHARLIE *takes chair from him and sets it down in front of desk.* RICK *puts lamp on desk, and both boys look around stage.*

17

JIM (*As if checking list on clipboard*): What else do we still need here?

RICK: Two more chairs for that table. (*Points right*)

CHARLIE: And do you have the record books for the angels?

JIM: Margo's bringing them.

RICK: Margo! Where did that girl disappear to?

JIM: Whose idea was it, anyway, to have this dress rehearsal on Christmas Eve afternoon? We know our parts. (*MARGO, in high spirits, "dances" in, carrying three record books, her own playscript, and a cardboard suit box. She wears a Santa Claus hat, beard, and red jacket.*)

MARGO (*Clowning*): Ho, ho, ho! How are all the good little children? (*Puts books and box on table*)

JIM: Take off the disguise, Margo. We know you.

RICK (*As MARGO takes off the hat, beard, and jacket*): Why the ho-ho-ho outfit?

MARGO: It's for you to wear at my party tonight. (*Puts Santa costume in box*) Miss Wayne let me borrow it from the wardrobe department.

JIM: Well, I'm off to get those two chairs. (*Exits*)

RICK (*Backing away from MARGO*): I'm not going to wear any Santa rig.

MARGO: Rick, you promised.

RICK: I'd feel kind of silly.

CHARLIE: That figures.

MARGO: Come on, let's get this rehearsal started. If we want to win the award at the Community House Festival, our pageant has to be really smooth. (*JIM brings in two straight chairs and puts them at table.*)

CHARLIE: I haven't even finished all my Christmas shopping yet!

MARGO: You think *you're* busy? I have dozens of cookies to decorate for my party.

RICK: Cookies! Is that all you're having to eat?

MARGO: Wait till you see. Practically every good thing you've ever heard of. (*Proudly*) A real spread. (BETSY *comes in wearing a white angel robe.*)

BETSY: Everybody's in costume but Emily. (*Looks around*) Where is she?

MARGO: Not here.

RICK: Somebody help me carry in the Window of Heaven, and we'll be ready.

CHARLIE: I'm your man. (*He exits with* RICK.)

JIM: Oh-oh. I forgot the music rack for the Heavenly Choir! (*Goes out*)

MARGO (*Sitting at table*): I hope nobody needs any prompting tonight.

BETSY: Me, too. You're lucky you can read your part.

MARGO: I could rattle it off anyway. (MISS WAYNE *enters.*)

MISS WAYNE: Hello, Margo—Betsy. Is everyone ready to start the rehearsal?

MARGO: Hello, Miss Wayne. The boys will be back in a minute with the last few items.

BETSY: Hello, Miss Wayne. Gosh, I certainly am nervous.

MARGO: Don't worry. We're sure to walk away with the award. Don't you think so, Miss Wayne?

MISS WAYNE: I hope so, since you've all worked so hard. But, after all, it's *giving* the pageant that's important.

MARGO: Just the same, we'll win. Won't it be wonderful to get a special drama award for Christmas?

MISS WAYNE: Very nice indeed. Is the stage all set?

MARGO: Just about.

BETSY: Have you seen Emily around?

MISS WAYNE: She ran out to do some shopping for Mary Sue.

MARGO: Who's Mary Sue?

MISS WAYNE: Her little sister. She's in the hospital—broke her arm when she fell on the ice last week.

BETSY: Poor little kid. It's a shame.

MARGO: If Emily isn't back soon, we'll have to start without her. She's only one of the choir angels, anyhow.

MISS WAYNE: Margo, I think you read your lines a little too fast in yesterday's rehearsal.

MARGO (*Sharply*): *I* did?

MISS WAYNE: Maybe not so much too fast as . . . well . . . too lightly—as if you weren't giving enough thought to what you were saying.

MARGO (*Stiffly*): I'm sorry.

MISS WAYNE: You were good, but put a little more feeling into it, and you can be better. (*Goes left*) I'll round up the angels for you. (*Goes out left*)

MARGO (*Annoyed*): "Put a little more feeling into it!" Does she want me to burst into tears?

BETSY: You know she didn't mean that. (*After a pause*) I wonder what's keeping Emily.

MARGO: Who cares? (*Happy again, she gets up.*) Betsy, I have a stunning new dress for my party!

BETSY: That's nice.

MARGO: And I expect to get a string of real pearls to go with it—I've been working on Dad.

BETSY: All that, and a big party, too?

MARGO (*Grandly*): The entire cast of the pageant's invited. You're coming, aren't you?

BETSY: I wouldn't miss it for anything. (EMILY *enters, carrying a bag.*) Hi, Emily. We've been looking for you.

EMILY: I hope I haven't held things up.

MARGO (*Unpleasantly*): Emily, you picked a fine time to go shopping. (*As they talk,* JIM *comes in with a music stand and puts it up right.* RICK *and* CHARLIE *carry in and set up the "Window of Heaven," a large wooden frame.*)

EMILY (*Opening the bag*): I bought a doll for Mary Sue. (*Holds up doll*)

BETSY: How cute! She'll just love it.

MARGO (*Indifferently*): Pretty.

BETSY: Is Mary Sue feeling better now?

EMILY: The doctor told my grandmother that Mary Sue could probably come home from the hospital this afternoon.

BETSY: I'm so glad! (MARGO *ignores* EMILY *and* BETSY. *She takes out her compact and begins to powder her nose.*)

EMILY: I've been to visit Mary Sue every day and my heart just aches for the poor little kids who have to stay in the hospital at Christmastime.

BETSY: Are there many of them?

EMILY: You have no idea, till you see the children's ward. The nurses try to cheer them up, but they're so busy. It's the volunteer workers who are such a wonderful help with the little ones. (*Puts doll back into bag*)

MARGO: Emily, are you coming to my party tonight?

EMILY: I'm looking forward to it. I won't be able to stay very late—I want things to be ready for Mary Sue's Christmas. Dad works late, so Gram and I will have to take care of all the preparations. (MISS WAYNE *comes in, followed by* MRS. CAREY.) Hello, Miss Wayne, Mrs. Carey.

MISS WAYNE: Emily, Mrs. Carey would like to see you.

MRS. CAREY: Yes, Emily, you see. . . .

EMILY (*To* MRS. CAREY): Are you going for Mary Sue now, Mrs. Carey? It's so nice of you to drive her home. . . .

MISS WAYNE (*Breaking in*): Emily, Mrs. Carey has something to tell you. Why don't you both go to my room to talk?

EMILY (*Suddenly anxious*): Mary Sue's all right, isn't she?

MRS. CAREY: Oh, yes, she's all right. (MISS WAYNE *takes* EMILY *out.* MRS. CAREY *is about to follow when she stops and turns.*) I've just thought of something I'd like to ask you young people.

MARGO: Ask *us?*

MRS. CAREY: Yes. I wonder if some of you could come caroling tonight at the children's ward.

BETSY: Oh, Mrs. Carey, we'd really like to, but . . .

MARGO: But it's just impossible. We're getting ready now
to rehearse for the pageant we're putting on at the Community Festival.

MRS. CAREY: Could you come after the Festival? The children are so excited on Christmas Eve that they just can't
go to sleep early.

MARGO: Afterward, everyone's coming to a Christmas party
at my house.

MRS. CAREY (*Disappointed*): Oh, I see. Well, it was just a
thought. (*She goes out.*)

BETSY: It *is* too bad we can't go.

MARGO: Look, Christmas is fun time, isn't it? And what's
more fun than a party? Forget all this sob stuff. (ALICE,
ENID *and* MAC *come in, wearing white robes.*)

ALICE: How much longer do we have to wait around?

MAC: I'm beginning to sprout wings!

ENID: That'll be the day! (*They sit at the table with* MAC
in the center. EMILY *re-enters sadly.*)

BETSY: Is something wrong, Emily?

EMILY: The doctor says he'll have to keep Mary Sue in the
hospital a few more days. (*Sighs*) I guess you'll have to
get along without me in the pageant.

CHARLIE: But why?

EMILY: Well, I have to go to the hospital now with Mrs.
Carey. I'll be spending Christmas Eve there with Mary
Sue and all the other little ones who have to stay.

BETSY (*Genuinely sorry*): That's too bad.

EMILY (*To* MARGO): I'm sorry, Margo, but I guess I'll have
to miss your party, too.

MARGO: I'm sorry.

BETSY: Has Mary Sue been told yet?

EMILY (*Unsteadily, her voice breaking*): No, and I just hope she doesn't cry. (*Exits quickly*)

ALICE: Poor little Mary Sue.

ENID: I'd hate to spend *my* Christmas Eve in a hospital.

RICK (*Considering*): I suppose we *could* go there caroling after we give the pageant.

MARGO: No! What about my party?

BETSY: Maybe we could have the party at the hospital for the children.

RICK: With me in the Santa Claus outfit!

BETSY (*Enthusiastically*): We could buy little gifts, and round up some refreshments. (*Looks toward* MARGO) You said you have dozens of cookies.

RICK: Let's take them along to the children's ward!

MARGO (*Growing angry*): You must be out of your mind!

BETSY: I have another idea. What would you think if we gave our pageant for the children, too?

ALICE: Instead of at the Community House?

BETSY: There are so many other entries, we won't be missed at all.

JIM: Now, wait a minute. We've worked all month on this—

BETSY (*Breaking in*): Think how happy we could make the children.

ENID: But it just isn't practical. There wouldn't even be a stage in the children's ward.

JIM: What would we do about all the props?

CHARLIE: How could we rig up the lights?

BETSY: We'd manage somehow.

MARGO (*Impatiently*): That's ridiculous! We have to go to the Community House if we're interested in getting the award.

RICK (*Thoughtfully*): Maybe that award isn't so important.

BETSY: We've all been thinking too much about *getting.* Christmas is *giving,* isn't it?

MARGO (*Angrily*): So now I'm being preached at!

RICK: Please, Margo, don't be angry. Think about it.

MARGO: Don't you want to come to my party—any of you?

BETSY (*Kindly*): You know we've all been counting on it, Margo. But I really think this would be a better way to celebrate Christmas.

MAC: What would Miss Wayne say? We'd have to ask her.

BETSY: You know Miss Wayne would leave this decision up to us. She's always said it was *our* Christmas project.

CHARLIE: If it's O.K. with Miss Wayne, I vote to move the show to the hospital!

ALICE: I'm sure the rest of the cast will feel the same way. Let's do it!

ALL (*Except* MARGO, *ad lib*): I'm all for it! Yes, yes! Great idea! (*Etc.*)

BETSY: Then tonight we play the children's ward! (*In loud voice*) Rehearsal is about to start! Places, everyone! Lights! Ready at the curtains! (*Pageant cast start to take places.*)

RICK: Margo, you're with us on this, aren't you? Say something.

MARGO: All right, I *will* say something. Go ahead and rehearse. Give the pageant at the hospital. And sing carols and have a party! (*With burst of anger*) But count me out! (*She slams her script down on table and storms out. They look after her in surprise as the curtain falls.*)

*   *   *

SCENE 2

TIME: *Christmas Eve.*

SETTING: *A room in the children's wing of a hospital, decorated for Christmas.*

AT RISE: CHILDREN *of various ages, dressed in bathrobes and slippers, are sitting in circle of small chairs.* EMILY *enters with* MARY SUE, *who has her arm in a sling, and also wears a bathrobe and slippers.*

EMILY: Come, we'll sit here with the children for a while, Mary Sue.

MARY SUE: Why?

EMILY: For a very special reason. (*They sit down as* MRS. CAREY *enters.*)

MRS. CAREY: Children, you're going to have a big surprise.

CHILDREN (*Ad lib*): What? Tell us! What is it? (*Etc.*)

MRS. CAREY: Something that will make you all very happy.

MARY SUE: I'm not very happy about staying in the hospital for Christmas. I'd rather be at home.

EMILY (*Patting her gently*): But I'm here, Mary Sue.

MARY SUE: When is our surprise coming?

MRS. CAREY: Any minute now.

EMILY (*To* MRS. CAREY): I still can't believe it. They're giving up their chance for the Festival award, and their party . . .

MRS. CAREY: Not giving *up*. As Betsy said when she talked to me on the phone, they're *giving*. What a difference!

EMILY: I'm so very glad. (BETSY, CHARLIE *and* JIM *come in.*)

BETSY: Hi!

CHARLIE: How are you doing, young ones?

JIM: You're all looking great!

CHILDREN (*Ad lib*): Hi! Hello! What's the surpise? (*Etc.*)

EMILY: It's grand of you to do this.

CHARLIE: Fun for us, too.

BETSY: The others are in the room next door, hurrying to get ready.

CHARLIE (*Looking around*): A few changes, and we'll be all set. (*As he takes the cloth from table and folds it*) Hope you don't mind, kids. This is part of the surprise.

JIM (*Removing small tree from desk*): We'll have to take this out, too. (*The boys take the things out.*)

BETSY: Don't worry, children. The boys will put the things back in time for the party.

CHILDREN (*Ad lib*): Party! Are we going to have a party? When? (*Etc.*)

EMILY: Pretty soon. But the very special part is coming first. They're going to put on a lovely Christmas pageant just for you!

CHILDREN (*Ad lib*): Hurray! How exciting! A pageant! (*Etc.*)

EMILY (*To Betsy*): Is Rick coming?

BETSY: Already here. And dressed as you-know-who.

EMILY: Oh, wonderful! And Margo didn't mind at all? (*There is a pause.*) Did she?

BETSY: Well, yes. That's the only thing we're sorry about. Margo won't be here.

EMILY: I've spoiled her plans.

BETSY: Not you—not you, at all. The rest of us wanted to do this. (JIM *and* CHARLIE *enter, with script and props.* JIM *puts record books on the table, one in front of each of the three chairs already there.* CHARLIE *puts a music stand in the corner.*)

EMILY: But . . . Margo's the Narrator.

BETSY: We hoped she'd change her mind—but I guess she won't.

EMILY: What are you going to do?

CHARLIE: Why couldn't Emily read the part? You know what it's all about, Emily. (*Hands script to* EMILY)

EMILY: Why . . . I suppose I do. (*Takes the script*) I guess I could read it. But I do wish Margo had come.

BETSY: So do we. (*Sound of jingling bells is heard from off-stage.*)

CHARLIE (*Pointing left*): Look, kids, look who's here! (RICK, *dressed as Santa Claus, capers in, with a big sack on his back. The children jump up, reacting with happy cries.*)

RICK: Ho, ho, ho! Here's old Santa Claus to find out if everybody's been good!

CHILDREN (*Ad lib*): Yes! I have! I'm good! (Etc.)

RICK: I'm glad to hear it, because I have a present for each one of you a little later on.

MRS. CAREY: But first, you're going to see a play. So pick up your chairs, children, and we'll all go sit over here. (*Each child picks up a chair and follows her to front of stage. JIM and CHARLIE exit, then re-enter with "Window of Heaven" and place it up center. EMILY takes a position at front of stage, script in hand.*)

BETSY: Goodness, I'm not in costume yet! Ready with lights, Charlie?

CHARLIE: One second. (*He, JIM and BETSY hurry off.*)

RICK: Have fun, kids, and Santa will soon be back. (*Starts left. MARGO comes in left.*) Margo!

EMILY: I'm so glad you're here. Now you can be Narrator.

MARGO: No, thanks, I'm not staying.

RICK: Then why did you come?

MARGO: An errand for Mother. (*Airily*) I didn't mean to interrupt things. (*There is a pause while EMILY and RICK look at MARGO, who half turns away.*)

RICK (*To EMILY*): All right: Let's start the pageant. (*Goes out left. MARGO looks around at the stage setting, then toward the children. After a moment, the stage lights dim and a spotlight shines on EMILY. MARGO goes out left.*)

EMILY: We're going to tell you a modern legend of what might be happening in a Council Room of Heaven tonight. It is based on the old story that the Star of Bethlehem shines in the sky every year on the eve of Christmas . . . shines in the sky if the people of earth care enough to lift up their eyes to see it. (*EMILY opens script and reads.*)

"In Heaven, as the angels prepared to celebrate Christmas, they appointed three angels to be on the Special Council. The Star of Bethlehem was brought out of the Vault of Precious Things by the angel Fidelia, who was Keeper of the Star. But the angels of the Council were deeply troubled concerning the Star, because they feared that the people of earth were no longer interested in it. Therefore, they sent unto earth three messenger angels to mingle with the people, learning what was within their hearts as they prepared for Christmas, somewhat in the manner of earth people who take polls before Presidential elections, and other matters which they consider important.

"The small city of Danfield was selected as a test city for these angels to visit. Now, on the eve of the celebration, the members of the Special Council come to their table to await the return of the messenger angels. . . ." (*Spotlight on* EMILY *goes out, but she remains standing there.* ALICE (EUDORA), ENID (JUSTINA) *and* MAC (JARIUS) *enter, wearing angel robes, and sit at the table; the spotlight shines down right.*)

JARIUS: The hour grows late, and the time approaches when we must begin the Christmas celebration.

EUDORA: That is so.

JARIUS: Still am I concerned about the Star.

JUSTINA: We share in your concern, O Jarius.

JARIUS: After nearly two thousand years, there are still people on earth whose hearts are filled with hatred and bitterness, people who snatch greedily for material things, people who turn their eyes away from the light in the sky. I fear they no longer care to celebrate in unison with the angels in Heaven.

EUDORA: And if they care not?

JARIUS: Then the Star of Bethlehem can no longer be lighted in the skies of earth. (FIDELIA *enters.*) Come forward, Fidelia, Keeper of the Star.

FIDELIA: I have come to tell you that the Star is ready for lighting.

JARIUS: The ceremony must wait until we hear the report of the messenger angels. Have they returned from the city of Danfield?

FIDELIA: The summons for their return has been sounded. Two of them even now approach the Gates of Pearl.

JARIUS: Go to the angel Malcolm, Director of the Heavenly Choir, and bid him have them ready to sing their hymns of praise.

FIDELIA: Please, O Jarius and Angels of the Council, let us light the Star as we have always done, for the sake of the people who look up.

JARIUS: Do you think there are any such?

FIDELIA: Those who desire the Star may have sent their petitions unto Heaven. I pray you, let me go and make inquiry. (*They confer together.*)

JARIUS: When you have spoken to the Director of the Choir, go also unto the angel Crispin in the Department of Communications, and ask if there have been any petitions for the Star. (*The light on the council table goes out as* FIDELIA *leaves.*)

EMILY (*Reading*): "The angel Fidelia left the Council Room and went first to Malcolm, Director of the Heavenly Choir." (*Spotlight shines up right and reveals* MALCOLM *arranging music on a stand. A few* ANGELS *are with him, humming softly.* FIDELIA *enters spotlighted area.*)

MALCOLM: What brings you here, O Keeper of the Star?

FIDELIA: I am come from the angel Jarius to bid you be ready for the hymns of praise.

MALCOLM: The choir is in readiness. How soon do we sing?

FIDELIA: We await the return of the messengers from earth.

MALCOLM: I pray that the report of the messengers be a good report.

FIDELIA: And I, also. (*The spotlight goes out as* FIDELIA *leaves.*)

EMILY (*Reading*): "Fidelia hastened unto the Department of Communications where the angel Crispin recorded petitions as they were received from earth." (*Spotlight shines up left, where* CRISPIN *sits at the desk talking on the telephone. There is a record book in front of him.*)

CRISPIN (*On phone*): Yes, Mrs. Bradley, I have made a note of your request. (*He hangs up as* FIDELIA *draws near.*) Welcome, Fidelia.

FIDELIA: Can you spare me a moment?

CRISPIN: Gladly. (*The telephone rings.*) Excuse me. (*Picks up receiver*) Yes? . . . Your request will be given consideration. (*Hangs up, writes in his book*) Another one asking for a white Christmas.

FIDELIA: Have there been many?

CRISPIN: Our record book is filled with their names. They want snow on the trees and on the hills, that their little world may look like a picture on a greeting card.

FIDELIA: Know they not that on the first Christmas the brown hillsides were bare of snow, and even for the sheep there was little grass?

CRISPIN: They have forgotten, if they ever knew.

FIDELIA: What other requests have you received? (MARGO *enters left, and remains standing down left.*)

CRISPIN: Some from little children asking for toys. We transferred them to another line. And just before you came, there was a call from a young mother-to-be, asking that her baby be born on Christmas Day. Hundreds of others have asked the same.

FIDELIA: Because the day is holy and beautiful.

CRISPIN: Oh, no. Because in certain cities the chief department store presents each Christmas baby with a large layette.

FIDELIA: Know they not that on the first Christmas there were only swaddling clothes?

CRISPIN: If they knew it once, they have forgotten.

FIDELIA: Have any of these petitioners mentioned the Star of Bethlehem?

CRISPIN: There have been no requests for the Star.

FIDELIA: None at all?

CRISPIN: Except from ministers and priests who are men of God, none at all. (*Spotlight goes out;* FIDELIA *leaves.*)

EMILY (*Reading*): "Sorrowfully, the angel Fidelia returned to the room where the angels of the Council waited." (*Spotlight shines on the council table, as* FIDELIA *draws near.*)

JARIUS: Approach, O Keeper of the Star, and make known your tidings.

FIDELIA: The Heavenly Choir is ready. But except from men of God, there have been no requests for the Star.

JARIUS: Why, O people of earth, why? Long ago, when the Wise Men saw the Star, they rejoiced with exceeding great joy. (CELESTA *and* AURELIA *come into the spotlighted area.*)

FIDELIA: Here are two of the messenger angels.

CELESTA: I, Celesta, am ready to make my report.

AURELIA: And I, Aurelia, also.

JARIUS: But what of Seraphina, the third angel?

AURELIA: We have heard naught from her.

JARIUS: Then we must proceed without her. Tell us, Celesta, what you saw on your visit to the small city of Danfield.

CELESTA: I saw a big parade heralding the arrival of Santa Claus to the chief department store. I saw giant toys, and huge floats which were graced by stars of the enter-tainment world.

JARIUS: But what of the Star of Bethlehem?

CELESTA: Of it there was no mention.

JARIUS: And you, Aurelia?

AURELIA: I saw a tall tree set up in the city square, and the Mayor himself pulled the switch that made it blaze with lights of many colors. Then did the Mayor make a speech unto the multitude.

JARIUS: And in that speech?

AURELIA: He praised the city of Danfield, and the City Council, calling them progressive men of great com-munity spirit.

JARIUS: But the Star?

AURELIA: He made mention of the star on the top of the tall tree, but no mention of the Star of Bethlehem. (*The angels confer, shaking their heads.*)

JARIUS: Did you seek further, going away from the crowds into the quiet places?

CELESTA: On the sidewalks of the city I saw young people laden with gay packages. I heard them talk of the price of the gifts they had bought, or of the gifts they hoped to receive.

AURELIA: I watched a woman count the Christmas cards which were sent to her. I heard her say with pride that the number was greater than any other person in the city had ever known. (SERAPHINA *enters spotlighted area.*)

FIDELIA: The third angel returns!

JARIUS: Why so late, O Seraphina?

SERAPHINA: I became so interested in the people of earth that I delayed overlong.

JARIUS: Let us hear your report.

SERAPHINA: I found many whose hearts were filled with

gladness: people who are busy tonight with preparations for the needy, children who made with their own hands little gifts of love.

JARIUS: These things are good.

SERAPHINA: The buyers and sellers are in the market places, yes. But surely there is no wrong in that? Gifts are a symbol of Christmas, and there must be those who sell what the giver would buy.

JARIUS: Well spoken, O Messenger Angel. But you have said naught of the Star.

SERAPHINA: I watched the Christmas preparations in one small house. I saw a man bring home a turkey, and his wife prepare it for the feast tomorrow. I saw her prepare pies and fruit cakes and cookies of many shapes and sizes. All of them seasoned with the love she bore her family, and love is a part of Christmas.

JARIUS: It is.

SERAPHINA: Verily, such love was in that home that when I heard the summons from Heaven, I was slow in taking my departure.

JARIUS: But was any mention made of the Star?

SERAPHINA: There were stars in the eyes of all in that house, and the music of Christmas was in their hearts.

JARIUS: You have not answered the question which was asked of you.

SERAPHINA (*After a pause*): The Star of Bethlehem was not mentioned. (*The angels confer, shaking their heads sadly.*)

FIDELIA: Please, O Jarius, give unto the people of earth just one more chance! Let us open wide the Window of Heaven, that each messenger angel may look down at a place of her own choosing! (*Again the angels confer.*)

JARIUS: It shall be as you ask. Let the Window of Heaven be opened!

CELESTA: It was said in the city that a certain woman was

to present unto her church a beautiful stained glass window. . . . (*Spotlight on the council table goes out. Two angels draw drapes back from "Window of Heaven" as spotlight shines on it.* MRS. TILLSTROM *sits in chair placed behind the window frame. A* REPORTER *stands near with a notebook and pencil.*)

MRS. TILLSTROM (*Importantly*): Will this article about me appear in the Sunday paper?

REPORTER: Yes, Mrs. Tillstrom. Your picture will be in the paper, too.

MRS. TILLSTROM: Of course you understand that I have no personal desire for publicity?

REPORTER (*Dryly*): Naturally not.

MRS. TILLSTROM: But the doings of our church must be reported for all to read.

REPORTER: Certainly.

MRS. TILLSTROM: You'll describe the stained glass window in great detail? Mention that it's the most expensive gift ever given to a church in this area.

REPORTER: Oh, yes.

MRS. TILLSTROM: The people in the other churches will be green with envy.

REPORTER: No doubt about it.

MRS. TILLSTROM: I want you to spell my name exactly right. Write it down as I tell you.

REPORTER: You can depend on me.

MRS. TILLSTROM: Mrs. Hilary Tillstrom. Spelled with only one "l" in Hilary. Two "l's" in the last name. (*As he writes.*) T-i-l-l-s-t-r-o-m. (*Two angels close drapes as spotlight on "Window of Heaven" goes out. It then shines again on the council table.*)

CELESTA: I'm sorry.

JARIUS: This woman is presenting a Christmas gift only for her own personal glory.

FIDELIA: But surely, surely, all are not like her!

JARIUS: Let us look from the Window of Heaven a second time.

AURELIA: I heard much praise of a certain television program presided over by a young woman named Netta Noble, who has a large audience in that city. . . . (*Spotlight goes out on the council table, then shines on the "Window of Heaven" as the two angels draw the drapes apart again. The same chair is still in place. In front of chair is a table with glassware on it and a banner reading:* JEWEL TONE PRODUCTS. NETTA NOBLE *sits at the table and the* ANNOUNCER *stands near.*)

NETTA: Now, after that commercial, where were we? Oh, yes. I was telling you about a new kind of Christmas list that all of us should make. Maybe it's too late for this year, but keep it in mind, will you? A list of what *not* to give us for Christmas!

ANNOUNCER: Leave it to you, Netta, to think of something like that.

NETTA: Take me, for instance. I hate gay little aprons with my name stamped on them. So why not tell my friends in advance?

ANNOUNCER: Why not, indeed?

NETTA: Slipper socks with wool flowers embroidered on them give me the willies.

ANNOUNCER: Then pass them along to me. I get cold feet when the bills come due in January! (*Laughs*)

NETTA: Oh, you! Now here, my friends, is my own list of what I *don't* want Santa to give me. No mink-topped can openers, and no solid gold toothpicks. No elephant bookends. And please, no real live elephants, either! Of course, there are some things I *do* like. A nice shiny Cadillac, for instance!

ANNOUNCER: Well!

NETTA: And a mink stole would be most acceptable. Our sponsor's product, too, which I consider quite heavenly

—all these beautiful jewel colors in glassware. (*Points to glassware on table*)

ANNOUNCER (*Indicating the glassware*): Hurry, folks! Just a few more shopping hours before Christmas. This amazing value in Jewel Tone glassware is for the Christmas season only. Make your friends, your family, yourself, happy with a set of rainbow-hued beauty! Only a few shopping hours left. Hurry! (*Spotlight goes out on the "Window of Heaven," as the two angels close the drapes. It then shines on the council table again.*)

AURELIA (*Sadly*): I, too, judged wrong.

JARIUS: Miss Netta Noble finds Christmas amusing. Her sponsor considers it an auction sale. (*Angrily*) Enough!

FIDELIA: But you promised that each of the messenger angels could try once more.

JARIUS: Let the Window of Heaven be opened for the third and last time.

SERAPHINA: I choose to see again that small house so filled with love. (*Spotlight goes out on the council table. Two angels open drapes on "Window of Heaven" as spotlight again shines on "Window." The table has been removed. The same chair is there, and MRS. CRANFORD is sitting in it with a book on her lap. Her little boy, DONNY, stands near with a large Christmas stocking in his hand.*)

DONNY: Mommy, will Santa Claus fill my stocking?

MRS. CRANFORD: Of course he will, Donny.

DONNY: Even if we don't have a fireplace?

MRS. CRANFORD: Santa always finds a way.

DONNY: I've been very good.

MRS. CRANFORD: Very good, indeed.

DONNY: Will Daddy see Santa when he comes home late from work?

MRS. CRANFORD: Maybe so.

DONNY: Will Daddy be very late?

MRS. CRANFORD: About midnight, I think.

DONNY: I wish he were here now.

MRS. CRANFORD: So do I, but he has to work. (JEAN *enters and joins group.*)

JEAN: I'm home!

DONNY: Hi, Jean.

MRS. CRANFORD: How was the caroling?

JEAN: Wonderful! And the sky was so clear! Mother, did you know that some people say that the Star of Bethlehem appears again on every Christmas Eve?

MRS. CRANFORD: So I've heard it said.

JEAN: I found myself looking up at the sky and wondering.

DONNY: Will Daddy see it when he comes home?

MRS. CRANFORD: If he looks up—and he *will* look up. (*Takes* DONNY *on her lap*)

DONNY: What *is* the Star of Bethlehem?

MRS. CRANFORD: What is it? (*Thoughtfully*) A star which led the Wise Men. A light in a dark sky. The light of faith in the hearts of people. (*Quoting*) "And lo, the star, which they saw in the east, went before them, till it came and stood over where the young child was."

JEAN: Do you think it will shine again tonight?

MRS. CRANFORD (*Softly*): I'm very sure it will. (*Spotlight on the "Window of Heaven" goes out, as the two angels close the drapes. It shines again on the council table.*)

FIDELIA: Now, O Jarius, what of the Star?

JARIUS (*Rising*): Let the Star of Bethlehem shine once again in the skies of earth! And may there be many who lift up their eyes, seeing it with the eyes of faith! (*The* ANGELS *of the Heavenly Choir, led by* MALCOLM, *begin singing refrain of "We Three Kings of Orient Are." At the same time a lighted star may appear high on the stage, if desired. When the singing ends, the pageant cast files out, humming softly. The lights come on full. The children applaud.*)

EMILY (*Seeing* MARGO): Margo, you're still here! (BETSY *re-enters.*)

MARGO (*Moving toward center*): I didn't intend to stay. But when the pageant started, I began to listen. For the first time, I really listened. Would you like to know why I came? Not to help. Simply because my mother insisted that I bring the cookies. Oh, yes, they're here. Boxes of them, in the other room.

BETSY: I'm glad. (*Slips off her angel robe, putting it on the back of a chair*)

MARGO: But while I listened . . . and thought about the children . . . I knew I'd been wrong about so many things. The Festival award doesn't seem important now. I did talk too much about *getting*. Even with the party. I was planning to *have* a party, not *give* one.

EMILY: So you stayed. Won't you stay a little longer?

MARGO: If you still want me. A while ago I said, count me out. But I don't feel that way any more. Will you please count me *in?*

EMILY: Oh, yes!

BETSY: Yes, Margo, yes!

MARGO (*Happily*): Then let's start the fun. (*To the children*) Come on! Come on, everyone! We're going to sing carols and have a party, aren't we? (*She takes a child's hand.*) What shall we sing first? (RICK, *in his Santa suit, comes in jingling bells and singing "Jingle Bells" and joins* MARGO, *who sings with him.* EMILY *and* BETSY *join the singing, too, as the children take it up. After one chorus, the other young people come in, without costumes now.* MARGO *starts a Christmas carol and they all sing. Curtain.*)

THE END

'Twas the Night Before Christmas

by Edrie Pendleton

Characters

FRED SAUNDERS   BILLY, *eight years old*
AGNES SAUNDERS   RUBY, *the maid*
BUD, *seventeen years old*

TIME: *Christmas Eve, around seven.*
SETTING: *The Saunders living room.*
AT RISE: FRED SAUNDERS *is standing on a wobbly stepladder hammering a nail in the doorframe for the Christmas wreath which is lying on the ladder. His wife,* AGNES, *is trimming the Christmas tree. She rummages through boxes of ornaments on the floor, now and then hanging a ball on the tree.*

FRED (*Singing*):
"Deck the halls with boughs of holly—" (*Banging his finger with the hammer*) Ouch! Why didn't Bud put up this wreath?
AGNES (*Soothingly*): Now, Fred, be calm. Remember it's Christmas. And I simply can't imagine where that Christmas angel could have gone!
FRED: Probably flown away somewhere.
AGNES: Nonsense—I'm sure I packed her carefully away in tissue paper—well, I'll just have to find her—(*She goes out left and the doorbell rings—also the telephone.* FRED *looks*

39

wild as he starts to get down the ladder. But the ladder is wobbly.)

FRED (*Calling*): Agnes—Agnes! (*She comes back with another box of decorations, and notices* FRED *see-sawing on the ladder.*)

AGNES: Look out, Fred, you're going to fall!

FRED (*Righting himself*): Never mind, Agnes, will you answer one or both of those bells? (*She sets the box down and goes around the ladder.*)

AGNES: I don't want to walk under it, Fred—I might have bad luck. (*Exits*)

FRED: If anybody has bad luck with this ladder, it's going to be me. (*The telephone keeps ringing and finally in desperation* FRED *gets down and rushes to it.*) Hello! . . . What? . . . Oh, yes, Mrs. Peabody. . . . What's that? . . . Merry Christmas?—Oh—er—yes, but it hasn't arrived at our house yet. . . . Is that all you wanted, Mrs. Peabody? . . . Well, that's very nice. . . . What's that? Christmas Eve is a busy time?—It certainly is! (*He hangs up and wipes his brow as* BILLY *enters left chewing vigorously. He has some cookies in one hand and a cupcake in the other.*)

BILLY (*With his mouth full*): " 'Twas the night before Christmas and all through the house, not a creature was stirring —not even a mouse."

FRED: Whose house are you talking about? (AGNES *has reentered with a large package during* BILLY'S *speech. She looks at him.*)

AGNES: Billy, stop eating Ruby's Christmas cakes and cookies. There won't be any left for company—and besides you'll be sick. You won't be able to eat any Christmas dinner tomorrow.

BILLY: Oh, yes, I will.

FRED: Was that package for me, Agnes?

AGNES: No, it's for all of us—from Aunt Hattie. Why should it be for you?

FRED: Well, I was expecting—

BILLY (*Looking at package*): From Aunt Hattie? Probably a vase again. (AGNES *puts package down with some others on the desk.* BUD *enters left carrying a large, odd-shaped bottle of cologne. He waves it at his mother who is at the tree again.* FRED *climbs back up on the stepladder.*)

BUD: Mom, can you help me wrap this present for Sally? I have to take it over—

AGNES: Well, I haven't wrapped all of mine, Bud—and right now I'm looking for the Christmas angel. What's the matter with your doing it?

BUD: I don't know—I have one wrapped all right, but every time I try to wrap this, it turns out to be a goofy-looking package—this funny shape—

BILLY: How many presents are you giving your old girl friend?

BUD: Never you mind— Mom, please—

BILLY: Aw, I know what you're giving her—a great big scrapbook so she can put all the wonderful snapshots you take in it—

AGNES: That doesn't look like a scrapbook—

BILLY: That's the other present—cologne—that junky stuff.

BUD: Junky? You listen here—(*He shows bottle*) Look, Mom, the girl at the store said it was a good kind. Do you think it's all right?

AGNES (*Coming over and looking at it*): Hmmm-m—pretty bottle—what does it say? "Je vous désire"—isn't that French for "I desire you"? (FRED *almost falls off the stepladder again.*)

FRED: What's that?

AGNES: Don't fall off the stepladder, Fred.

FRED: But he can't give a girl a present with a name like that—

BUD: Watch out, Dad, stand still—you almost made me drop it—

FRED: I wish I had.

BILLY: And get that stuff all over the house—we'd be asphyxiated—it smells awful—

AGNES: Billy—

FRED: Agnes, it's indecent.

AGNES: Oh, now, Fred, all the colognes have funny names—there's even one called "My Sin."

FRED: What's that?

AGNES: I don't think this is so bad—(RUBY *enters left*.)

RUBY: Mrs. Saunders, I'm going to make the stuffing for the turkey now so that bird will be ready to pop in the oven bright and early tomorrow morning.

AGNES: Oh, fine, Ruby.

RUBY: Yes'm, but I'm just wondering—what kind of stuffing's the favorite this year?

FRED: Old-fashioned sage dressing for me, Ruby—nothing like it.

BUD (*Quickly*): Chestnut, Ruby.

BILLY: With raisins, Ruby—

AGNES: Well, of course I always liked oyster but—

RUBY: Land sakes—how am I going to please everyone?

AGNES: Now, Ruby, you know there's no use asking—we go through this every year. Just use your own judgment.

RUBY (*Laughing, as she goes toward left exit.*): Guess I'll just have to stuff that bird piecemeal. (*As* RUBY *exits left, the doorbell rings.* FRED *tries to get off the ladder and* AGNES *starts for the door, right.*)

BILLY: I'll go, Mom. (BILLY *exits right center.*)

BUD: Mom, will you please wrap—

AGNES: All right, dear. Where's your paper?

BUD: On the dining room table. (BUD *and* AGNES *go out left and* BILLY *re-enters with a small package.*)

FRED (*Starting to speak, then breaking off as he sees package*): Was that for me?—no, no, I can see it isn't big enough . . .

BILLY (*He is tearing open package*): Big enough?—Listen,
Pop—

FRED: Billy, will you do something for me? Keep your mother
out of the room for a while—

BILLY: All right, I'll try, but first, Pop, I want to ask you—
(*Shows him small box*) This is Mom's present, see—the one
I got her—and it's a red necklace—

FRED: Fine—splendid—and you're very fortunate, son, to
have a present for her at all—it's more than I've got.

BILLY: How come, Dad?

FRED: Oh, I have some flowers and candy, but her real present
hasn't come yet. I have to call up the store—

BILLY: But, Pop, it's getting late—

FRED: You're telling me? Fortunately, the stores are open till
all hours on Christmas Eve—so if you'll just keep your
mother out of the room—

BILLY: O.K., Pop, but first I want to ask you—look—(*Holding up box*) Do you think Mom'll like this necklace?

FRED (*As he looks at necklace in box*): Of course she will.

BILLY: It cost an awful lot, Pop—I've been saving my nickels
ever since October.

FRED: Since October, eh? Your spirit of unselfishness amazes
me, son.

BILLY: What?

FRED: It would be nice if you could be that way all the year
round.

BILLY: I never thought of that.

FRED: Unfortunately, we're all the same, but it would be a
good thing to remember. Now, hurry up, Billy. Keep your
mother out of here.

AGNES (*Offstage*): That's a very pretty package, Bud.

FRED: There, you see? Your mother's coming back.

BILLY: I'll get her out again, Pop. Leave it to me. (*Calling*)
Mom, Mom . . .

AGNES (*As she appears in doorway*): What is it, Billy?

BILLY (*Walking toward her*): I want to show you Ruby's present.

AGNES: But I'm looking for the Christmas angel—

BILLY (*Putting his hand on her arm as if to lead her off*): Please, Mom. I have her present up in my room. It's a box of candy, and I hope it's all right.

FRED: Yes, son, you'd better get your mother's approval. (*Motioning to him to get* AGNES *out of room.*)

BILLY: Come on, Mom . . .

AGNES: All right, but if I ever get that tree trimmed—(*As they exit,* FRED *rushes to the phone.*)

FRED (*Watching the door as he picks up receiver*): Main 123, please . . . Hello, is this the Davis Specialty Shop? This is Fred Saunders . . . I'm calling about a package—yes, yes, I know you're busy—so am I—but when I stopped in this afternoon you said you'd look into it—but it isn't here yet . . . No—when I ordered what I wanted, you didn't have the right size : . . But you *didn't* deliver it last week —now, now, please, do I have to go over it again? . . . But tomorrow's Christmas! . . . Well, will you please check on it and I'll call you back. . . . All right, thank you. (*He hangs up and wipes his brow as* BUD *enters left, carrying two packages—the cologne and another package the shape of a suit box.*)

BUD: Hi, Dad.

FRED (*Turning to* BUD, *and speaking with desperation in his voice*): Bud, what am I going to do? Your mother's Christmas present has been lost.

BUD: Lost? But—

FRED: I ordered one of those negligee things for her—you know the kind she's always wanted—filmy material—like the ones they wear in the movies—glamorous! Now the store can't find it—they think they've delivered it—

BUD: Maybe it'll still come, Dad.

FRED: Maybe? It has to. Your mother had her heart set on this, and I finally whipped up courage to go in the lingerie department—have you ever been in the lingerie department?

BUD: I should say not, Dad.

FRED: Well, it's embarrassing—a man feels out of place, but I went through with it—and now after all that, it's lost. It isn't here, I tell you—(BILLY *re-enters eating cookies and cake again.*)

BILLY: Did you find Mom's present, Pop?

FRED: No—the store can't find any trace of it there.

BUD: Where'd you say you bought it, Dad?

FRED: At the Davis Specialty Shop.

BUD: It seems to me I remember taking a package from there last week—addressed to you—

FRED: What's that?

BUD: Sure—don't you remember, Billy? You were here—a package came for me at the same time.

FRED (*Angrily*): Why doesn't someone tell me these things?

BUD: But I have to get over to Sally's now, Dad, and—

FRED: Bud, wait—you don't take a step till you tell me where—

BUD: Billy knows, Dad.

BILLY: Sure—we put it in the guest room closet.

BUD (*Going out right center*): See you later.

FRED: Billy, will you please—

BILLY: I'll get it for you, Pop. (*He runs out left.* AGNES *re-enters left, carrying a box which she is looking through.*)

AGNES: Fred, would you believe it? I'm still looking for the Christmas angel.

FRED: I wish that was all I was looking for.

AGNES (*Fussing with the tree*): I don't think these lights are going to work right at all—and your wreath's cockeyed. Can't you hang it straight?

FRED: I haven't finished with it yet.

AGNES: But, Fred, don't you realize—there are millions of things to do—you've been fussing with that wreath for hours.

FRED: It seems to me you've been looking for the Christmas angel for hours.

AGNES: So I have . . . Fred, have you any money?

FRED: Money—money—on Christmas Eve?

AGNES: I bought Ruby a red silk dress, but we always give her some money too.

FRED: But you said you'd have enough to take care of that—

AGNES: I know, but then at the last minute, I saw some more things for the boys, and I sent some toys to the Children's Home. Oh, Fred, I do hope you have some money.

FRED: Well, maybe if I dig way down deep in my pocket— (*The phone rings, and* FRED, *with a desperate look at* AGNES, *answers it.*) Hello! What's that? . . . Well, Merry Christmas to you too! (*He hangs up.*)

AGNES: Who was that?

FRED: I don't know.

AGNES: You mean to say you didn't even ask—(BILLY *rushes in carrying a large suit box.*)

BILLY: I found it—I found it!

AGNES (*Brightly*): The Christmas angel?

BILLY: No—Pop, it's Mom's—

FRED: Shh-hhh—never mind. (*He takes it from* BILLY, *and holding it behind him, quickly backs toward the desk, depositing it.*)

AGNES: My—my, what are you so mysterious about, Fred?

FRED: Agnes, don't you have to go out of the room—or something? (RUBY *comes in left, looking belligerent, but she isn't really very cross.*)

RUBY: Mrs. Saunders, Billy has got to stop eating up my cakes and cookies.

BILLY: Who? Me?

RUBY: Of course, you—you've got a guilty conscience—that's what you've got.

BILLY: But I'm not eating a thing.

RUBY: Then it's the first time all day. Why that boy's made a hole this big (*Holding her hands to indicate large circle.*) in my cookies—and now he's started on the sandwiches I'm making for the boys and girls when they come round singing carols—

AGNES: Billy, I've told you—

BILLY: Sure, Mom—I kind of got over bein' hungry anyway.

RUBY: Well, all I've got to say is, if I was a boy and tomorrow was Christmas, I'd kinda watch my step. (*She starts out.*)

FRED: Ruby, don't you—er—want Mrs. Saunders' help in the kitchen? . . . That is, don't you want to ask her—(*He makes motions at her to get* AGNES *out of the room.*)

Ruby: What's that, Mr. Saunders?—Oh, sure—sure, I do. Mrs. Saunders, I wish you'd come and see if I'm making enough sandwiches—I've no idea.

AGNES: All right, Ruby—if this is a conspiracy to get me out of the room—(*She makes a funny face at* FRED, *as she goes out left, followed by* RUBY. FRED *quickly grabs the package from desk and looks at it.*)

FRED: Billy, my boy, this is it all right—"Mr. Frederick Saunders"—and it's from the Davis Specialty Shop. (*He begins to unwrap it.*) You don't know how relieved I feel.

BILLY: What is it, Pop?

FRED: It's a negligee—you know, one of those fancy affairs the women all like—(*He has box open now and takes the tissue paper off but is looking up at* BILLY *as he talks.*) Wait till you see it. (AGNES *re-enters just as* FRED *is about to lift out the present.*) Agnes—Agnes, you can't come in—it's your Christmas present—(*He has it in his hands now and realizes by the feel of it that it isn't what he thought it was. He holds a very large scrapbook in his hands.*)

AGNES (*Coming over*): My present? A scrapbook? But what will I do with that? Put our wedding pictures in it?

FRED (*Looking in the scrapbook; bewildered*): But this isn't it—I mean—

BILLY: I'll bet Bud got them mixed up, Pop. This is what he was going to give Sally.

FRED: No—no, he was giving her "My Sin" or—

BILLY: What you talking about, Pop?

FRED: Or "I Desire You"—some silly name—he was giving her cologne.

BILLY: No, but a scrapbook, too—don't you know I said—

FRED: But how could he have mixed them up? This package is addressed to me—Mr. Frederick Saunders—

AGNES: Well, Fred, Bud is named after you—or is that too long ago for you to remember?

FRED: Why can't he put Junior after his name then? (*He starts toward door rear.*)

AGNES: Fred, where are you going?

FRED: I don't know—out shopping—

AGNES: Now, Fred, it's too late, and besides you have to get that wreath straight—

FRED: You want me to climb this ladder again—the way I feel now—(*But dazedly he goes up a step or two.* BUD *enters right center, all smiles, carrying a box that looks as though it might contain a tie.*)

BUD (*Walking around the ladder*): Look what Sally gave me —and boy, you should have seen her—she's wondering what's in the boxes I took her. She's all excited—the whole house is, in fact—her dad just fell off a stepladder—

FRED (*He almost falls off again*): What's that? (*Regaining his balance and coming down to* BUD. *Slowly with emphasis.*) That's all very interesting about Sam Burton and the stepladder—but if you don't mind, I'd like a word with you.

BUD: What? Sure! What's the matter, Dad?

FRED: Nothing—nothing except—what have you done with your mother's Christmas present?

BUD: Mother's Christmas present—nothing, Dad. Why would I—

FRED (*Indicating scrapbook*): What is that? Will you kindly tell me?

BUD: Why, that's my scrapbook—that I gave Sally—that I was going to gi—I mean—hey, Dad—I don't get it. What happened?

FRED: Nothing, son—nothing at all, except that I had a present for your mother—something she's had her heart set on—lo, these many years.

AGNES (*Interested*): Well!

FRED: And now you have given it to Sally.

BUD: I—I have? You mean I got the boxes mixed up?

FRED: Exactly.

BUD: Well, I'm sorry, Dad, but—but—is it something Sally will like?

FRED (*Exploding*): Something she'll like? I don't know, and I don't care. All I know is it was a very expensive negligee—

AGNES: A negligee? Fred, you did get it for me after all. How wonderful!

FRED: Wonderful? What's wonderful about it? It's gone— (*Desperately searching for words*)—gone with the sweet perfumes of Araby—to his gal, Sal.

AGNES: Dear me, so it has. . . . Oh, but there must be some way— Bud, can't we get it back?

BUD: Why, sure—sure, we can. Sally won't open it till tomorrow—I put great big stickers on the package—"Don't open until Christmas." . . . Billy, why don't you run over and take the scrapbook and explain to her—

FRED: Oh, why—why, yes. (*He begins stuffing the scrapbook back in the box.*)

BILLY: I don't see why I have to unscramble his mistakes—

AGNES: Somebody will have to do something. Billy, it's Christmas Eve.

BUD (*Persuasively*): Sure—and all you have to do is—is take this package over there, and well—say there's been a mistake—it's easy.

BILLY: If it's so easy, why don't you do it?

BUD: All right—I'll call her up and explain first . . . (*Going to phone*) Then you won't have to open your mouth. (*Picking up receiver*) Maple 203, please.

AGNES: What color is it, Fred?

FRED: Never you mind. If we ever rescue this thing from the clutches of the younger generation—at least you can still be surprised at the color.

BUD: Hello? I want to talk to Sally—oh, it *is* you, Sally. I guess I'm sort of excited. I wanted to tell you—I wanted to explain—

AGNES: Now, Bud, get to the point.

BUD: You see, that package I left for you—the long flat one, not the little one—what's that? . . . You—you've what? . . . You've opened it? Well, you can't do that. I mean— oh. . . . Oh . . . (*Putting hand over mouthpiece and turning to others.*) She's opened it. (*There are expressions of consternation on the faces of* FRED *and* AGNES. BILLY *grins mischievously.*) Yes . . . yes. . . . You do? . . . It does? (*To others.*) It fits her. . . . It is? (*To others.*) It's the color of her eyes. . . . What? Well, I—I—er—I don't know how I ever thought of it either. (*Quickly*) Well, I have to hang up now. . . . Goodbye, Sally. (*He hangs up.*)

FRED: But why on earth didn't you tell her—

BUD: I couldn't, Dad. She's crazy about it. If you'd have heard her rave—I didn't have the heart—

AGNES: Well, at least I know. Sally's eyes are blue. It was blue, wasn't it, Fred?

FRED: Blue, yes. Azure blue.

AGNES (*Forgetting a moment that it's gone*): Oh, Fred, how could you think to pick just the color I like?

FRED: To tell you the truth, I asked the young lady—(*Walking about mincingly like a model*) she was modeling it—

AGNES: Oh—

FRED: I asked her if she would like it for Christmas, and she looked rather surprised, but smiled and nodded at me so I thought, well, you'd like it too.

AGNES (*Laughing*): Why, Fred! She must have thought—

FRED: Why—why—what do you mean? Agnes, you don't think she *did* think—

AGNES: Of course I think she did think. Who wouldn't think?

FRED: Well, I—I—it's ridiculous, and it's beside the point. It's not proper for Bud at his age to be giving a thing like that to that child of Sam Burton's. Why, the idea—think of it—"My Sin" and a negligee.

BUD: But it wasn't "My Sin." It was—(*Giving it in bad French*) "Je vous désire"—in French that means "I desire you"—oh-h, boy . . . it does sound—(*Breaking off*) Dad, will I be compromised or something?

BILLY: Sure. You'll have to marry the girl . . .

BUD: Quiet, you. . . . Mom, what'll I do?

AGNES: I don't know, son. . . . What will *I* do without my negligee? (*The phone rings and they all jump.*)

FRED: Another Merry Christmas—I'll get it. . . . I'll make short work of whoever . . . (*At phone. Lifting receiver.*) Hello! Who? Oh, Sam—Sam Burton. How are you? I hear you just fell off a stepladder. . . . What's that? Sam, what are you shouting about? . . . My son what?

BUD: Is he mad at me for something?

FRED: Gave your daughter an improper present? Well, I'll be— That's the last straw!

BUD: He—he's mad about the negligee?

FRED (*Turning from phone*): Can you imagine that? (*Into*

phone again.) You listen to me, Sam Burton—in the first place that negligee wasn't even meant for your daughter. . . . It was a present for my wife—and you have a lot of nerve calling up here—I say it was a present for my wife! Bud mixed up the packages—and if anyone has a right to feel put out—huh? What's that? You're laughing? You think it's funny? (*Beginning to laugh too.*) Well, maybe it is, at that. . . . Agnes, he's laughing.

AGNES: I can laugh too, if I'm going to get my negligee . . .

FRED (*Into phone*): Fine—fine—we'll send Billy right over to pick it up—

BILLY: Hey—

FRED: And he'll bring something else for Sally. . . . Merry Christmas, Sam—we'll see you tomorrow. (*He hangs up.*)

BILLY: Hey, Pop, you mean I have to—

FRED: Hurry, son—(*Handing him package with scrapbook*) —and don't argue. It'll only take you a few minutes—

BUD: But, Dad, what's Sally going to think—

FRED: Now, don't you start. . . . Run, Billy.

BILLY: Oh, all right. (*He runs out right center.*)

BUD (*Looking woebegone*): Of course I'm glad Mom's going to have her present, but Sally'll be pretty disappointed.

FRED (*All cheerful*): Listen, son—smile—smile. It's almost Christmas—Merry Christmas.

BUD: She may even be mad—and well—a man doesn't want his best girl mad at Christmas.

FRED: Now—now—don't worry—everything's fine. Wonderful time—Christmas.

BUD: I notice you didn't feel—

FRED: Why, I feel wonderful now. Agnes, I'll bet I can get that wreath straight in two shakes—(*He climbs up the ladder.*)

AGNES: I hope so—and then we can get that ladder out of here. Oh, dear, but I don't know what I'm going to do. The tree just doesn't look right without the Christmas angel—(RUBY *appears in doorway at left with several Christmas packages, one large one.*)

RUBY: Is that Billy boy around?

AGNES: No, Ruby.

RUBY: Well, I've been wanting to give you these—to put under the tree. There's a few little things for all of you—

FRED (*Getting down from ladder*): Ruby, you shouldn't have—

RUBY: And then this here big one's for that Billy boy. Mad as I get at that child, I sure think a lot of him.

AGNES: Ruby, thank you—(*Taking presents and putting them under tree*)—and you mustn't forget to hang your sock up on the mantel tonight—

RUBY: I won't—and I'm all done with the sandwiches, so bring on those "caroleers."

AGNES: Good.

RUBY (*Looking toward* FRED): You through with that ladder, Mr. Saunders? I'll take it. (*With one sweep of her arm she collapses the ladder, tucks it under her arm and goes out left.* BILLY *rushes in right center, carrying a large flat box.*)

BILLY: Here it is, Pop—

FRED (*Taking it*): Wonderful—wonderful, Billy.

AGNES: Oh, Fred—let me see—

FRED (*Shaking finger at her and placing package under tree*): Now—now—mustn't open till Christmas.

BUD: What—what did Sally say?

BILLY: She didn't say anything. I just saw Mr. Burton, and look what he gave me. (*He is eating candy again.*)

AGNES: Are you eating again?

BUD (*Sadly*): If Sally didn't even show up, she must be pretty angry.

BILLY (*Sing-song*): Sally's mad and I'm glad. . . . (*The phone rings and* BUD *rushes to it.*)

BUD: Hello—Sally? Oh, gosh, I—what? You what? . . . You like the scrapbook? . . . You don't know how relieved

I am. . . . Yes . . . yes, I guess you're right. . . . Well, I'll see you in a little while, Sally. We're supposed to start caroling at seven-thirty. . . . O.K., goodbye. (*He hangs up, all smiles.*) She likes it—she likes it—she said she guessed the negligee was really too old for her, after all.

AGNES: Oh, she did, did she?

FRED (*Sitting down in easy chair*): Agnes, I am ready to start enjoying Christmas.

AGNES: You are? Well, until I find the Christmas angel— (RUBY *enters left carrying the Christmas angel.*)

RUBY: Speak of angels, and you hear the rustle of their wings. Mrs. Saunders, here it is.

AGNES (*Descending on her*): The Christmas angel! Ruby, where on earth did you find—

RUBY: Right where you put it last year, Mrs. Saunders. When I got down that big cut glass bowl we always use for Christmas, there she was.

AGNES: Why, of course—I remember. We forgot to put her away with the rest of the things, so I thought she'd be safe in the punch bowl—well, let's put her on the tree right away. (*She reaches for a chair and is about to get up on it.*)

BUD: Hey, Mom, let me—look out—you'll break your neck.

AGNES: Well, I wouldn't want to do that—not at this point when Christmas is about to begin—(BUD *takes the angel and places it on top of the tree.*) That's perfect.

FRED: It's what that tree needed—the finishing touch.

BILLY: Can't we have it lit up now? I'm going to turn off some of these lights. (*He goes around turning off lights.*)

AGNES: Now—I hope the tree lights all work. (*She switches tree lights on. There are "Oh's" and "Ah's" from everyone as they look at tree.*)

BUD (*After a pause*): Gosh, there—there's something about Christmas that kind of gets you, isn't there? (*Voices off in the distance sing "God Rest You Merry, Gentlemen." BUD turns quickly.*) It's the carolers, and I ought to be with them—what'll they think?

FRED: Well, go on, son—get your voice in there.

BUD: O.K.—well—I'll see you later—Merry Christmas! (*He rushes out right center.*)

AGNES (*Calling*): Bring them all in for sandwiches, Bud.

RUBY: Well, I'd better hustle some food in here if that crowd of young'uns is coming, and you all must need some sustenance too.

BILLY: Ruby, can't I help? I'll put the plates on the tea wagon for you.

RUBY: You sure can, boy—you run right on out and get the big sandwich plates off the top shelf for me.

BILLY: O.K. (*He exits left.*)

RUBY: Land sakes, the spirit of Christmas must be here for sure the way that boy runs to help—

AGNES: Yes, Ruby, it seems we all appreciate each other more when the spirit of good will toward men is with us—

FRED: That's right, Ruby, and while I think of it there's no better time than Christmas Eve to tell you how much we think of—well—how much we love you—

AGNES: You needn't be embarrassed about it, Fred—of course we love Ruby. (*She smiles at* RUBY *and then at* FRED.)

RUBY: I know you do (*Her voice sounds tearful.*), and all I can say—well, all I can say is— (*She takes a handkerchief from her apron pocket and dabs her eyes and hurriedly exits left.* AGNES *and* FRED *look at each other and smile.*)

FRED (*Sprawling in easy chair. Smiling*): "God's in His Heaven— All's right with the world."

AGNES (*Going back of him and leaning over and kissing him on the forehead*): Yes, dear—Merry Christmas. (*The carolers are right outside the Saunders' home now and begin singing "Silent Night, Holy Night."*)

AGNES: Listen . . .

FRED: Beautiful. . . . Can you hear Bud?—That voice of his—it has qualities that are—well—(*Carried away*)— Well, Agnes, it sounds almost angelic.

AGNES: No, Fred.

FRED: What do you mean, no?

AGNES: No, Fred—he sounds too much like you. (*They smile and he reaches up and pulls her down to him and kisses her.*)

FRED: You win. . . . Merry Christmas! (*The voices of carolers up on "Holy Night" as the curtain falls, and continue to end of song.*)

THE END

Merry Christmas, Crawfords!

by Mildred Hark and Noel McQueen

Characters

JOHN CRAWFORD
ALICE CRAWFORD, *his wife*
MYRA CRAWFORD, *15*
TED CRAWFORD, *13*   *their*
JANET CRAWFORD, *11*   *children*
BOBBY CRAWFORD, *8*
MAILMAN
BILL COLEMAN, *electric light repairman*
HELEN COLEMAN, *his wife*
JIMMY COLEMAN, *their 8-year-old son*
GRACE SAUNDERS, *a neighbor*
FRANCES SAUNDERS, *11*
LARRY SAUNDERS, *16*
MR. BASCOLM, *Mr. Crawford's boss*
MRS. BASCOLM
TEEN-AGERS

TIME: *Late afternoon, the day before Christmas.*
SETTING: *Crawfords' partly furnished living room. On rear wall center, there is a fireplace with mantel. Partially trimmed Christmas tree stands right, with lights strung on it, but unlighted. Ladder stands near tree, and two cartons sit next to it on floor. A small radio and a telephone are on table right and a television set left.*
AT RISE: MYRA *sits on floor, pinning up hem of curtains*

at window right. TED *sits on chair near phone, holding receiver to his ear.* JANET *and* BOBBY *are trimming tree.*

MYRA (*Getting up from floor after pinning up second curtain*): There, I've pinned up our old curtains. That will have to do till we can shorten them. At least the living room will look a little respectable for Christmas.

JANET (*Hanging ornament on tree*): And we have a Christmas tree, anyhow, if we don't have anything else. (*She steps back, looking at tree.*) Even if the trimmings are skimpy. . . .

BOBBY: Yeah, but Janet, where *are* all our decorations? We had lots more last year.

JANET: I don't know, Bobby. They must have gotten lost during the moving. If only I could find that box with the prettiest balls!

TED (*Into phone*): Hello. . . . Hello. . . . But I *have* been waiting, and this is important. (MR. CRAWFORD *enters left, holding out small Christmas angel.*)

MR. CRAWFORD: Myra, look what I found for our tree.

MYRA: Dad, the Christmas angel! Where in the world did you find it?

MR. CRAWFORD: With the kitchen pots and pans. I was unpacking them, and I found the angel in that old percolator we never use.

JANET: Oh, good! Let me have her, Dad. She goes right on the top of the tree. (*Takes angel, climbs ladder and puts angel on top*)

MR. CRAWFORD: There, that makes it look more like home, doesn't it? And what about the lights? Did you call the electric company, Ted?

TED: That's what I'm doing now. But I'm just waiting. They keep switching me from person to person.

MR. CRAWFORD: I can't understand it. I called them three times today and they were supposed to be here this morning. Well, tell them they've got to do something. It'll be getting dark and we can't be without lights for Christmas.

BOBBY (*Sadly*): The tree won't look right without lights.

MR. CRAWFORD: Tell them you're talking for me, Ted. I've got to find the big roaster or we won't be able to cook the turkey tomorrow. I've come across everything else— the old iron pot we use for camping, the waffle iron, the ice cream freezer (*As he goes off left*)—everything but the roaster!

MYRA: Poor Dad.

TED (*Into phone*): Hello . . .

BOBBY: We may not even have any turkey.

MYRA (*Motioning toward* TED): Shh-h-h.

TED (*Into phone*): Hello, I'm speaking for Mr. John Crawford. We've just moved into a new house and you were supposed to send someone to turn on our lights. It's 123 Acorn Street. . . . But you have all that information and you've got the order. The gas company and the phone company were here yesterday. . . . Oh. . . . You're what? . . . You're closing? . . . But what if the man doesn't come? . . . What'll we do? . . . Where can we call? . . . Oh, you think what? . . . Oh, I see. . . . What? . . . Well, yes, Merry Christmas to you, too. (*He hangs up.*) What nerve! She said Merry Christmas.

JANET: Merry Christmas without any lights?

TED: Oh, she says if he has the order, he'll get here. She thinks the snow may have delayed him.

BOBBY: But if he doesn't come, we won't have any lights on our tree.

MYRA: Tree lights? We won't have any lights at all! We'll be in total darkness.

JANET: Total darkness for Christmas! Can you imagine anything more depressing?

TED (*Sighing*): If you ask me, this whole holiday's depressing.

MYRA: Come on, Ted. We have to keep our spirits up for Mom and Dad's sake. They must feel just as bad as we do—in a strange town, without any of their old friends.

TED: Yes, I guess you're right. About the only person they've met is Dad's new boss.

JANET: That old Mr. Bascolm. All he could talk about was the Bascolm Manufacturing Company.

BOBBY: He's like Mr. Scrooge. Spoiling our Christmas.

MYRA: At least Dad has a good job there.

JANET: But why did it have to start now? I wish we could have waited until after the holidays to move.

MYRA: We couldn't, though. Dad's job starts the first of the year, and we were lucky to find this house and get moved in before then.

TED: It certainly is a mess, though. (*He is looking out window at right.*) Anyway, it looks like Christmas outside with all the fresh snow.

MYRA (*Looking out; wistfully*): Yes, don't the houses look pretty with snow on their roofs and the decorations out front? And look, the mailman is still delivering packages all up and down the street.

BOBBY: I guess he won't be delivering any packages to the Crawford house.

JANET: Packages? We won't even get any Christmas cards. There wasn't time to tell anyone about our change of address.

TED: The post office has our new address, so they'll forward our cards and packages eventually.

BOBBY (*Sadly*): Eventually—when is that? I wanted some presents for Christmas.

MYRA: There will be a few presents, Bobby. We didn't send all of them through the mail.

BOBBY: Oh, sure, the ones we brought for each other in

our suitcases—but what about Mom and Dad's presents for us? And Grandma and Grandpa's? The post office doesn't know where those boxes are.

TED: It's too bad they're lost, but maybe the post office will find them after the Christmas rush is over.

JANET: That's no fun.

BOBBY: Yeah. And after Christmas, they won't even be *Christmas* presents.

MYRA: I guess it won't seem the same, Bobby, but . . . (*She looks out window.*) Look, there's company arriving for Christmas across the street. They've got suitcases.

BOBBY (*Looking out*): I'll bet it's their grandpa and grandma.

JANET (*Sniffling*): Our Grandpa and Grandma are thousands of miles away—they won't get here on time.

TED: Come on now, Janet, cheer up, and put the rest of the stuff on the tree. Try to hang things that will cover that bare spot on the side.

JANET: Oh, all right, but I don't see why we couldn't at least have had a better tree. (*She hangs more ornaments.*)

BOBBY: You can't even buy a decent Christmas tree in this town.

MYRA: You can't buy a decent tree anywhere at the last minute, Bobby.

BOBBY: At home you could. Dad always took us to at least six places before we chose one.

MYRA: Yes, but that was at home—in the city. We don't know where to look for trees here in the suburbs.

BOBBY: Suburbs. I hate the suburbs! (MRS. CRAWFORD *enters left, carrying small box.*)

MRS. CRAWFORD: What's that, Bobby?

BOBBY: I said, I hate the suburbs.

MRS. CRAWFORD (*Cheerfully*): Why, Bobby, we've only been here one day. Give the new town a chance. (*Looking around*) Why, you kids have done wonders. The curtains look much better, Myra. And the tree looks great! You've done a fine job of decorating it. And I have a surprise for you. I found the box with the best Christmas tree balls.

JANET: Oh, Mom! (*Taking box*) Now we can really make the tree look nice.

MRS. CRAWFORD: Of course you can. And cheer up, Bobby, the Crawford family is going to have a Christmas dinner in spite of everything. Your father found the big roaster and now I'm going to make the stuffing for the turkey. (*She goes off left.*)

BOBBY: Oh, boy! Turkey with stuffing.

TED: Good old Mom. All she has to do is throw a few cheerful words around and things seem more like Christmas.

MYRA: Yes. (*Looking out right*) And—and look, the mailman is coming with a big package!

BOBBY: He is?

JANET: The presents!

BOBBY: I'll go! I'll go! (*He starts toward front door, right.*)

MYRA (*From window*): Never mind. I was wrong. He's taking the package to the house next door.

TED: Well, let's get the rest of the decorations on the tree. Open the box, Janet.

JANET (*Untying box*): O.K. (*She opens box; in dismay*) Oh, no! (MYRA, TED and BOBBY *rush over and look into box.*)

MYRA: Oh, dear, they're all broken!

BOBBY (*Shaking his head*): All busted! What's the use of trying to have Christmas when everything goes wrong?

JANET: Let's turn on the radio. Maybe if we listen to some Christmas carols we'll get into the right mood.

BOBBY (*Brightly, going to radio and turning it on*): That's a good idea!

TED: It would be a good idea if we had any electricity.

BOBBY (*Turning radio off*): Nuts. I forgot about that. We can't use the radio or the TV set. (MRS. CRAWFORD *enters left with hat and coat on.*)

MYRA (*Surprised*): Why, Mom—are you going out?

MRS. CRAWFORD (*Smiling*): Yes, I am.

MYRA: But I thought you were going to stuff the turkey.

MRS. CRAWFORD: No, I'm letting that go till this evening. In fact, we're letting everything go till this evening. Your father and I decided that straightening the house wasn't nearly as important as Christmas presents.

BOBBY: Presents?

MRS. CRAWFORD: Yes, we're driving over to the shopping center and shop like mad till the stores close.

TED: Hooray—Merry Christmas!

OTHERS: Merry Christmas! Merry Christmas! (MR. CRAWFORD *enters left, in hat and overcoat.*)

MR. CRAWFORD: Merry Christmas!

ALL (*Together*): Merry Christmas, Dad!

MR. CRAWFORD: I may look like Dad to you, but in fact, you are gazing at Mr. and Mrs. Santa Claus! We are about to climb into our sleigh and our trusty reindeer will whisk us away to the North Pole. And when we return—the Crawfords will have a Merry Christmas, indeed! (*He starts right with* MRS. CRAWFORD. *Phone rings. They stop and turn.*)

TED (*Laughing*): Better wait, Mr. Santa Claus, this may be for you. (TED *picks up phone.*) Hello? . . . Merry Christmas. . . . Oh, yes, sir. (*Holding out phone*) It *is* for you, Dad. It's Mr. Bascolm.

MRS. CRAWFORD (*Puzzled*): Mr. Bascolm? What in the world can he want with you on Christmas Eve?

BOBBY: It's old Mr. Scrooge!

MR. CRAWFORD: Shh-h, Bobby, he'll hear you. (*Taking phone from* TED) Hello, Mr. Bascolm. . . . Why . . . why. . . . Well, of course we're not very straightened around yet, but my wife and I were just going out to do a bit of last-minute Christmas shopping. . . . Yes. . . . Yes, we were just going out the door. . . . An—an office party? . . . Well—well . . . that's very nice of you to invite us, Mr. Bascolm, but I'm really afraid . . . Yes. . . . Yes, well, as I said we really have to do some shopping. Things have been a bit rushed, you know, and—but Mr. Bascolm, we just can't. . . . Well, of course, my wife will be glad to talk to Mrs. Bascolm. (*Putting hand over phone; to* Mrs. Crawford) He wants you to talk to Mrs. Bascolm. There's a party at the office, and—

Mrs. Crawford: But John, you know we can't go. I don't want to go. I—

Mr. Crawford: I know, I know, neither do I, so you tell her. He's putting her on now. (*Listening in phone*) Yes. . . . Hello, Mrs. Bascolm, here's Mrs. Crawford. (*Holding phone to* Mrs. Crawford)

Mrs. Crawford (*Taking phone*): Hello, Mrs. Bascolm. My, that is kind of you and your husband to want us to come to the party, but—but (*Weakly*)—but Mrs. Bascolm . . . Yes. . . . Yes. . . . Every year . . . all the office employees. . . . Well, of course, but—yes. . . . Yes, Mrs. Bascolm. Yes, I understand, and we'll be seeing you. . . . Goodbye. (*She hangs up phone.*)

Mr. Crawford: You—you didn't say we'd go?

Mrs. Crawford: What else could I say? They have it every year. All the office employees will be there. They are there right now waiting to meet us.

Mr. Crawford: Oh—oh—so they are waiting. (*He sighs.*) Well, then I suppose there's nothing else to do. We'll have to go right over.

Bobby (*Almost in tears*): But—but what about our presents?

Mrs. Crawford: Bobby, we'll make it up to you. (*Turning to* Mr. Crawford) Oh, John, it isn't fair. All our Christmas plans are being spoiled because of your new job. I almost wish you still had your old one and we were back in the city.

MR. CRAWFORD: I know just how you feel. I'm disappointed, myself, but it's too late now—we have to go through with this party. (*To children*) Sorry, kids—I was wrong when I introduced you to Mr. and Mrs. Santa. (*With wry smile*) We're just Mr. and Mrs. Crawford, going to an office party.

BOBBY (*Angrily*): That rotten office! They ought to call it the Scrooge Manufacturing Company. They ruined our Christmas.

MRS. CRAWFORD: Oh, Bobby! I don't want to go to this party—but—but, I guess we have to go.

MR. CRAWFORD: Let's get it over with, dear. Come on. (MR. *and* MRS. CRAWFORD *cross to right exit.*) Goodbye!

MRS. CRAWFORD: Bye! (*They start to exit.*)

CHILDREN (*Calling, ad lib*): Bye! Have a good time! Hurry home! (*Etc.*)

MR. CRAWFORD (*Turning*): Oh, Ted—if the man ever gets here about the lights, you know where the fuse box and the main switch are.

TED: Yes, Dad. I'll show him.

MR. CRAWFORD: Thanks. We'll see you as soon as we can. Bye. (*They exit.*)

TED: Poor Mom and Dad. I guess they feel even worse than we do. And who knows if the man from the electric company will ever get here?

JANET: I don't know if I even care. (*Almost crying*) And —and no one could feel worse than I do.

BOBBY: Me too.

MYRA: But—it doesn't seem right to be miserable on Christmas, just because we've moved to a new place. Christmas ought to be everywhere.

BOBBY: But there ought to be presents.

TED: Oh, it isn't just the presents, Bobby. Christmas is more than just presents.

MYRA: Of course. It's—it's a kind of a feeling you get. And that feeling is made up of lots of things like—well, Christmas means surprises and secrets and sharing, and doing things for people and having them do things for you. Other years we've had all these things—friends and neighbors running in and out—

JANET: That's because we were back home. I agree with Mom. I wish we were back there right now. This afternoon I'd be going over to see Lizzie Slater's Christmas tree and tomorrow they'd all come over to see ours.

BOBBY: Sure, and I'd probably go sledding in the park with Tommy McGinnis. I miss Tommy.

TED (*Laughing*): I thought you were mad at Tommy. Last time you went out sledding you had a fight.

BOBBY: Well, here, there's not even anyone to fight with.

MYRA (*Laughing a little*): I know just what you mean. We've lost all our real friends. I was going to the holiday dance with Charlie, and now I don't know a single boy in town, so—well, even if they do have a dance, no one will ask me. (*Knock on door is heard.*)

TED: Well, I guess we'll get some lights, anyway. (*Crosses to door right and opens it, revealing* MAILMAN, *holding large package with torn wrapping paper*)

MAILMAN: You people expecting a package from out of town?

TED: A Christmas package! Is it really for us?

MAILMAN: The wrapping is so torn that all I can make out is the name of the street and (*Pointing*) over here it says from Mr. and Mrs. G . . . I can't make out the rest.

MYRA: Granger—that's Grandma and Grandpa's name.

MAILMAN: Granger, huh? I guess that must be it. Glad I found you in time. (*Putting down carton and holding slip and pencil out to* TED) Sign here.

TED (*As he signs*): I certainly will.

MAILMAN (*As he goes out right*): Merry Christmas! (BOBBY *pulls carton into middle of room.*)

BOBBY (*Excitedly*): Presents! We've got some presents!

JANET: Grandma and Grandpa's presents. They got here after all!

BOBBY (*Starting to rip open carton*): Let's take them out and put them under the tree.

TED: Now, wait, Bobby. Do you think we ought to, Myra, before Mom and Dad get home?

MYRA: No, I don't. We all wanted a surprise, and now we've got one. Let's save it to surprise Mom and Dad, too, when they get home.

TED: I agree.

MYRA: And this package has given me an idea. There must be other things we can do to surprise Mom and Dad. Let's try not worrying about ourselves so much and think of other things we can do to make it a Merry Christmas for Mom and Dad.

TED: I have an idea. (*He goes to carton near tree and takes out handful of Christmas cards.*) Here are some of last year's cards Mom saved. They'll look just as good as new ones if we stand them around the room. (*He stands cards on mantel.*)

MYRA: It makes it seem more like home already!

JANET: I want to put some around, too. (*Picks up handful of cards and looks left*) How about on top of the television set?

TED: That's fine. (*Puts more cards on mantel*) Bobby, why don't you put some on that table near the window?

BOBBY: O.K. (*Takes cards from carton and stands them on table at right*) I like this one with the big fat Santa.

MYRA: Why, the whole room looks more Christmasy. You know what? Mom was worrying because she hadn't had time for mince pies. But I'm going to make some Christmas cookies.

BOBBY: Cookies? You mean in the shape of stars and lambs and angels?

MYRA: Why not? Dad was unpacking the kitchen stuff and the cookie cutters must be there somewhere.

TED: I'd better get to work, too. I'll unpack all those cartons in Mom and Dad's room and put as much in place as I can. Will they be surprised!

JANET: May I help cut out the cookies?

MYRA: Maybe. But first you'd better finish the tree and get these boxes and the ladder out of the way.

JANET: All right, I'll hurry. (*She starts putting things on tree again.*)

BOBBY (*Looking out window right*): Hey, guess what? The electric company truck is outside! And here comes the man!

TED: Terrific! (*Goes right toward door*) Now our Christmas will really get started. We can have lights on the tree. . . . (*Opens door and admits* BILL COLEMAN, *who enters with toolbox*) Hello! We sure are glad you're here.

BILL (*Gruffly*): Is this the Crawford family? (*As* TED *nods*) Sign here. (*Holds out order book and pen*)

TED: But what's this for? We still don't have any lights, so why should I sign?

BILL: Just to show that I made the call.

TED: But what about the lights?

BILL: I've got an order just to hook 'em on, and there's no wire running from the pole out back.

MYRA: But that's terrible. Can't you run a wire?

BILL: Not today I can't. There's too much ice and snow on the pole to do it with my equipment. You'll have to wait until after Christmas.

JANET (*Sadly*): No lights after all.

BOBBY (*Almost crying*): Now our tree's no good.

JIMMY (*From offstage*): Hey, Dad! Dad! (JIMMY *rushes in; to* BILL) Hey, Dad, come out and look at my new sled!

BILL: Hold it, Jim. You can't come running into strange houses this way without being invited. What's the idea?

JIMMY: I saw your truck outside, so I knew you were here. Mom gave me my sled early because of the snow.

BILL: Oh, she did, did she? (*To others*) My son's just excited. Sorry that he bothered you this way. We'll be going now—I'll be back after Christmas to make the hookup. (*Turns to go with* JIMMY)

BOBBY: Just a second! (*They turn around.*) Could I—that is, would you let me try your sled?

JIMMY: Sure!

BOBBY (*Excited*): Neat-o! Oh, but we all have to plan a Christmas surprise for Mom and Dad.

MYRA: No, Bobby, I think going out for a while is a good idea. And sledding—why, that'll be just like home. There'll still be plenty for you to do when you get back.

BOBBY: O.K. Wait till I get my jacket! (*Rushes off left*)

TED (*To* BILL): I hope this is all right with you, Mr.—

BILL: My name's Coleman—Bill Coleman. We live just a few doors down the street. Sure, let the boys go sledding. (BOBBY *re-enters, wearing jacket.*)

BOBBY: Hey, Jimmy, does your sled steer?

JIMMY: Of course it does! I'll show you. (*Boys rush out right.*)

BILL: Well, see you after Christmas. (*Exits*)

MYRA: I guess it's not Mr. Coleman's fault about the lights, but he didn't try very hard, did he?

TED: Never mind. I'll go downstairs and see if there are any candles or flashlights in the basement. (*Exits left.*)

MYRA (*Looking out window right*): The boys are off in the snow with Bobby pushing the sled. Maybe he won't mind so much about the lights if he has fun sledding. (*Crossing left*) Guess I'll go to work on the cookies. Finish up the tree, will you, Janet?

JANET: O.K. (MYRA *exits left.* JANET *starts to trim tree.*

There is a knock on door. JANET *crosses to door and opens it, revealing* FRANCES.)

FRANCES: Hi. My name's Frances Saunders, and I live in the next block.

JANET: Oh, did you come over to get acquainted?

FRANCES (*Stepping inside, leaving door open*): No, I came over to get that Christmas package. (*Pointing to wrapped box*) It's our presents from Grandma and Grandpa.

JANET (*Startled*): Why—why, it is not! It's *our* presents from Grandma and Grandpa.

FRANCES: No. We asked the mailman, and he said he must have made a mistake and delivered it here. My big brother is coming over for it.

JANET (*Backing toward carton*): Well, you—you can't have it. (FRANCES *dodges around* JANET *and grabs string on carton.*)

FRANCES: We can too have it. It's ours! (JANET *also grabs string. They tug back and forth.*)

JANET (*Shouting*): It's ours, I tell you, it's ours! The mailman said so.

MYRA (*Rushing in left*): Janet, Janet—what's going on here?

JANET: She says this is their Christmas package, and it can't be.

MYRA: Let go of those strings. Both of you. (*As they let go, to* FRANCES) Now, who are you? What's your name?

FRANCES (*Excitedly*): I'm Frances Saunders and the mailman said our package was left here, and—and—(*Looking toward open door where* LARRY *has just appeared*) —and this is my brother, Larry. Larry, they won't let me have it.

LARRY (*Stepping in*): Frances, be quiet. You shouldn't have come here without me in the first place.

MYRA (*To* LARRY; *coldly*): Would you mind telling me

what's going on? I suppose you must be this girl's brother.

LARRY: Yes—I'm Larry Saunders. You see, we've been expecting the Christmas box that always comes from our grandparents, and when we asked the mailman about it, he said he probably left it here by mistake. (TED *enters left.*)

MYRA (*Pointing to package*): Ted, they say this is their package, not ours!

TED: Oh, they do? (*Going to box and pulling off string*) There's an easy way to find out. We'll look at the packages inside. (*He opens box, takes out package in Christmas wrappings, and reads tag.*) "To Mother, from Grandpa and Grandma."

JANET: See?

TED (*Taking out two more*): Oh-oh. (*Reads*) "To Frances from Grandpa and Grandma," and here's one to Larry.

FRANCES: There, what did I tell you?

JANET (*Stubbornly*): But it says from Grandpa and Grandma.

MYRA: But, Janet, lots of families have grandparents—

JANET (*Tearfully*): It's not fair. They were all the presents we had.

TED: It is too bad all right, but if they're not ours, they're not ours. Well, take 'em away, Larry.

JANET (*Crying*): Just everything has gone wrong. The Christmas tree balls were all broken, and then. . . .

FRANCES (*Interrupting*): Oh, who cares about a few Christmas tree balls? (*She rushes out, right.*)

LARRY (*Picking up box*): I don't know what's gotten into Frances. She doesn't usually act this way.

MYRA: I guess she's upset.

LARRY: Well, I suppose. But it's too bad you got the package first and—and had to be disappointed.

TED: It can't be helped. We just moved here, you see, and

none of our presents have come in the mail yet. The post office says they're lost. We wouldn't have minded about the package, except—well, we didn't have time to get ready for Christmas.

LARRY: Yeah, I understand. (*Going to door, with package*) Well, so long.

TED (*Closing door*): So long—Merry Christmas. (JANET *is sniffling a little.* TED *and* MYRA *stand looking at each other sadly.*)

MYRA (*Almost crying*): Oh, Ted. . . . (BOBBY *rushes in, right. His jacket is torn and dirty.*)

BOBBY (*Heatedly*): Say, where's that guy going with our presents from Grandma and Grandpa?

TED: They're not ours, Bobby. It was a mistake.

BOBBY: A mistake? But . . .

MYRA: Bobby Crawford, what have you been doing? Your clothes are a mess.

BOBBY: Oh, nothing very much. I—I had a fight with Jimmy.

TED: What?

BOBBY: Well, he said I wasn't as strong as he was because I came from the city. So we had a fight, and I washed his face with snow.

TED: But, Bobby, you shouldn't have done that. You—

MYRA: You picked a fine person to fight with, Bobby. Now Mr. Coleman will be furious with us, and we'll never get any lights.

JANET (*Looking out window*): And here comes that Frances, running up our walk. I don't want to see her again.

MYRA: Now, Janet, take it easy. We're getting in wrong with our neighbors as it is. (MYRA *opens door just as* FRANCES *appears in doorway, holding cardboard box.*)

FRANCES (*Holding out box*): See? I knew you didn't have to worry about a few Christmas tree balls. I ran home and told my mother, and she sent me right back with these. We've got lots of extras we never use. (*Holds out box to* MYRA)

MYRA (*Taking box*): Why—why, Frances, that's so nice! Janet, look!

JANET (*Peering into box*): Oh, they're beautiful! You— you mean we can use them on our tree?

FRANCES (*Excitedly*): Of course. And that isn't all. Everybody is coming to help.

MYRA: What do you mean by that?

FRANCES: When I told Mother how sad you all were when we took your—I mean, our presents away from you, she looked sort of cross the way she does sometimes when she's thinking. And then she said, "Why, it's terrible, just terrible!"

TED: But they *were* your presents.

FRANCES: That isn't what she meant. She said people who move into a new house always need help to get settled. And here we've all been thinking about our own Christmas and doing nothing about your family. Larry wants to help, too. He said we should all come over here and cheer up our new neighbors. (*To* MYRA) I think he mostly meant you!

MYRA (*Smiling*): He—he did?

FRANCES: Yes, and he's gone to get some of his friends, and Mother's on the way over, too. (*To* JANET) And . . . and may I help you finish decorating your tree?

JANET: Of course, Frances! (*They go to tree and hang balls on it.*)

TED: Well, if all the neighbors are coming to help, it sounds as though we may have surprises for Mom and Dad after all.

MYRA: You're right. But there's so much to do that I don't know where to begin.

FRANCES: You won't have to worry about that when my

mother gets here. She's the best organizer in town. Every year she organizes the voters' drive, and the PTA fair.

TED: That's quite a recommendation! (*Knock on door is heard.*) That must be your mother now. (*Opens door;* MRS. SAUNDERS *hurries in, carrying bulging shopping bag.*) Hello. You must be Mrs. Saunders.

MRS. SAUNDERS: Yes, I am. I just put a few things into this bag on my way out of the house.

BOBBY (*Looking into bag*): Mm-m-m! Oranges and cookies and candy!

MRS. SAUNDERS: Wait a minute! These are for Christmas —you can't eat them now.

MYRA (*Laughing*): That's right, Bobby. (*Going to* MRS. SAUNDERS) It's so good of you to come, Mrs. Saunders. I'm Myra Crawford, and this is Ted, and Janet, and Bobby—with the appetite.

MRS. SAUNDERS: We'll get acquainted as we work—there isn't much time. Where are your parents?

MYRA: Oh, they had to go to an office party where our dad has a new job.

MRS. SAUNDERS: Office party on Christmas Eve! Why, that's terrible. I'll bet you're hardly unpacked.

TED: We straightened up this room as well as we could, but the rest of the house is still kind of upset.

MRS. SAUNDERS: Naturally it is. I saw the moving van here yesterday, and I meant to come over, but there was so much to do that it slipped my mind. Well, when the others get here, you two will have to show them what things have to be moved, and how to arrange the rooms. Now, what about getting things ready for your dinner tomorrow?

MYRA: Oh, we've got a turkey, and Mom is going to stuff it when she gets home.

MRS. SAUNDERS: After the party? Nonsense. She'll be too

tired. We can take care of that right now. Is your phone in yet?

TED: Yes, it's right there. (*Points*)

MRS. SAUNDERS (*Going quickly to phone and dialing*): Helen is the best cook in town. She'll have that turkey ready for the oven in no time. (*Into phone*) Hello, Helen. . . . Yes . . . yes, I'm over at the home of that new family at 123, and they need a turkey stuffed for tomorrow. . . . Yes, that's what I said. . . . Then you'll be over? Yes. (*Laughs*) Then you're already acquainted with part of the family? . . . All right, hurry over. We haven't much time. (*Hanging up phone*)

MYRA: What did you mean, she's acquainted with our family?

MRS. SAUNDERS (*Smiling*): She says that Bobby, here, washed her son Jimmy's face with snow—and it hasn't been so clean in weeks!

BOBBY: You mean—she wasn't mad at me?

MRS. SAUNDERS: She didn't sound angry when she told me about it. (LARRY *and* TEEN-AGERS *are heard laughing and talking offstage.*) That must be Larry and his friends coming now. (TED *opens door.* LARRY *enters, followed by* TEEN-AGERS.)

LARRY: Now, one, two, three.

TEEN-AGERS (*Together*): Merry Christmas, Crawfords!

MYRA: Merry Christmas! Oh, this is wonderful.

LARRY: Merry Christmas, Myra.

MYRA: Merry Christmas, Larry.

MRS. SAUNDERS: Never mind the Merry Christmas until after we've done our work. Ted, you take some of this crew with you and put them to work.

TED: O.K. I guess the first thing is to lug a lot of stuff down to the basement, so that we can put the dining room furniture in place.

LARRY: Lead the way! (TED, LARRY, *and several* TEEN-

AGERS *exit left, laughing and talking.*)

MRS. SAUNDERS: Now, Myra, what needs to be done upstairs?

MYRA: Well, the bedrooms are still a mess, and there are linens to be put on the shelves, and the rugs can be unrolled, too, as soon as we get enough space cleared. (*She exits left, followed by other* TEEN-AGERS, *all talking happily.*)

MRS. SAUNDERS: Well, that's a start. Bobby, why don't you take that stepladder and put it away somewhere?

BOBBY: All right. (*He folds ladder and carries it off left.*)

MRS. SAUNDERS (*To* FRANCES *and* JANET): And when you girls finish with the tree, take both these cartons to the basement.

JANET: We will, Mrs. Saunders. Your Christmas balls do make the tree look better. If only we had lights.

MRS. SAUNDERS: You mean to say your lights aren't turned on?

JANET: No. Mr. Coleman was here and he says he can't fix them.

MRS. SAUNDERS: That's too bad. But, if Bill Coleman can't fix them, nobody can. We'll have to get you some candles for the mantel before it gets dark. (*Knock on door is heard.* MRS. SAUNDERS *opens it, letting in* HELEN COLEMAN, *carrying wrapped pie, and* JIMMY, *carrying candlesticks with candles.*) Oh, good, Helen, glad you came so fast.

HELEN: Hello, Grace. Glad to help.

MRS. SAUNDERS: And, Jimmy, we were just saying we needed candles for the mantel.

JIMMY: Dad said there were no lights here, so Mom said to bring these. (*Hands candlesticks to* MRS. SAUNDERS)

MRS. SAUNDERS: Thank you—they'll be just fine. (*She puts them on mantel.*)

BOBBY (*Rushing in left*): Wow, are they getting things straightened out in a hurry! (*Seeing* HELEN *and* JIMMY) Oh—hello.

HELEN: Hello, Bobby. Why did you run away so fast when I came out on the front porch at our house?

BOBBY: Well, I—I thought you'd be mad because I was fighting with Jimmy.

HELEN: Oh, I don't suppose it's the last fight you two will have. But I wanted to give you this mince pie to bring home.

BOBBY: Mince pie?

HELEN: Yes, I heard you telling Jimmy your mother wouldn't have time to make any and we had three.

BOBBY (*Taking pie and holding it up*): Hooray! Look, Janet! We've got mince pie for Christmas! (*He puts it on table.*)

JANET: I—I guess we're getting almost everything for Christmas. (*Tree lights come on.*) Oh, look—the lights are on!

BOBBY: The lights are on!

FRANCES (*Looking at tree*): It's beautiful!

MRS. SAUNDERS: Yes, there's nothing as beautiful as a Christmas tree, I always say.

JANET (*Picking up carton*): Let's take the cartons out and tell everyone to come and look at the tree.

FRANCES: All right. (*Picks up other carton and runs off left behind* JANET)

JANET (*From offstage*): Everybody come and see the tree! The lights are on!

MRS. SAUNDERS: And Bill said he couldn't fix them. Was he trying to fool somebody?

HELEN: No, he was serious when he talked to me—I guess he managed, anyhow. Well, I can't stand here looking at the tree if I'm going to get that bird stuffed before their parents get home. (*She turns toward kitchen, just as* JANET *and* FRANCES *re-enter left, with* MYRA, TED, LARRY, *and* TEEN-AGERS *following them. All exclaim as they see tree. Front door opens and* MR. *and* MRS. CRAWFORD *enter, followed by* MR. *and* MRS. BASCOLM. MR. BASCOLM *carries large package wrapped in Christmas paper.*)

MR. CRAWFORD: What's this? We have company!

BOBBY (*Rushing forward*): I'll say, Dad. They're straightening up the whole house, and Mrs. Coleman brought a mince pie, and Mrs. Saunders some cookies and candy, and Mrs. Coleman is going to stuff the turkey and—and wow, you've got a present!

MR. CRAWFORD: Just a minute, Bobby! One thing at a time. Will someone please tell me what's been going on here?

MRS. SAUNDERS: Well, I guess I'd better, as I've been sort of organizing things. I'm Grace Saunders and you must be Mr. and Mrs. Crawford, and I recognize Mr. and Mrs. Bascolm from pictures I've seen in the paper. The rest of us are just neighbors who have come in to help your family get comfortable in time for Christmas.

MRS. CRAWFORD (*Almost crying*): Why—why—if that isn't the nicest thing I've ever heard of in all my life. I don't know how to thank you.

MR. CRAWFORD: I've already made one speech today, to thank Mr. and Mrs. Bascolm and my new friends at the office. They insisted we go to what they called an office party, but it was really just an occasion for them all to give us a present for the family. So I'll just say what I said before. It's pretty wonderful to move to a new job and a new home, feeling that you'd lost all your old friends, and then to find—well, that you have many new friends all around you. Thank you all. (*Everybody applauds.*)

MR. BASCOLM: Well, I'd applaud, too, if I could put this package down.

MRS. CRAWFORD: Of course! Let's put it right under the tree.

MRS. BASCOLM: My, your tree is beautiful.

MRS. SAUNDERS: And the lights just came on—we don't know how, because Bill Coleman said he couldn't fix them. (BILL *enters left*.) Why, Bill! How did you do it?

BILL: I really didn't do much except tell Mr. and Mrs. Brady next door that there were no lights here, and I couldn't run a line from the pole. So they said to run one from their meter for a day or two. They're too old to get out much, but they told me to come in and say Merry Christmas to you from them.

MRS. CRAWFORD: Of all things! Just everybody is making Christmas nice for us. I can't believe it.

BOBBY: Boy, I like the suburbs. (*Everyone laughs*.)

MR. BASCOLM: It seems to me that I've heard that voice before. (*Laughing*) Yes, sir, it was when I called on the phone today. I distinctly heard him say, "It's old Mr. Scrooge."

BOBBY: Well—well—I—I—

MR. BASCOLM (*Pretending to be angry*): Yes, young man? What have you got to say for yourself?

BOBBY: Well, I—I—

JIMMY: Mr. Bascolm, what he meant was that you are a real good guy like Scrooge in the end of the story.

BOBBY: Yes—yes, that's right, Mr. Scrooge—I mean, Mr. Bascolm.

MR. BASCOLM: Oh. (*Indicating* JIMMY) I take it this boy is a friend of yours.

BOBBY: Him? (*Giving* JIMMY *playful shove*) Sure. He's Jimmy Coleman. He's my buddy. (*All laugh*.)

MR. BASCOLM: Well, that's fine. You stick with him and

you'll do all right. And as long as I'm the nice Mr. Scrooge, I'll say *(Waving arm to include everyone)*—God bless us every one!

ALL: Merry Christmas! *(Curtain)*

THE END

The Christmas Revel

by Claire Boiko

Characters

TOWN CRIER
TOM ⎫
JOAN ⎪
HARRY ⎬ *village children*
JILL ⎪
BETSY ⎪
NAN ⎭
OTHER BOYS AND GIRLS
WILL
KATHERINE DE MONFORT
WALTER DE MONFORT
LADY JOYCE LUCY
LORD THOMAS LUCY (*Lord of Misrule*)
MAID
FOOTMAN
MAYOR
TITANIA (*Queen Elizabeth*)

SCENE 1

TIME: *Christmas afternoon, 1578.*

SETTING: *A village square in Warwickshire, England. If desired, the scene may be played before the curtain.*

AT RISE: TOM, JOAN, HARRY, JILL, BETSY, NAN, *and*
OTHER BOYS AND GIRLS *enter, singing to the tune of*
"Greensleeves."

CHILDREN (*Singing*):
Oh, once upon a time, in England
Lord and commoner mingled so;
On Christmas Eve with yule log blazing
And candles all aglow.
Green, green were the holly branches,
Green, green the mistletoe,
Green, green the pine and laurel
Once in the long ago . . .

TOWN CRIER (*Entering*): Hear ye! Hear ye, good citizens
of Warwickshire! His Lordship, Sir Thomas Lucy, of
the Manor Charlecote, announces a Christmas revel!

CHILDREN: Merry Christmas, town crier!

TOWN CRIER: Merry Christmas, children! Have you heard
the news? A Christmas revel is held at Charlecote this
very evening.

JOAN: Oh, that's nothing to us, crier. That's for ladies with
their noses in the air, and for gentlemen in fine ruffs
and doublets.

TOWN CRIER: Not so. Not so at all, Miss Snippet. 'Tis for
all the people of this village and especially for the children.

CHILDREN (*Ad lib; happily*): The children? A revel? For us?
(*Etc.*)

BETSY (*Shyly*): Do you say it is for all of us?

NAN: Even for me?

TOWN CRIER: Especially for you. This is a special revel—
not like any before it. (*He motions them to draw near.*)
Hear me well. Her Ladyship is having a doll contest.

JILL: Dolls? What sort of dolls?

TOWN CRIER: All sorts of dolls. Rag dolls, wooden dolls,

china dolls and paper dolls. For the best doll brought to the revel, there will be a prize.

CHILDREN: A prize, a prize!

JOAN: And pray, what is it?

TOWN CRIER: A bag of gold sovereigns, that's what.

CHILDREN (*Ad lib; excitedly*): Gold pieces! Prizes! Sovereigns? (*Etc.*)

TOM: Forsooth, this is a contest for girls.

HARRY: His Lordship should have a contest for the boys.

TOWN CRIER: He has. Indeed, fellow, he has. Are there any lads here who are well spoken and have a courtly manner?

BOYS (*Ad lib*): Me! Me! I have! (*Etc.*)

HARRY: Here, town crier. I am Harry of the Duck Farm. The whole town knows how courteous and quick-witted I am.

TOM: No, town crier, take me. I am called Tom. (*Striking a pose*) I speak pure pear-shaped tones.

BOYS (*Interrupting each other*): Take me . . . take me . . . (*Etc.*)

TOWN CRIER (*Holding up his hand for quiet*): Wait upon my words, lads. Each of ye who wishes to enter will be the champion of a doll put in the contest by a girl.

TOM: I must speak for a *doll?*

TOWN CRIER: You must.

TOM: Oh, fie! I withdraw.

TOWN CRIER: There's another bag of gold in it, boy—

TOM: I'll do it!

BOYS (*Ad lib*): And I. And I! Me, too! (*Etc.*)

TOWN CRIER: Good villagers, I must tell my news in other places. Come one and all with your dolls and champions, or not, as you please, to the great hall at Charlecote this evening when dusk falls.

BETSY: Must we bring anything—gifts or tokens?

TOWN CRIER: Only your merriest heart, child. And now farewell. (*He bows and exits, calling*) Hear ye, hear ye!

CHILDREN: Farewell! Farewell!

GIRL: Let us be off to find our dolls and champions.

BOY: Aye. Come! We must practice our speeches. (OTHER BOYS AND GIRLS *exit.* TOM, JOAN, HARRY, JILL, BETSY, *and* NAN *gather in a group at center.*)

JOAN: A doll contest. Fancy that! I shall enter it, for I have a fine doll made for me by my grandmother. 'Tis a muslin moppet, embroidered in scarlet, with two buttons for eyes. She is dressed in a linen frock with wool tassels.*

TOM: Very fine. Tell me, do you have a champion in mind?

HARRY: Here now, she looked plainly at me, didn't you, Joan?

JILL: Come, Harry of the Duck Farm. I'll have you for my champion. My doll is made of smooth cedar wood, all painted like a courtier, and dressed in leather with a pair of buckled boots. It has arms and legs that move. What say you to that?

HARRY: Why, that's a sporting kind of doll, Jill! I'll champion that one. Wait until you hear how I beat the air with my silver words.

TOM: Ho, ho. You'll quack like your ducks, Harry. Listen to me, Joan. I've been to school for a whole month. I've already learned a poem. (WILL, *a boy of fourteen, enters left, carrying a box.*)

HARRY (*As* WILL *steps forward*): I know you. You live at Stratford, don't you, fellow? Your name is on my tongue. . . . Will, that's it, isn't it?

WILL: That's what I am called, true enough.

---

* Other dolls may be substituted throughout play, if appropriate changes in descriptions are made.

TOM: Yes, I've seen you in the town, too. Your father's a glover— What's the last name? Ah, I have it. Tremble-staff. Will Tremblestaff.

HARRY: No, you dolt, 'tis Quiverlance. Will Quiverlance.

WILL: 'Tis neither, but I'll not tell you at all. Then when you think of it, you'll remember me better.

JOAN (*Impatiently*): Come along, Tom, we've work to do. Let us be off. (*She takes his arm, and they exit.*)

JILL: There—you see, Harry. They've nipped in already to get ahead of us. Now come along, and mind you, we'll take the shortcut home. (*She takes his coat sleeve and pulls him after her as she exits. WILL looks after them, puzzled. He shakes his head.*)

BETSY: We could be part of that contest, Nan!

NAN: But we've no doll, Betsy.

BETSY: We have that strange little figure Father gave us —the Italian doll.

NAN: The one with strings attached, the marionette? Is she a doll?

BETSY: She's like a doll, and surely no other girl will have a doll that walks and sits and moves her head.

NAN: But where will we find a champion? We know not one lad who would help us.

WILL (*Crossing over to the girls*): I beg your pardon, ladies, pray—

NAN: Why, he addresses us as if we were ladies of the court. My name is Nan, if it please Your Lordship.

BETSY: Fine ladies we are, dressed in rags. I am Betsy Os-borne. We're orphans, the two of us. We live with Old Granny.

WILL: No! I mistook you for ladies of the court of Raggle Taggle. Now, if it please you, tell me the way to Charle-cote Hall. I must deliver a box of gloves to Her Lady-ship.

BETSY: 'Tis up the hill and down the hill and left through a grove of willows.

WILL: Well told, Lady Betsy. Thank you. (*Hesitating*) Will you be entering a doll in the contest at the Christmas revel?

NAN: We could, we surely could.

BETSY: But we can't.

WILL: What kind of riddle is this—"We could, we could, but we can't—"?

NAN: We have a doll. Our father was a sea captain but he was lost in a shipwreck. Once he went on a trip to Naples and brought us back a curious doll with strings upon it. It moves and dances when you pluck the strings.

BETSY: But we know no boy who would be a champion for us.

WILL: I think you are mistaken. You do know a boy who would champion the doll. Now think—

NAN (*Putting her hands to her head*): I'm thinking.

BETSY (*Shaking her head sadly*): We know of no one.

NAN: Tell us, who might he be?

WILL: Do you see no one in front of your nose?

NAN: You.

WILL: Well, then—and what am I?

NAN: A boy.

BETSY: *You* would be our champion? But you scarcely know us.

WILL: It would give me great pleasure to be champion to the noble ladies of the Raggle Taggle Court.

BETSY: I do not know what to say—

WILL: Then I'll write your speech. Say, "Thank you, generous sir. I accept your gracious offer."

NAN: Wait, wait! (*To* BETSY) We do not know what kind of champion this lad will be! Why, he might swallow his words or forget himself.

BETSY: Shush, Nan. He seems nimble enough with words. What would you have him do—brag and boast like Tom or Harry?

WILL: What say you, ladies?

BETSY: I say, "Thank you, generous sir—"

NAN: "I accept your gracious offer."

WILL: Good! I'm at your service, good my ladies. Now— here's the plot. Let me come with you to see the doll and work her strings. I'll plan my speech on the way to Charlecote, using the doll as an audience to practice on. Then, I'll leave her on the mantel at Charlecote Hall, ready and waiting for me this evening when I enter the lists as her champion. Is it agreed?

BETSY and NAN (*Jubilantly*): Agreed!

BETSY: Let us be off.

NAN: This way, noble Will. This way— (*They exit triumphantly, followed by* WILL, *as the curtain falls.*)

* * *

SCENE 2

TIME: *Later that afternoon.*

SETTING: *The Great Hall at Charlecote.*

AT RISE: *A* FOOTMAN *is standing on a ladder hanging holly about the room.* LADY JOYCE LUCY *rushes about the room, with her* MAID *following her.*

LADY JOYCE (*Perturbed, to* MAID): Oh, why did that town crier have to come near here? Now my niece, Katherine de Monfort, will insist on entering the doll contest!

MAID: But it is a contest open to everyone, my lady.

LADY JOYCE: It really should be only for the children of the village, and that headstrong girl will spoil it for them by entering her doll. No doubt her cousin Walter, who is here, is behind this. He is insufferable!

KATHERINE (*From offstage*): Aunt Joyce, Aunt Joyce!

LADY JOYCE (*Sighing*): Alas, I'm sure she heard the town crier's announcement, and now there will be no way to stop her.

MAID: Perhaps His Lordship will be able to help you.

LADY JOYCE: You're right. He's the only one strong enough to handle her. Come, let us go find him this moment. (LADY JOYCE *and* MAID *go to exit right and reach door just as* KATHERINE *bursts in, followed by* WALTER.)

KATHERINE: Aunt, why did you not tell me of the doll contest? (*Pushes past* LADY JOYCE *and* MAID, *with* WALTER *close behind her.*)

LADY JOYCE (*Moving back to center; feigning innocence*): Contest? Oh, the *doll* contest. It must have slipped my mind, my dear Katherine.

WALTER (*Pompously*): You forgot us, Aunt, your own flesh and blood? Surely this revel is not intended simply for the common village children. Are we to pine and languish for lack of amusement?

LADY JOYCE: Come, come! Surely you and Katherine have no need of contests. You shall both sit among the revelers.

KATHERINE (*Stamping her foot angrily*): But I *want* to enter the contest, and indeed I *shall* enter. I have a fair china doll with eyes that open and close. She must win the prize. She *must,* I say!

WALTER: And gentle Katherine has chosen me to be her champion. I have already written a speech of presentation. 'Tis full of clever conceits, and pretty phrases. We must win, Aunt.

LADY JOYCE: What shall I do? Of course, you would win. That is not the point, children. 'Twould not be fair for my own noble flesh and blood to enter and win a contest for village children. Oh, where is your Uncle Thomas? He must help me with this matter.

KATHERINE (*Sneakily*): Uncle Thomas is so stern a man, Aunt. He is not kind and generous as you are.

WALTER (*Flatteringly*): I shall mention you in the speech, dear Aunt. I shall make you a benefactress.

LADY JOYCE: No, no, no. 'Tis a matter of principle. 'Twould not be fair at all. I must say nay.

KATHERINE (*Angrily*): Do not say nay, Aunt. Do not! (*She pretends to hold her breath.*)

LADY JOYCE: Now then, Katherine, pray hold your temper. You are becoming red in the face.

WALTER (*Smugly*): See what you have done, Aunt. Katherine will hold her breath until she swoons. I have seen her do it many times.

LADY JOYCE (*Shaking* KATHERINE): Katherine. Ho, niece —dear niece. Pray, stop. Stop!

WALTER: You should not have crossed her wishes, Aunt. She will hold her breath until she turns blue! (*A knock at door right is heard.*)

LADY JOYCE (*To* MAID): Go! Answer the door whilst I call His Lordship. (MAID *crosses to the door, admitting* WILL, *who carries a marionette and a box.* KATHERINE *continues to puff out her cheeks.* LADY JOYCE *crosses left and calls*) My lord! My lord! Come hither.

MAID (*Crossing to center with* WILL): 'Tis the lad from the glover's at Stratford, my lady.

LADY JOYCE: Oh, interruptions, interruptions! Fie. . . . What shall I do? Go, girl. Fetch His Lordship this instant. (MAID *exits left.* LADY JOYCE *takes a fan, fans herself violently.*)

WILL (*Examining* KATHERINE *curiously*): Has she the mumps, fellow?

WALTER (*Stiffening*): I'll thank you not to call me "fellow." I am the Viscount Walter de Monfort. This is my noble cousin, Katherine.

WILL (*Laughing*): Your noble cousin Katherine has uncommonly plump cheeks. Does she store nuts in them, like a squirrel?

LADY JOYCE (*Fanning* KATHERINE): 'Tis not a laughing matter, boy. The girl will make herself ill. She is holding her breath, and I fear she will turn blue.

WILL: Oh, well—if 'tis a cure Your Ladyship needs, why I know a certain remedy.

WALTER: Indeed? The likes of you—?

LADY JOYCE: Oh, I would be so grateful if you could help her.

WILL (*Standing to one side of* KATHERINE, *arms extended and fingers pointed*): I have a small sister at home. She likes to hold her breath when things do not go her way. This is how I cure her. (*He tickles* KATHERINE *so suddenly that she lets out all her breath, and giggles. Then furious, she turns on* WILL.)

KATHERINE: Oh! Churl! Varlet!

WILL (*Amused*): Are you trying to guess my name? Try again.

KATHERINE: A plague upon you, villain. (LORD THOMAS *enters left.*)

LORD THOMAS: Here now, what's the noise?

LADY JOYCE: My lord, 'tis Katherine. I have said she must not enter a doll in the contest, and she will not listen.

LORD THOMAS: She will listen to me. Now, then, Katherine. We will have no more of this nonsense. Do you hear me?

KATHERINE: Aye, sir.

LORD THOMAS: And you, Walter?

WALTER (*Hastily*): Oh, I had no part in this, sir. 'Twas all Katherine's imagining.

LORD THOMAS: Both of you shall leave your aunt in peace. It is my wish that you shall observe the revel, but you shall take no part in it.

BOTH: Yes, Uncle.

LORD THOMAS: Off with you, then. (*They exit left.*)

LADY JOYCE (*To* WILL): Well, fellow. We've had no time for you. What have you in the box?

WILL: Gloves you ordered from my father, Your Ladyship. (*He gives her box.*)

LADY JOYCE: This is the boy who cured Katherine when she held her breath.

LORD THOMAS: Did you, lad? I must reward you well.

WILL: Your Lordship, I ask but one small boon. I am champion of this doll. (*He holds out the marionette.*) May I but leave her upon your mantel for her owners?

LADY JOYCE (*Taking the doll*): A strange little minikin. Leave her, boy. No one shall harm her. (*She puts the doll on the mantel.*)

WILL (*Bowing*): Farewell, Your Ladyship.

LADY JOYCE: Farewell, boy. (*He exits right.*) An odd boy, indeed. He did not want a reward. I did not think to ask his name.

LORD THOMAS: Never mind. The sun is going down. We must costume ourselves for the revel. I will put on the robes of the Lord of Misrule, and you, madam, must be certain that all is well with our special guest and her ladies.

LADY JOYCE: I'll go at once and see to her. Will it not be a wonderful surprise? Why, they'll talk of the excitement of Charlecote for years to come. (*They exit left. After a moment* KATHERINE *and* WALTER *re-enter stealthily.*)

KATHERINE (*Beckoning* WALTER *to come to center*): Hssst, Walter. Come here now.

WALTER: Oh, Katherine—pray, let us stay out of trouble. No more schemes and plots, please, Katherine.

KATHERINE: Pasty face! (*She pokes him in the back.*) Is that a spine I see, or a wet noodle? Where's your courage, Walter? Let me tell you this: We *shall* enter the contest!

WALTER: What, after Uncle has forbidden us to enter?

KATHERINE: We must. Something strange is afoot. This afternoon I saw gilded carriages arriving at the east wing of this very hall. Ladies and gentlemen in velvet cloaks went through the door, and someone all wrapped in furs and satin robes arrived, and they bowed to her. Mark my words, someone high and mighty from London is here. I mean to see her.

WALTER: How?

KATHERINE: I have a plan. (WALTER *groans.*) We shall not enter the contest as Katherine and Walter de Monfort. We shall don rags and tatters, and wear masks.

WALTER (*Turning up his nose*): Rags and tatters indeed!

KATHERINE: Aye. I shall be Plain Kate, the forester's daughter, and you shall be Dirty Walt of the Peat Bog.

WALTER: Dirty Walt of the Peat Bog! Oh, no, Katherine, you go too far.

KATHERINE: Too far for a pretty speech and a bag of gold?

WALTER: Well—

KATHERINE: 'Tis settled then. (*She catches sight of the doll on the mantel.*) Ho—what's this? (*Takes down the doll to look it over*)

WALTER: A doll, methinks.

KATHERINE: Toad brain! I can see it is a doll. But who left it here? Look—it moves when I lift the strings.

WALTER: Gadzooks. The hands wave as if the little thing were alive.

KATHERINE: Look! I'll make her dance a tarantella. (*She moves the doll faster, tangling the strings.*) Oh, help! The strings are tangled.

WALTER: Oh, fie! What have you done? (*He takes small knife from his scabbard*) Here's my jeweled dagger. I'll cut the strings loose. (*Cuts strings*)

KATHERINE: Oh, you cabbage. You've cut the strings that move her. Now see— (*She holds up the doll. Most of the*

strings hang limply down.) 'Twill not dance any more.
What have you done?

WALTER: What have *you* done? 'Twas you who took the
doll and tangled the strings. Let us go quickly hence. I
feel a calamity coming.

KATHERINE: So do I. (*She replaces the doll and walks close
to* WALTER, *staring intently*) Swear to me, Walter, never
to tell a living soul of this, or I shall send the bony
Witch of Endor to ride upon your back when the moon
is full.

WALTER (*Trembling*): I s-s-swear.

KATHERINE: Good. Let's be gone. (*They exit, as the curtain falls.*)

*   *   *

SCENE 3*

BEFORE RISE: *There is a brief musical interlude.*

TIME: *Christmas night.*

SETTING: *Same as Scene 2. Benches are placed about the
room, and there is a dais set beside the fireplace.*

AT RISE: *Village children are seated on the benches, the
girls holding their dolls.* OTHER BOYS AND GIRLS *sit on
the floor.* NAN *and* BETSY'S *marionette is on the mantel.*
LADY JOYCE, MAYOR, TITANIA, *who wears a mask, and*
LORD THOMAS, *who is dressed as the* LORD OF MISRULE,
sit on dais. TITANIA *holds basket containing two bags of
gold sovereigns.* WALTER *and* KATHERINE, *who sit behind village children, wear masks and peasant costumes.*
KATHERINE *holds a china doll.*

LORD OF MISRULE (*Capering down center*): A Merry
Christmas to you, one and all!

---

* If desired, additional Christmas program material may be added to
the following scene.

ALL: Merry Christmas, my Lord of Misrule.

LORD OF MISRULE: Welcome to this house. Today we shall have none of pomp and rank, but lord and servant, highborn and commoner, shall eat, drink, and play together as if all were born to the same parents. We shall tease out Christmas from his hiding place with songs and merriment. I do proclaim that frowns and tears shall be banished, and solemn words shall hide in the cellar with the cobwebs. Come one, come all, give us a cheer to shake the welkin! For now we bring in the monarch of the forest, the mighty yule log. (*All cheer, as* FOOTMAN *and* TOWN CRIER *enter with yule log, which they carry to center.*)

Ho, children, sit upon the yule log and wish us good luck in the coming year. (*Several children sit on the log and sing a short carol.*)

Well done, my cheery songsters. (*He takes firebrand from fireplace and holds it up.*) Roll the yule log into the fireplace. (FOOTMAN *and* CRIER *do so.*) Here's a firebrand I hold from last year's log, to light our way to Christmas. (*He "lights" the fire, as all applaud.* NOTE: *A red light may be used to simulate fire.*) Now, before we go to the groaning board, is there not something we have forgotten to attend to?

CHILDREN: The contest—the contest—

LORD OF MISRULE: Oh, to be sure, the contest. We shall have dolls of all kinds and descriptions this very evening. And to present them, we shall have young lads, like the gladiators of old, to fight for their puppets, not with swords, but with words. Now, let us hear the champions exclaim, proclaim and declaim for their ladies fair of wax or wool. Will the first champion rise and make his presentation. . . . (JOAN *hands her doll to* TOM, *who takes it and hesitantly comes forward.*)

JOAN (*In a loud whisper*): Bow! (TOM, *confused, curtsies.*)

No—that was a curtsy. Bow! (Tom *bows so low he is in danger of toppling, and* Joan *rushes to help him regain his balance, prodding.*) Speak!

Tom (*Opening his mouth, and shutting it several times*): My lord. My ladies. My lord. My ladies.

Joan (*Angrily*): Go on!

Tom: I have before me in this hand a-a-a—

Joan: Doll, dolt.

Tom: A doll dolt. That's it—a doll.

All (*Good-naturedly*): Hurray!

Tom (*To* Joan): I said what it was, can I go now?

Joan: No. Tell them about it.

Tom: I have before me in this hand a doll, made of the finest—ah—

Joan: Muslin.

Tom: Muslin. This same doll has garments woven of the softest—ah—

Joan: Linen.

Tom: Linen. This same doll has a face. (*He holds the back of the doll toward the children. They laugh, and* Tom *quickly turns doll around.*) And the face is embeedered—

Children: What?

Tom: Embordered—

Children: What?

Joan: *Embroidered*—

Tom: That's what it is. (*He takes a deep breath.*) That's all, so please you. (*He sits down, cringing as* Joan *shakes her finger at him*)

Harry (*Guffawing*): Did you hear that? And he's been to school a month!

Lord of Misrule: Next champion! (*Before* Harry *can object,* Jill *thrusts her doll into his hands and pushes him forward. He looks around and gulps.*) What is your name, lad?

HARRY: 'Tis Harry of the Doll Farm. No, 'tis Doll of the Harry Farm. Oh, fie! 'Tis Harry Farm of the Duck Doll. Oh!

LORD OF MISRULE: And what do you wish, Harry?

HARRY (*Miserably*): I wish I were dead.

JILL: Speak, Harry.

HARRY (*He clears his throat and speaks in falsetto*): Ladies and gentlemen. (*Looks around; now in normal voice*) And others. (*Children laugh.* HARRY *continues in singsong.*) Please to cast your eyes upon this fine wooden duh—duh—

JILL: Doll, Harry.

HARRY: I have it—duck. See how the joints of this duck move with hardly any—squeaking. And look how 'tis all dressed in leather that has hardly any cracks. If you should want for yourself a duck that will last you a lifetime, buy yourself a duck like this . . . like this . . . like this . . .

JILL: Finish, Harry.

HARRY (*Desperately*): How do I finish? (*He thinks, then suddenly says*) Ah . . . ah . . . amen! (*He sighs with relief and sits down, as* JILL *snatches doll.*)

LORD OF MISRULE: Well and religiously spoken, Harry Duck. And now, have we another champion? (KATHERINE *hands her doll to* WALTER.)

WALTER (*Stepping forward with confidence*): Here, sire.

LORD OF MISRULE: Ah, a masked stranger. Give your name to us, stranger, that we may be acquainted with you.

WALTER: 'Tis Dirty Walt of the Peat Bog, sire. I speak for Kate, the forester's daughter.

LORD OF MISRULE: Speak, then.

WALTER (*Bowing in courtly fashion and speaking fluently*): My lords, my ladies, children of the village, and servants of the house. (*He holds up a china baby doll beautifully dressed in christening clothes.*) I shall champion the cause of this china doll, made by a craftsman in London. See her bisque head, as smooth and milky as that daughter of an oyster, the pearl. (*He makes doll open and shut her eyes.*) Behold how she is like a real child —with eyes so cunningly emplaced in their orbits that they open and close to a lullaby. The clothes are fashioned of the most downy silk, spun by Minerva, and dyed by the nymphs who guard the rainbow. Surely, there is no other doll in England made like this. Therefore, I beg you, lay the wreath of victory upon the doll of Kate, the forester's daughter. (*He bows right and left, and smiles smugly, and takes his place beside* KATHERINE.)

LORD OF MISRULE: Well spoken, lad. And now, have we concluded with our champions?

BETSY: No, Your Lordship. There is yet another.

WILL (*Coming forward and taking marionette from mantel*): 'Tis I, Your Lordship, come to champion the doll of Betsy and Nan Osborne.

LORD OF MISRULE: Champion away, then.

WILL (*Holding the doll behind his back*): Good Christmas revelers, I champion a doll of such talents that it would stagger the mind. Fancy this: a doll that can sit and stand, walk and dance, clap and wave.

CHILDREN (*Excitedly*): Show us!

WILL: At a motion of my hand, this doll will merrily nod, or gravely shake her head.

CHILDREN: Let us see her.

WILL: Since you one and all desire the sight of this prodigy —here she is! (*He brings the marionette out from behind his back and tries to move the strings, but the doll will not work.*)

CHILDREN (*Murmuring; ad lib*): He said it would move. His doll is broken. I wanted to see it move. (*Etc.*)

WILL: Why—what is this? She moved this afternoon. (BETSY *runs to* WILL.)

BETSY: What will we do now?

NAN (*Beginning to cry*): All is lost, lackaday!

WILL (*Putting the doll aside*): Poor useless bauble. (*He puts his finger to his head, thoughtfully.*) Ladies and gentlemen, did I not tell you of a marvelous creation that could walk and dance?

CHILDREN (*Ad lib*): Yes! Where is it? Forsooth, you did, lad. (*Etc.*)

WILL (*Pulling* NAN *along with him*): That manikin was but a wooden fraud. I have the true creation here. (NAN *catches on and plays along.*) See here—the stringless marvel, a living doll, a miraculous mite. (*He holds* NAN'*s hand out to the audience.*) Examine, I beg you, this well-made bit of skin and bone. Do you see a seam anywhere? Is there mayhap a rough peg, or a nail in this elbow? (*Holds her hair out*) Look at this hair. Why 'twould take a wigmaker a hundred years to make strands like that. Now watch you well. (*To* NAN) Close your eyes, doll. (*She does so, and continues to follow instructions.*) Open your eyes, doll. Wink. Walk, doll. Faster. (*She runs around the stage.*) Dance. (*She dances back to him.*) There. Do you see? An obedient slave.

NAN (*Pertly*): I am *not* an obedient slave!

WILL: Aha, a *talking* doll. The pigwidgeon even talks back to her master. Is there another doll in all the universe like this? Here is the empress of all minikins, a warm-blooded dandiprat, winsome of smile and saucy of mind. If it please you, judges, award the prize to this bantam original, of which dolls are but fanciful shadows, this immortal . . . mortal *child.* (*He bows,* NAN *curtsies, and there is much applause as they return to their seats.*)

LORD OF MISRULE (*Rising*): Come, judges, let us put our

heads together and see which doll and which champion shall win the prize of gold. Strike up a song, children. (*Children sing short carol, as* LADY JOYCE, MAYOR, *and* TITANIA *rise and confer with* LORD OF MISRULE. *As carol ends, all but* LORD OF MISRULE *take their seats.*) 'Tis done. Our most mysterious and sovereign fairy queen will present the prizes this evening. But first, how many of you clamor to know the identity of the person behind the mask? Who can she be, this most mysterious Titania?

CHILDREN (*Ad lib*): Tell us! Who can she be? Who is the fairy queen? (*Etc.*)

LORD OF MISRULE: If it please you, gracious magical majesty, divest yourself of that concealing mask, and reveal yourself to us now. Stand, good citizens. (*All stand as* TITANIA *slowly takes off her mask.*)

CHILDREN (*In surprise and awe, ad lib*): Queen Elizabeth! England's fair queen! Your Majesty! (*Etc.*) (*Ladies all curtsy, and men bow.*)

QUEEN ELIZABETH: A most merry Christmas to you, good subjects. I am indeed your queen, come to join you in this frolic. In this basket I have two bags of golden sovereigns, one for the champion whose speech most charmed and impressed us, and one for his remarkable doll. One champion, one doll stood out above all the rest. (*Pause*) Which were they?

CHILDREN: Tell us!

QUEEN ELIZABETH: The champion is . . . is . . . why, by my troth, we know not his name.

TOM (*Rising*): My name is Tom, Your Highness.

HARRY (*Rising*): Harry of the Duck Farm, Your Majesty.

WALTER (*Rising*): Dunderheads! (*Boys sit.*) Her Majesty would have none of your stammers. (*He smiles pompously.*) My name is—er—Walt of the Peat Bog, Your Highness.

QUEEN ELIZABETH: Sturdy lads, and true, all of you. But

this champion came last. (WALTER *sits.*) He had so quick a wit, and so silver a tongue, that we all voted without hesitation to award him the prize.

BETSY: The last champion? Oh, Will, 'tis you.

NAN: We've won, Will, we've won!

QUEEN ELIZABETH: Stand forth, lad, and receive your prize — (WILL *comes forward with* NAN *and* BETSY. *He kneels, and they curtsy.*) Rise, champion of the doll and receive these golden sovereigns from thy Sovereign. And tell me, what is thy name?

TOM: I remember! I remember, Your Majesty. 'Tis William.

QUEEN ELIZABETH: William what—

TOM: William What! That's it. William What!

HARRY: No, Your Highness. 'Tis a strange name. William —William—Shivertimbers!

QUEEN ELIZABETH: Take then, thy tribute, William Shivertimbers. (*She hands him the bag.*) And take thou, thy tribute, Nan Osborne. (*She gives other bag of sovereigns to* NAN.)

WILL, NAN *and* BETSY (*Bowing*): Thank you, Your Majesty.

KATHERINE (*Pushing her mask to her forehead and rising*): 'Tis not fair!

LADY JOYCE: Forsooth! 'Tis Katherine! (WALTER *pulls* KATHERINE's *mask down, and pulls her to the seat again. She pulls her mask back up.*)

KATHERINE: 'Tis not fair, I say. He won by trickery, the scurvy knave.

LORD OF MISRULE: Hold your tongue, Kate. (*He pulls off their masks.* WALTER *tries to hide behind* KATHERINE.)

KATHERINE (*Loudly*): He won by trickery and trumpery, I say. He had no doll.

LORD OF MISRULE: He had a doll ere you arrived on the scene, I'll warrant. What say you to that, Walter?

WALTER (*Fearfully*): I only meant to free the doll that Katherine tangled. I didn't mean to cut it apart, truly.

LORD OF MISRULE: Shame, shame on you both. As for trickery, what think you of two scamps who disobey their uncle and try to win a contest clad in tatters and masks? Eh, Katherine? Is that not deceit? Is that not trickery? (*He collars them and takes them down left.*) Away with you now. To the kitchen with you. You shall do no more harm to Will Shivertimbers.

QUEEN ELIZABETH: Will Shivertimbers. Marry, 'tis a strange name.

WILL: 'Tis not my true name, Your Majesty. They have not remembered aright. My name is William, indeed. But my surname is Shakespeare. Therefore I am your obedient servant, William Shakespeare.

KATHERINE (*Tossing her head*): Shakespeare. William Shakespeare, forsooth! A lowborn rascal, I call him. Tell me this—in a hundred years who will remember "William Shakespeare"? (WALTER *and* KATHERINE *start left, then pause at door.*)

QUEEN ELIZABETH: *I* will remember you, lad. And so shall all of us. For, by my troth, I do believe you have a keen and rich imagination. One day, when you are grown to be a man, I'll look for you in London. Mayhap you'll be an actor, or write books. When I am at court, someone will present you to me, as a fellow of rare talent. I'll look into those deep gray eyes and say—"Ah yes, I know this Shakespeare. Now, where have I met him before?" And then I shall think of this revel, this merry Christmas revel at Charlecote, and I will say to myself, "Ah, yes. I met young William Shakespeare once . . . upon . . . a . . . time . . ." (*All hold positions as children sing.*)

CHILDREN (*Singing*):
Oh, once upon a time, in England

Lord and commoner mingled so;
On Christmas eve with yule log blazing
And candles all aglow.
Green, green were the holly branches,
Green, green the mistletoe,
Green, green the pine and laurel
Once in the long ago . . .
(Curtain starts to close as children repeat last line.)
Once . . . in . . . the . . . long . . . ago. *(Curtain)*

THE END

Puppy Love

by Helen Louise Miller

Characters

MR. BRADLEY
MRS. BRADLEY
MIKE
VALERIE
JUDY
CRYSTAL AVERY
MR. WINTERS

TIME: *Christmas Eve.*
SETTING: *The living room of the Bradley home.*
AT RISE: JUDY *is addressing some last-minute cards and* VALERIE
is wrapping gifts.

VALERIE (*Impatiently*): There! The string broke! I don't see
how Mother manages to turn out such artistic packages. Mine
always get lumpy and the string is either too long or too short.
I think I'll leave this one for her.

JUDY: No fair! Remember, this Christmas we're doing things
Dad's way. A job for everyone and everyone on the job!
Mother's job is the dinner. Yours is gifts, and mine is cards.
Let's each stick to her own department.

VALERIE: You get off easy compared with me.

JUDY: What's so easy about mailing cards for a family of five?

I've worn my fingers off to the elbow and what do I get? Nothing but complaints.

VALERIE: And no wonder. You're sending the same cards to everybody. Dogs . . . nothing but dogs.

JUDY: I think dog cards are cute.

VALERIE: But they're not suitable for everybody, Judy. You should try to make the cards suit the people.

JUDY: I do. Cocker spaniels for Mother's friends; hunting dogs for Dad's crowd; police dogs for Mike's gang; scotties for yours and wire hairs for mine. Besides, I get plenty of cards I don't like, so if some people don't like these, we're even. It has something to do with the law of averages.

VALERIE: You talk like Dad. Everything's system with Dad since he's after his new job. He even thinks he can systematize Christmas. (*Taking one of her packages to* JUDY's *table.*) Would it be too far out of your department to hold your finger on this string while I tie the knot?

JUDY: Oh, sure. That's just cooperation. There!

VALERIE (*As she ties knot*): Thanks. How are you coming with your cards? Why, Judy Bradley! You've sent a card to Crystal Avery from Mike.

JUDY: And why not?

VALERIE: Why not? You ask me "why not" when they haven't been speaking for a whole week!

JUDY: That's none of my business. Here's Mike's list, and there's Crystal's name, as big as you please. So naturally I sent her a card.

VALERIE: But that list was made out before the fight. Don't you think Mike will be mad?

JUDY: I don't think. I just follow orders. I stick to the lists. If they're not right, it's not my worry.

VALERIE: You're terrible.

JUDY: I am not terrible. I'm just practical. Besides, I think it's silly to be mad at your best girl at Christmas time. Now he won't get any present.

VALERIE: And neither will she. Oh, Judy, it *is* silly. Mike and Crystal always had such fun together. I wish they'd make up.

JUDY: Wishing won't make it so.

VALERIE: But what else can we do?

JUDY: Plenty.

VALERIE: Like what?

JUDY: Like sending Crystal a card—or a present.

VALERIE: A present! I wouldn't dare!

JUDY: It would probably fix everything.

VALERIE: But she'd find out Mike didn't send it.

JUDY: Maybe yes—maybe no. Anyhow, nothing ventured, nothing won, is the way I look at it.

VALERIE: But what could I get at this late date? The stores will close in another hour. What could you suggest?

JUDY: That's your department. Remember, I stick to cards.

VALERIE: Oh, Judy, you're so provoking. Now, you've put this idea in my head, and left me high and dry with it. (MIKE *enters with an armload of greens which he dumps on the floor.*)

MIKE: Well, here they are! Where do you want 'em?

VALERIE: That's not in our department. You're in charge of decorations.

MIKE: That only includes cutting and hauling. It doesn't mean I have to put them up.

VALERIE: Oh, yes, it does.

MIKE: Says who?

VALERIE: Says Dad. He's the boss. The rest of us just take orders.

MIKE: Oh, yeah?

JUDY: Yeah. And how about closing the door? It's wide open, and you know how Dad feels about heating all outdoors.

MIKE: Shut it yourself. That's not in my department.

JUDY: Oh, dear! I sometimes wonder if Dad's efficiency is all it's cracked up to be. Somehow it just doesn't go with Christmas.

VALERIE: Well, paying the bills is Dad's department, so somebody better shut the door. If he doesn't land his new job we'll all be out in the cold.

JUDY: Very well. I'll shut it. But you'd better get that mess cleared away before Mother comes home. (JUDY *exits*.)

MIKE: I'll take it down cellar and sort it out.

VALERIE: That's a good idea. The tree stand's down there some place.

JUDY (*Calling*): Mike! Valerie! Look! Look what I have! (*Enters carrying a puppy*.) Bless his little heart! Isn't he a darling?

VALERIE: Oh, Judy! He's precious! Where did you get him?

JUDY: Right on our doorstep.

MIKE: Gee, he's a cute little tyke. What's your name, fella?

JUDY (*To the dog*): Tell him you don't have a first name yet, but as of now, your last name is Bradley.

MIKE: Bradley! Ha! You don't think we're keeping him, do you?

JUDY: I most certainly do. All my life I've wanted a puppy for Christmas, and now I have one.

MIKE: And what about the rest of us? Don't you think I've wanted a puppy for Christmas, Easter, and George Washington's birthday ever since I was so high? But did I ever get one?

VALERIE: As long as we live in the Carlton Apartments, Judy, you might as well forget about pets. If Dad lands his new job maybe we'll move.

JUDY: But this is different. This puppy came straight from Heaven.

MIKE: Like fun! He walked up Milford Avenue.

JUDY: That's not what I mean. He was sent to us by Fate.

MIKE: Tell that to Mr. Carlton, and ask him about our lease.

VALERIE: It's no use, Judy. I'd love to keep the little fellow too, but it's out of the question.

JUDY: But what will we do with him? We can't put him out in the cold.

MIKE: Well, I know what I'm going to do with him. Give him to me. (*Reaches for dog.*)

JUDY (*Pulling away*): No, no. Keep away from him. What are you going to do with him?

MIKE: Feed him. Give him to me, Judy, and I'll see that he gets some chow. (*Takes dog.*) Come on, Poochie, we'll see if we can find you some nice warm milk. (*Exit.*)

VALERIE: He's darling.

JUDY: Oh, Val, can't we keep him?

VALERIE: I'm afraid not, Judy, but he sure would make a wonderful Christmas present for somebody.

JUDY: Yeah. For somebody who didn't live in a hateful old apartment house.

VALERIE: For somebody who liked dogs.

JUDY: Val! I've got it! Let's give him to Crystal. She doesn't live in an apartment. And she loves dogs!

VALERIE: We could tie a big red bow around his neck.

JUDY (*Getting card from table*): And here's the perfect card to go with it.

VALERIE: Here's the ribbon. There's enough for a good-sized bow.

JUDY: What shall we write on the card? I guess we won't dare to sign Mike's name.

VALERIE: Mercy no! That would be forgery. Just write "Merry Christmas."

JUDY: I'll take it over, and she can draw her own conclusions.

VALERIE (*Watching as she writes*): Two r's in "Merry." You're a dreadful speller.

JUDY: Spelling doesn't matter at Christmas time. I'll go fix him up. (*Exit.*)

VALERIE: I know this isn't in our department, but Christmas is a wonderful time to meddle in other people's business. (*Doorbell*) Now who in the world can that be? (*Goes to door.*) Why, Crystal Avery! This *is* a surprise!

CRYSTAL (*Entering with* VALERIE. *She carries two packages.*): Oh, Val, is Mike in?

VALERIE: Yes, do you want to see him?

CRYSTAL (*Drawing back*): Heavens, no! No, indeed! I'm just stopping by with this fruit cake. Mother wanted me to bring it over . . . and I thought if Mike were out, I'd stay for a few minutes. But since he's in, I'd better go.

VALERIE: Nonsense! He's down in the cellar fixing the Christmas greens. And what if you should run into him? It's high time you two made up.

CRYSTAL: Oh, I know, Valerie, I'd love to . . . but . . . you know how hard it is to make up, once you start not speaking.

JUDY (*Entering with puppy now wearing red bow and tag*): Look! Isn't he a picture? Oh, Crystal! When did you arrive?

CRYSTAL: Oh, how precious! Where did you get him? What's his name?

JUDY: Well—er—he isn't exactly ours. He's a present.

CRYSTAL: A present? For whom?

VALERIE: For you, Crystal.

CRYSTAL: Oh, no! Not for me!

JUDY: Yes, for you. Do you like him?

CRYSTAL: Like him? I adore him . . . only . . . only . . . well . . . who sent him to me?

JUDY: Can't you guess?

CRYSTAL: Oh, girls! This is wonderful! Absolutely wonderful. Now I can give in and not be mad any more. I can even leave this present for Mike.

VALERIE: You have a present for Mike?

CRYSTAL: Of course, I've been expecting we'd make up any minute, and I wanted to be prepared. Here, (*Hands package to* JUDY) give this to Mike, will you?

JUDY: But he'll be up here any minute. You can give it to him yourself.

CRYSTAL: Oh, no. I don't want to see him just now. I have a feeling he'll be over later this evening.

JUDY: I have a feeling you're right.

VALERIE: It will be wonderful to have you back in the family, Crystal.

JUDY: And the puppy will be part of the family too.

CRYSTAL: The puppy! Oh, my goodness! How awful!

VALERIE: What's the matter?

CRYSTAL: Oh dear! This is terrible.

JUDY: What's terrible?

CRYSTAL: The puppy!

VALERIE: What's terrible about the puppy? I thought you liked him!

CRYSTAL: I do. I love him. But I can't take him.

JUDY: For heaven's sake, why not? You don't live in an apartment.

CRYSTAL: No, but it's Mother. She's allergic to dogs. Gets hay fever if one sets foot in the house. I've never been allowed to have a dog. (*Hands him back to* JUDY) Here, take him! And explain to Mike, will you? He'll understand. At least, I hope so.

VALERIE: At least, he'll understand you're not mad any more.

CRYSTAL: And that's the most wonderful thing in the world. Well, I must fly before he catches me here. Merry Christmas, everybody.

GIRLS: Merry Christmas.

CRYSTAL (*At door*): And Merry Christmas to you, Doggie. I'll send you the biggest bone I can find tomorrow. (*Exits*)

VALERIE: Well, what do you know about that?

JUDY: I know we still have this puppy on our hands, and I love it.

VALERIE: Better take him back to the kitchen till we can decide what to do with him.

JUDY: I've already decided. Of course, if somebody claims him, we'll have to return him, but for now, I'm keeping him!

VALERIE: I wish it were just that easy. It's a good thing, after all, that Crystal couldn't take the dog. We'd better advertise for the owner. (*JUDY exits.*)

MIKE (*Entering with small tree in stand*): There! How do you like the tree?

VALERIE: It loks nice, Mike. By the way, somebody was here just a minute ago.

MIKE: I thought I heard voices. Who was it?

VALERIE: Crystal.

MIKE: Crystal! What did she want?

VALERIE: She brought you a present.

MIKE: Oh, no. You're kidding.

VALERIE: No, I'm not, Mike. Honest. Here it is. (*Hands him package*) She left it for you.

MIKE: Well, I'll be doggoned! You mean to tell me she's not sore any more?

VALERIE: It doesn't look that way. You don't go around buying presents for people you're sore at.

MIKE: Oh, I wouldn't say that. I was sore at her, and yet I bought her a present.

VALERIE: You did?

MIKE: Sure. I've been expecting to make up and I wanted to be prepared. I'll take it right over. Gee, this is swell! This is great! I knew she couldn't hold out . . . not over Christmas.

Women are always sentimental when it comes to Christmas.

VALERIE: And dogs.

MIKE: Dogs? What do dogs have to do with it?

VALERIE: Well, Crystal saw the puppy, and somehow, I just
can't explain how, but *somehow,* she got the idea you intended
the puppy for her Christmas gift.

MIKE (*Laughing*): That's a good one! Mrs. Avery would
sneeze her head off at sight of a dog. But the only thing that
matters now is that Crystal and I have made up. If the puppy
had anything to do with it, I'll buy him a bone as big as his
head for his Christmas dinner. So long. . . . Tell Mother
I'll bring Crystal along home to help trim the tree. (*Exit.*)

JUDY (*Enters*): The puppy is sound asleep. I made him a bed
under the stove and he's good as gold.

VALERIE: Judy, dear, there's no use setting your heart on this
puppy. Dad would never hear of it.

JUDY: What's the matter? Doesn't he have a department for
dogs?

VALERIE: Oh, don't talk like that, Judy. Dad loves dogs as much
as anybody else. It's just that we've always lived in apartments
and there's no place for a dog.

JUDY: And besides, dogs aren't efficient. Dad has no time for
anything that isn't efficient. Look how he has Christmas organ-
ized. You in charge of gifts. Mike in charge of decorations.
Mother in charge of food. He's trying to run Christmas the
way he runs the factory.

VALERIE: It's only because he wants to get the new job. If he
can impress Mr. Winters with his efficiency he'll get to be the
new superintendent and things will be much better all around.
We might even get a house of our own.

JUDY: Oh, fiddlesticks on Mr. Winters. I hate him.

VALERIE: That's silly, Judy. You've never even seen Mr. Winters. (MRS. BRADLEY *enters in time to hear last sentence.*)

MRS. BRADLEY: Well, you're going to see Mr. Winters sooner than you expect. I just stopped at the factory to pick up your father, and his secretary told me he's on his way out to the house with Mr. Winters in tow.

GIRLS: Good grief! Not on the day before Christmas!

MRS. BRADLEY: That's the way I feel about it ... . but it's too late now! If only he had called me. Good heavens! Look at this room. Judy, clear away that card table. Valerie, straighten up that sofa. I'll go make some tea. This house doesn't show much evidence of efficiency. Look at that tree! Not even trimmed. Where's Michael?

JUDY: He's made up with Crystal. I guess he's over at her house.

VALERIE: He said he'd be bringing her over later to help trim the tree.

MRS. BRADLEY: I hope it's much, much later, after Mr. Winters goes. Please, girls, try to make the room look decent. And as soon as you can, come help me in the kitchen. (*Exit*)

JUDY: This is awful! Poor Mother! Imagine Dad dragging Mr. Winters out here today of all days. Doesn't the man have a home?

VALERIE: Business is business, you know.

JUDY: Yeah, I know. And Christmas is Christmas! (*There is a scream from the kitchen and* MRS. BRADLEY *runs in.*)

MRS. BRADLEY: Valerie! Judy! Come quick! There's a strange dog in the kitchen. Help me get it out of here!

JUDY: Oh, dear! It's not a strange dog, Mother. It's the puppy.

MRS. BRADLEY: What puppy?

VALERIE: Judy found a puppy on the doorstep and brought it in out of the cold.

MRS. BRADLEY: Well, get it out of here. Your father will have a fit!

JUDY: I thought Dad liked dogs.

MRS. BRADLEY: Not in the apartment! It's breaking our lease. Old Man Carlton is just looking for a good excuse to get rid of us anyhow. Judy, you've got to get that dog out of here.

JUDY: But Mother! I can't put him out this minute.

MRS. BRADLEY: Yes, you can. Right this minute. Before your father . . .

MR. BRADLEY (*Off stage*): Just put your things in the hall closet, J. W., and make yourself at home.

MRS. BRADLEY: It's too late! They're here. (MR. BRADLEY *and* MR. WINTERS *enter.*)

MR. WINTERS: I hate to impose on your hospitality the day before Christmas, Bradley. I know how much confusion and extra work there is at this season of the year.

MR. BRADLEY: Oh, my family takes Christmas in its stride, J. W. A job for everyone and everyone on the job, I always say. Mary, this is Mr. Winters, President of Winters, Incorporated.

MRS. BRADLEY: How do you do, Mr. Winters?

MR. WINTERS: I was just telling your husband I hate to intrude at this time, Mrs. Bradley, but he assures me you always have everything under control.

MRS. BRADLEY: Well, you know how things are at Christmas, Mr. Winters.

MR. WINTERS: Exactly. And are these young ladies your daughters?

MRS. BRADLEY: Yes, this is Valerie, Mr. Winters.

VALERIE: How do you do, Mr. Winters?

MR. BRADLEY: And this is our youngest, Judy. Judy, this is Mr. Winters.

JUDY: Good afternoon, Mr. Winters.

MR. BRADLEY: We believe in division of labor at this house,

J. W. Judy is in charge of the cards this year. Valerie has the gifts and Mike has the decorations. (*Notices the tree*) Er— I see Mike hasn't finished his job. Where is he?

MRS. BRADLEY: He and Crystal will be in later, dear, to trim the tree. It's still quite early, you know.

MR. WINTERS: And that last-minute hustle and bustle is all part of the Christmas excitement, isn't it?

MRS. BRADLEY: It certainly is. If you'll excuse me, I'll see about the tea things.

MR. WINTERS: Now don't go to any trouble, Mrs. Bradley.

MRS. BRADLEY: Just some tea and fruit cake, Mr. Winters, in honor of the occasion. (*Exit*)

MR. BRADLEY: Sit down, J. W., and make yourself comfortable. Well, girls, is everything ready for the big day?

JUDY: Not quite, Dad. I still have some last-minute cards.

MR. BRADLEY (*Frowning*): Quite a few I should say.

MR. WINTERS (*Chuckling*): I always get a flock of cards the day after Christmas. And I see you're still wrapping Christmas packages.

VALERIE: Yes, there's no end to it with such a large family. (MIKE *and* CRYSTAL *enter,* MIKE *pulling* CRYSTAL *by the hand.*)

MIKE: Sure you're going to stay for supper, and we'll trim the tree afterwards. Oh, excuse me, for bursting in like that, Dad. I didn't know you had company. We just came in to tell you the good news: Crystal and I have made up. We're going to all the Christmas dances together.

MR. BRADLEY: I'm glad to hear it. It's nice to see you again, Crystal, after a whole week. J. W., this is our little neighbor and my son's girl friend, Crystal Avery.

CRYSTAL: How do you do, Mr. Winters?

MR. WINTERS: Merry Christmas, Crystal, and Merry Christmas to you, young man. I suppose this is Michael?

MR. BRADLEY: Yes, this is my son. Mike, you better run out in the kitchen and see if you can help your mother bring in the tea things.

JUDY: Val and I will help too. (*All the young folks exit except* CRYSTAL.)

CRYSTAL: I brought a box of tree lights, Mr. Bradley. Mike said yours were on the blink. I'll see if I can plug them in.

MR. BRADLEY: Do you need any help?

CRYSTAL: Oh, no, thanks, I can manage. (*Wraps string of lights around tree and plugs them in.*)

MR. WINTERS: These modern girls are real mechanics.

CRYSTAL (*As tree lights go on*): Well, that's fine. They actually work.

MR. BRADLEY: They look very nice, although it's not like Michael to let the tree lights go till the last minute.

MR. WINTERS: Now it really looks like Christmas. (MRS. BRADLEY *and young people enter with trays of tea and cakes.*)

MIKE: Gee, that looks swell, Crystal.

MRS. BRADLEY: Put the tray on the table, Mike. Crystal, I'll ask you to do the honors. (CRYSTAL *takes place at tea table.*)

MR. WINTERS: This is really wonderful! A typical family group. Bradley, you are to be congratulated. There's just one thing lacking.

MR. BRADLEY: Name it, and we'll see what we can do, J. W.

MR. WINTERS: An old-fashioned Christmas Carol. Don't you think we could manage a verse or two of *God Rest You Merry, Gentlemen?*

MR. BRADLEY: I think we could oblige. What do you say, kids? Let's give it a try! (*They start to sing the carol, but before they have proceeded very far, there are loud and persistent howls from the kitchen.*)

MR. BRADLEY: What in the name of saints is that?

MIKE: What, Dad? I didn't hear anything.

Mr. Bradley: Then you're deaf as a post. Listen. (*More howls.*)

Mr. Winters: Why, it sounds like a dog . . . Quite a young dog, I should say!

Mrs. Bradley: Oh, dear! It's that wretched puppy!

Mr. Bradley: A puppy? In our kitchen? Michael, what does this mean?

Judy: It doesn't mean anything, Dad. It's just a puppy.

Mr. Bradley: Well, go get him. Get him right away. (Judy *exits.*)

Crystal: Oh, wait till you see him, Mr. Bradley. He's adorable.

Mr. Bradley: You've seen him?

Crystal: Oh, yes, and I think he's the most wonderful dog in the world. There! Look at him! (Judy *brings puppy in.*) Look at his big, red bow!

Mr. Winters (*Laughing*): Well, bless my soul, Bradley! It looks as if we've stumbled on a surprise. Look, the little fellow wears a tag! (*Reads tag*) Merry Christmas, it says! Merry Christmas! I'll bet my hat, this puppy is your Christmas gift from that wonderful family of yours! (*More laughter.*) Take him, Bradley! Take him! And a wonderful present, I call it. I'd give my whole year's salary to have my family give me a present like that.

Judy: Here he is, Dad, and Merry Christmas!

Mr. Bradley (*Holding dog*): Well, I'll be doggoned!

Judy: Isn't he wonderful, Dad?

Valerie: Do you like him, Dad?

Judy: Oh, Daddy, can we keep him?

Mr. Bradley: But what about Mr. Carlton?

Mr. Winters: Thunderation! Who is Mr. Carlton?

Mr. Bradley: Our landlord. There's a clause in the lease about animals.

Mr. Winters: Who cares? What's a lease to you, Bradley?

Starting next year you'll be our new superintendent, and no doubt you will want to make some change in your living quarters. An apartment is no place for three children and a dog!

MR. BRADLEY: Do you mean it, J. W.?

MR. WINTERS: Mean it? Of course, I mean it. You're just the man we need for the job. I don't mind telling you at first I thought you were a trifle hipped on the subject of efficiency and organization. Oh, not that efficiency and organization aren't important within limits, of course. But when I see you tonight, here in this house with your family, I see you have other qualities as well. A man who loves his home, his wife, his children, and has room in his heart for animals . . . that's the kind of man we can use on our staff, Bradley. So congratulations and Merry Christmas.

ALL: Merry Christmas, Dad!

MRS. BRADLEY: Congratulations, dear, and thank you, Mr. Winters. This has made a wonderful Christmas for us all. Now shall we sit down and have our tea?

JUDY: And let me take that puppy, Dad, I'll put him out in the kitchen.

MR. BRADLEY (*Sitting down with dog on lap*): Take him out in the kitchen? You'll do nothing of the sort. I'll have you know the kitchen is not this little fellow's department. From now on, he's an executive in his own right and he shares this easy chair with me. How about it, J.W.?

MR. WINTERS: How about it? It's a case of puppy love, if I ever saw one. You're made for each other! Now let's try another verse of that Christmas carol and see if we can get both of them to join in the chorus. (*All begin to sing as curtain falls.*)

THE END

Visions of Sugar Plums

by Anne Coulter Martens

Characters

MR. BENSON
MRS. BENSON
EDDIE, *13, their son*
DENA, *15* } *their two daughters*
KIM, *11*
BRUCE, *16, Dena's friend*
AUNT VINNIE

TIME: *Two nights before Christmas.*
SETTING: *The Benson living room. A lighted Christmas tree stands down right. A dress box is on the coffee table.*
AT RISE: KIM *stands on a stepladder near the decorated tree.* EDDIE *is in the corner up left. He is hammering on a small table, as* KIM *recites "A Visit from St. Nicholas" very dramatically.*

KIM (*Reciting*):
   " 'Twas the night before Christmas, when all through the house
   Not a creature was stirring, not even a mouse. (*Goes up a step on ladder*)
   The stockings were hung by the chimney with care,
   In hopes that St. Nicholas soon would be there." (*Goes up another step*)

EDDIE: Cut out the dramatics!

KIM:

"The children were nestled all snug in their beds,
While visions of sugar plums danced in their heads."
(She takes a step and pantomimes a sleeping child.)

EDDIE: You're laying it on too thick, Kim. *(Hammers, and apparently hits his finger)* Ouch!

KIM: I'll bet you put that nail in crooked.

EDDIE: How can I keep my mind on my work with you talking so loud?

KIM: I have to say it loud so they'll hear me in the back of the auditorium. My teacher said so.

EDDIE: I wish your teacher had to listen to you practicing.

KIM: What are you doing, Eddie?

EDDIE: Fixing this table so it will hold my aquarium.

KIM: But you don't even know if you're going to get one for Christmas.

EDDIE: If I keep on hinting to Dad, he'll buy me one. *(Hammers)* What are you hinting for?

KIM: Oh, I don't know.

EDDIE: You must want something special.

KIM: Dad always buys me something nice, and so does Mother. I think I'd rather be surprised. *(DENA comes in left with a small package of mistletoe, a hammer, and tacks.)*

DENA: Kim, I need that ladder.

KIM: Why? *(Dramatically)*

"When out on the lawn there arose such a clatter
I sprang from my bed to see what was the matter."
(Makes a springing motion)

EDDIE: Watch it, or you'll spring into mid-air.

DENA: Come on, Kim. I need the ladder to tack up some mistletoe.

EDDIE: Bruce is coming over, so Dena is setting traps.

DENA: Don't be ridiculous.

EDDIE: Ha!

DENA: The legs on that table still look wobbly.

EDDIE: Too many bosses around here.

DENA: Kim, get down.

EDDIE: I'll bet you won't catch Bruce in one of your traps.

DENA: All I want is for him to get the *idea* of mistletoe, so he'll think of inviting me to the New Year's Eve dance.

EDDIE: That makes sense? (*Apparently hammers his finger again*) Holy mackerel!

DENA: Keep that up, and you won't have any fingers left.

KIM: Maybe the hammer's out of order. (*She giggles, and* DENA *laughs*)

EDDIE (*Disgusted*): Girls! All they do is giggle. (MR. BENSON *comes in left with a newspaper in his hand and sits in an easy chair.*)

KIM:

"Away to the window I flew like a flash,

Tore open the shutter and threw up the sash." (*Makes motion*) How am I doing, Dad?

MR. BENSON: I had hoped you were through practicing.

KIM:

"The moon on the breast of the newfallen snow

Gave a luster of midday to objects below."

DENA (*Firmly*): Below! (*Indicates that* KIM *is to come down*)

KIM: Oh, all right. (*Comes down*) If I make a mistake tonight, you'll be sorry.

EDDIE: *Who'll* be sorry? (DENA *moves the ladder to the doorway left, just as* MRS. BENSON *is coming in with some Christmas cards in her hand.*)

MRS. BENSON: This place is like an obstacle course. (*Sits at the desk and begins to address envelopes*)

DENA (*To* KIM): Hand me up a sprig of mistletoe when I'm ready, will you?

KIM: O.K. (*Eagerly*) Know what I'm wearing in the school program tonight? (*She dashes to coffee table at center, on which is a dress box. She takes out a long nightgown and a nightcap and holds them up.*) See? So I'll look sort of old-fashioned when I recite.

MRS. BENSON: Cute.

DENA: Now hold the ladder, Kim. (KIM *does so as* DENA *climbs ladder.*)

KIM:

"When what to my wondering eyes should appear
But a miniature sleigh and eight tiny reindeer,
With a little old driver, so lively and quick,
I knew in a moment it must be St. Nick!"

MR. BENSON: Does this never end?

KIM: It's a long poem, and I have to keep saying it. Sometimes my mind just goes blank.

EDDIE: Is that something new?

KIM: Mother, how can you stand him?

MRS. BENSON: It's my legal duty to stand all of you. And please, I'd like to finish these last-minute cards before Aunt Vinnie gets here.

KIM: I expect Patty any minute. She's bringing something important.

MRS. BENSON: Is she going to be in the Christmas program?

KIM: Not this year. Her father just came home from the hospital so she wants to spend as much time as she can with him. (*Turns to her father*) Patty has a surprise for *you*, Dad.

MR. BENSON (*Looking up from his paper*): Eh? What's that?

KIM: You'll find out.

MR. BENSON: What happened to the sports section of this paper?

EDDIE: I may have left it in the dining room.

MR. BENSON (*Annoyed, getting up*): How many times do I have to tell you not to do that?

EDDIE: O.K., O.K., so I'm a delinquent.

KIM:

"More rapid than eagles his coursers they came,
And he whistled and shouted and called them by name.
'Now Dasher! Now Dancer!—' "

(DENA *hammers a tack for mistletoe*)

MR. BENSON: All I ask is a little consideration. Just one little bit of consideration. (*Goes out left, carrying newspaper*)

MRS. BENSON: Aunt Vinnie will be here any minute, so let's have some order by the time she arrives.

DENA: We'll be finished in a minute. (*To* KIM) Hand me some mistletoe. (KIM *does so.* DENA *hangs it and gets down from ladder*) I just barely remember Aunt Vinnie. She's sort of sweet, isn't she?

MRS. BENSON: Oh, yes. But not all the time. She's always prided herself on being very frank, and if things don't suit her, she speaks right out.

DENA: I'm glad you invited her.

MRS. BENSON: This is the first time she'd have been alone at Christmas, and I knew she'd be unhappy all by herself.

KIM:

" 'Now, Prancer and Vixen!
On, Comet! on, Cupid! on, Donder and Blitzen!' "

MRS. BENSON: Quiet, Kim, please!

DENA: I'm sure Aunt Vinnie will love our tree and the decorations.

KIM: It makes a person feel so good to do something for someone else at Christmas.

EDDIE (*Looking up from table*): Oh, is that so? Then why did you ask me to dry the dishes when it was your turn?

KIM: Because I had to practice for tonight.

MRS. BENSON (*Rummaging through desk*): I can't find my stamps. Did anyone take them?

DENA: I think I left them on the kitchen table.

MRS. BENSON: These last-minute cards are such a nuisance.

DENA (*As MRS. BENSON gets up*): Mother, do you know if Dad has done his Christmas shopping yet?

EDDIE (*Going to his mother*): He always waits till the very last day, doesn't he?

MRS. BENSON: He always has.

EDDIE: And there's only one day left now.

DENA (*Going to her mother*): Didn't he mention anything to you about his shopping?

MRS. BENSON: Not a word.

DENA: Then we'll have to go right on hinting at what we want.

KIM: Why do you have to hint, Dena? I think Christmas is nicer when . . . well . . . you just give people something because you *want* to, and they give you what *they* want to give.

EDDIE (*Indicating KIM*): Little Miss Goody-Goody doesn't believe in hinting. She likes surprises.

DENA: Sometimes the surprise is that you get the *wrong* thing!

MRS. BENSON (*Amused*): Surely it's the thought that counts, and not the gifts.

EDDIE: You must be kidding!

DENA: If I don't get a little transistor radio, I'll just die!

EDDIE: I just have to get an aquarium. Why else does Dad think I'm fixing this table?

DENA: He hasn't asked why you're doing it?

EDDIE: Hasn't said a thing.

DENA: Please, Mother, give him the message!

MRS. BENSON: Your father likes to do his own shopping. I don't interfere with him.

DENA (*Sighing*): Then it's back to the hinting.

EDDIE: Tonight's our last chance. (*Works on the table again*)

KIM: I still think Christmas is more fun when you don't know what you're getting.

DENA: Suppose he gives you a doll?

KIM: I'm too old for dolls!

DENA: See what I mean? *Then* what would you do?

KIM (*Slowly*): I guess I'd just say thank you, and tell him I loved it.

DENA: You *are* a baby. (*To* EDDIE) We'll keep hinting! (DENA *moves desk chair to door up right and hangs up more mistletoe.* MRS. BENSON *goes out left.*)

KIM (*Climbing ladder*):
 " 'Twas the night before Christmas, when all through the house . . ."

DENA: Do you have to start at the beginning?

EDDIE: She forgets it if she doesn't.

KIM: I do not!
 " 'Twas the night before Christmas when all through the house,
 Not a creature was stirring, not even a mouse.
 The stockings were hung . . ."
 (AUNT VINNIE *comes in up right, carefully avoiding* DENA's *chair. She wears a coat and carries a small suitcase and knitting bag.*)

AUNT VINNIE: Hello! I knocked but no one answered, so I just came right in. I'm your Aunt Vinnie.

KIM: Aunt Vinnie! (*Gets down from the ladder and runs to hug her.*)

AUNT VINNIE: Sure enough. You must be Kim. My, how you've grown. And Dena and Eddie, too!

DENA (*Getting down from chair*): We're so glad to see you, Aunt Vinnie.

EDDIE: Let me take your coat and suitcase. (*He takes them from her.*).

AUNT VINNIE (*Looking around*): I knew I'd find plenty of Christmas spirit in this house.

DENA: My goodness, yes, we're just bursting at the seams.

KIM: Doesn't it give you a good feeling inside when Christmas is so close?

AUNT VINNIE: Yes, it does—every year.

KIM (*Leading her to sofa*): I made some of my Christmas presents, Aunt Vinnie, and there's one for you! (AUNT VINNIE *sits on sofa*)

AUNT VINNIE: I can hardly wait to see it.

KIM: You'll *have* to wait. That's one of the nicest things about Christmas.

AUNT VINNIE: You young ones go on with your work and don't let me stop one little thing.

EDDIE: I'll tell Mother and Dad you're here, and be right back. (*Goes out left, carrying her coat and bag*)

AUNT VINNIE: What a beautiful tree!

KIM (*Proudly*): I helped decorate it.

DENA: Lots of my friends have bigger ones. (*Climbs on chair and works on mistletoe*)

KIM (*Teasingly*): She means Bruce's family. He's her boy friend. All we hear is Bruce, Bruce, Bruce.

AUNT VINNIE: Oh?

KIM: That's why she's putting up the mistletoe.

DENA: Honestly, children are just impossible!

KIM: Guess what, Aunt Vinnie. I'm going to be in the school program tonight.

AUNT VINNIE: How nice.

KIM: Wearing a long nightgown.

AUNT VINNIE: Mercy me!

KIM: My teacher says she's sure I won't be nervous. But if I am, a little bit, I'm supposed to look right at my parents and recite my lines to them.

AUNT VINNIE: An excellent idea.

KIM: I can't look at Dena and Eddie, because they might make me start laughing. But anyway, I'm glad they'll be there.

DENA: Kim, there's something I forgot to tell you.

KIM (*Ignoring her; happily*): I guess this is just about the most important night in my whole life!

AUNT VINNIE: I'm sure it is.

KIM: My poem's very, very long, and I want my family to be proud of me.

AUNT VINNIE: They will be. (EDDIE *enters left.*)

EDDIE: Mom and Dad will be right here.

DENA: Aunt Vinnie, before Dad comes in, I'd better tell you this. If Eddie and I talk in a peculiar way, we have our reasons.

EDDIE: We'll be hinting, so Dad will buy us the right gifts.

DENA: He always, always, does his shopping the day before Christmas.

AUNT VINNIE: I see.

DENA: If we don't get what we really want, it will just spoil Christmas.

AUNT VINNIE: Will it?

DENA: So if you hear me talking about a transistor radio, that's why.

EDDIE: And I want an aquarium, so I'm fixing a table for it.

DENA: Only one more shopping day left.

EDDIE: And Dad still acts as if he's deaf in both ears.

KIM: Shall I recite my poem now, so Aunt Vinnie can hear it?

DENA *and* EDDIE: No!

KIM: I don't always start at the beginning. (*Recites*)
"The children were nestled all snug in their beds,
While visions of sugar plums danced in their heads;
And Mamma in her kerchief, and I in my cap—"

(MR. BENSON, *with part of the newspaper, and* MRS. BENSON, *with some stamps, come in left.*)

MRS. BENSON (*Hugging* AUNT VINNIE): Aunt Vinnie, I'm so happy to see you!

MR. BENSON: Like old times, when you used to visit when I was a little boy. (*Gives her a hug*) I remember how you used to bawl me out if my manners weren't the best.

AUNT VINNIE: I haven't changed a bit, but I hope your manners have! (*They laugh*)

MR. BENSON: Let's hope so! (*Sits in chair with his paper*)

AUNT VINNIE: I was saying to the young ones, this is where I'll find real Christmas spirit. Right?

MR. BENSON: You bet!

MRS. BENSON: You don't mind if I finish up one or two Christmas cards? (*Gets chair and sits at desk*) Sometimes I wish people would just give up the idea.

AUNT VINNIE: I'm sure you don't mean that. (*Taking out knitting*) You all go right ahead with what you were doing. I'll just work on my knitting and enjoy being here with you. (DENA *whispers to* EDDIE, *as* KIM *puts finishing touches on tree.*)

EDDIE (*Going to his table*): I'd better get this table finished (*Loudly*) in case I get an aquarium for Christmas.

DENA: I'd love to have one of those little transistor radios. (*They look toward their father, who is hidden behind the paper*)

EDDIE (*Loudly*): Transistor, did you say?

DENA: All my friends have them. I think they're just darling.

EDDIE: It's fun to watch fish, and take care of them. If you happen to like that kind of thing, and I sure do.

DENA (*Loudly*): You're interested in an aquarium, Eddie?

EDDIE: I'll say I am!

DENA: Maybe you'll get one for Christmas.

EDDIE: Who'd ever think to give me *that?*

DENA: Maybe somebody will.

EDDIE: Maybe somebody will think of giving you a transistor radio.

DENA: Oh, do you really think so?

KIM: It's time I put my outfit on. (*Slips nightgown over her head*) Now, the cap.

DENA: Wait a minute. (*Takes cap*) Let me pin some mistletoe on top.

EDDIE: Do you plan on wearing it when Bruce gets here?

DENA: Maybe. (*Gets a pin from desk drawer and pins a sprig of mistletoe on cap*)

KIM: It's my cap! (*Puts it on*)

DENA: Then I won't let you borrow my transistor—if I get one.

KIM: Oh, all right, you can wear it if you get desperate.

DENA: I'm not desperate. Bruce isn't the only boy in the world.

EDDIE: You sure look funny in that outfit, Kim. I'll bet you'd scare the fish in my aquarium—if I had one.

KIM: Would somebody please tell me the time?

DENA (*Consulting her watch*): Just a little after seven.

KIM: Then I can go over my poem once more. (*Goes to ladder*)
    "The children were nestled all snug in their beds,
    While visions of sugar plums danced in their heads."
    (*Thoughtfully*) What *are* sugar plums, really?

AUNT VINNIE: I suppose they're candy, or something sweet. Anything nice and special, you might say.

DENA: Like a transistor?

EDDIE: Or an aquarium? (*The doorbell rings*)

KIM (*Leaving the ladder*): I'll get it. It must be Patty. (*Goes out up right*)

DENA: It certainly can't be Bruce this early.

MRS. BENSON (*To* AUNT VINNIE): The young ones are going to sing carols at the school program.

DENA: Not me, I'm not singing.

EDDIE: Why not? You're part of the program.

DENA: I'm going to tell Bruce I have some shopping to do, and then walk him past the charm bracelet counter. Maybe he'll get the hint.

EDDIE: Hey, Mom, if Dena's not going to sing, why do I have to?

MRS. BENSON: You promised the director you would.

EDDIE: We won't be missed. I have to stay home and finish this table.

DENA: He *has* to go, doesn't he, Mother?

EDDIE: Not if *you* get out of it! (KIM *comes in with a large cardboard box.*)

KIM: It was Patty.

MRS. BENSON: No time to come in?

KIM: She was in a hurry to get home. She's so happy to have her father home from the hospital. But she brought something for you, Dad, and she said thanks very much. (*Puts the box on his lap*)

MR. BENSON (*Getting up, box in hand*): What is it?

KIM: You'll never guess!

MR. BENSON: Am I supposed to open it now?

KIM: Of course, open it. (MR. BENSON *opens the box and takes out jacket of a red Santa Claus suit.* KIM *sits up on the ladder to watch.*)

MR. BENSON: What on earth is it?

KIM: A Santa Claus suit. Patty's father always used to play Santa for our Christmas program, but he can't this year because he's been sick. So I said you'd be glad to do it.

MR. BENSON (*Bellowing*): Me?

MRS. BENSON: An excellent idea.

DENA: You'll look adorable, with a few pillows in front.

MR. BENSON: That'll be the day, when I make a fool of myself in public ho-ho-ho-ing.

EDDIE (*Holding his stomach*): Ho! Ho! Ho!

KIM: Please, Dad. We need you.

MR. BENSON: You'll have to find somebody else.

KIM: At almost the last minute?

MR. BENSON: It's out of the question. (*Puts box on coffee table*) Besides, I plan to go bowling in a few minutes. Aunt Vinnie, you won't mind, will you?

AUNT VINNIE: Of course not.

MRS. BENSON (*To* MR. BENSON): Oh, dear, aren't you going to the Christmas program to hear Kim recite? I just can't make it. My club's having an executive meeting tonight.

KIM (*To her mother*): But I thought you were coming to see me.

MRS. BENSON: I thought your father was.

KIM: And you're not coming either, Dad?

MR. BENSON: There comes a time when a man has seen just too many Christmas programs. (*Sits down with newspaper*)

MRS. BENSON: You'll do just fine, Kim.

KIM: Dena?

DENA: I have plans for Bruce.

KIM: Eddie?

EDDIE: Sorry, sis. My table isn't finished yet, so I'd better stay here and work on it.

MRS. BENSON (*Going out left*): I really ought to put on my coat and dash. And don't worry, Kim. You'll be very good, I know. (*Exits*)

KIM (*Forlornly*): Nobody's coming? (*Goes to ladder and sits on it. Doorbell rings.*)

DENA (*Happily*): Bruce! (*Goes out right*)

KIM: Not Mother or Dad, not Dena or Eddie . . .

EDDIE: After all, it's just a poem—not such a big production.

KIM (*In a small voice*): I think it is. (DENA *comes in with* BRUCE.)

DENA: Aunt Vinnie, this is Bruce.

AUNT VINNIE: How do you do, Bruce?

BRUCE: I'm glad to meet you. Hi, Mr. Benson. (MR. BEN-SON *nods*.) Say, Dena, that's a nice tree.

DENA: But sort of small.

BRUCE: Sometimes they're prettier than the great big ones. (*To* EDDIE) Dena tells me we're going to skip the caroling.

EDDIE: Plenty of others will be there. They won't miss us.

BRUCE: I'd really like to go.

EDDIE: Are you kidding?

BRUCE: We've always had fun. And I hate to let the director down.

DENA: He'll manage. My shopping's *important*.

BRUCE: Isn't the caroling important, too?

DENA: How could it be?

MR. BENSON (*Looking at his watch*): Getting late. (*Goes out left*)

DENA (*Standing in doorway right*): Do you like our other decorations, Bruce?

BRUCE (*Beside her*): What's that stuff up over the door?

DENA: Mistletoe, silly.

EDDIE (*Mimicking* DENA): Silly.

DENA: Oh, go to the kitchen and nibble on some Christmas cookies!

EDDIE: Trying to get rid of me?

DENA: Could be. (*At doorway, looking at mistletoe*) Pretty, isn't it, Bruce?

BRUCE: Sort of. (KIM *still sits forlornly on the ladder.* DENA *sighs and tries again.*)

DENA: Your cap's cute, Kim. May I try it on?

KIM: If you want to. (*Hands her cap*)

DENA: A sprig of mistletoe on top. Imagine! (*Takes cap and puts it on her head*) Look, Bruce.

BRUCE: A new idea. Hey, what was that about Christmas cookies?

EDDIE: They're all out in the kitchen.

BRUCE: Am I invited to nibble?

DENA: Sure. (*Puts cap on coffee table, sighing, and goes left*) Want some, Kim?

KIM: No, thanks.

DENA: Anything the matter?

KIM: You're *all* going someplace else?

DENA: Right.

KIM: But who's going to clap for *me?*

EDDIE: They always clap.

KIM: But for me, specially? (EDDIE *shrugs.*)

EDDIE (*To* BRUCE): The cookies have raisins in them.

DENA: And nuts. (*She,* EDDIE *and* BRUCE *go out left.*)

AUNT VINNIE (*Getting up*): You'll excuse me a moment, Kim? I'll be right back.

KIM: Sure. (AUNT VINNIE *goes out left.* KIM *sits on the ladder a moment, sighs, then picks up the bottom of her long nightgown and dabs at her eyes, then climbs to top of ladder. She puts her arms down on the top of the ladder and rests her head on them.* AUNT VINNIE *comes in followed by* MR. *and* MRS. BENSON, *who have their coats over their arms, and* DENA, BRUCE *and* EDDIE)

MRS. BENSON: What's so important, Aunt Vinnie, that you have to talk to all of us at once? We're in a hurry.

MR. BENSON: Is something wrong?

AUNT VINNIE: Don't you really know?

DENA: If it's anything I said . . .

AUNT VINNIE: I've always been one to speak my mind frankly, even when people won't like what they'll hear.

MRS. BENSON (*Anxiously*): If we've done anything . . .

AUNT VINNIE: It's what you're *not* doing. When I came here I was sure I'd find some real Christmas spirit. But none of you has any . . . except Kim. (KIM *raises her head.* AUNT VINNIE *turns to* DENA *and* EDDIE.) You laugh at her reciting, but you're just like the children in the poem—visions of sugar plums dance in your heads. That's all Christmas means to you. Sugar plums!

DENA (*Defensively*): You mean just because we were sort of hinting?

MR. BENSON (*Angrily*): Sort of! For three whole weeks I've heard nothing but hints, because you know I've always done my shopping the day before Christmas. Well, this year I did it early! (*Goes out left*)

DENA: Dad's really angry!

EDDIE: Maybe we overdid our hints.

KIM: Sometimes other things matter more than presents.

EDDIE: Like what?

KIM: Never mind. (MR. BENSON *comes in left, carrying a small box and a large carton.*)

MR. BENSON: Here are your sugar plums! (*Puts boxes on coffee table*) Transistor radio, and aquarium. Since this is all Christmas means, you may as well have them a couple of days early! (DENA *and* EDDIE *look at him, then at the gifts, stunned.*)

DENA: Oh, Dad!

EDDIE: Now?

AUNT VINNIE: Don't you know that Christmas means giving, not getting? And not just the giving of gifts. Giving of yourself, too. (DENA *and* EDDIE *stand near the coffee table.* DENA *picks up small box, but puts it down without opening it.*)

DENA: Very nice.

EDDIE: Real great.

MR. BENSON: Now I suppose you're happy?

DENA: I ought to be.

EDDIE: Me, too. But . . . I don't know.

DENA: Thanks, Dad.

MR. BENSON (*Shortly*): You're welcome. (*Sits in chair, opens paper angrily and reads*)

MRS. BENSON: Kim, why are you still sitting up there?

KIM: I don't feel like getting down.

MRS. BENSON: What's the matter, dear?

KIM: Nothing.

AUNT VINNIE: There are those with eyes, who see not, and with ears, who hear not. Don't any of you *realize* about Kim?

KIM: Please don't tell them.

DENA: What about her?

KIM: I'll be all right by myself.

DENA: Up on that ladder?

KIM: Up on the school platform, too.

EDDIE: Feeling nervous about your poem?

KIM: I'm O.K.

AUNT VINNIE (*To the others*): There are better things to give than gifts that can be bought with money. But if you don't understand, I won't say any more. (*They all look at one another and then at* KIM. MRS. BENSON *sits on sofa, and watches others thoughtfully.*)

DENA (*To* KIM): You look so . . . *alone* up there.

KIM: It doesn't matter.

BRUCE: But it does matter. I've thought so all along.

DENA: I think I begin to see. Kim . . .

KIM: Never mind.

DENA: You want *us* to be at the program.

BRUCE: Of course she does.

EDDIE: In the caroling group.

DENA: Is that it?

KIM: I know you're busy.

DENA: Not that busy. I can spare time to hear my own sister recite her poem!

EDDIE: Me, too, kid.

BRUCE: Now you're talking.

KIM (*Gratefully*): Oh, will you really come?

DENA: You bet we'll be there! (*Sound of carolers singing is heard from offstage.*)

EDDIE: Let's get our coats! (*He and* DENA *hurry out left*)

KIM (*Happily*): I'm so glad. (*Gets down off the ladder*) Aunt Vinnie, Aunt Vinnie, thank you! (*Hugs her aunt*)

MRS. BENSON: Listen to the carolers. It really sounds like Christmas now. (*They listen for a few moments.* BRUCE *picks up the nightcap and looks at it.*)

BRUCE: Nice.

AUNT VINNIE: Yes, isn't it?

BRUCE: I like the decoration. (DENA *and* EDDIE *come in left wearing their coats.* DENA *carries another coat which she gives to* KIM. BRUCE *puts the cap on* AUNT VINNIE'*s head. Then he gives her a quick kiss on the cheek.*) That's for being a great gal! (*Turns to* DENA) Think I don't know what mistletoe is for? I'll show you—at the New Year's Eve dance! (*Takes* DENA *by the hand and leads her right*) See you later, young one.

EDDIE: Don't be late, Kim. We're going to clap like crazy!

DENA: Especially for you! (*She,* BRUCE *and* EDDIE *go out right.*)

KIM: For *me*. And I thought they didn't care at all.

AUNT VINNIE: Of course they care.

KIM: I'd better get going. They want us there early. (AUNT VINNIE *puts the nightcap on* KIM'*s head.*) But, oh dear, where are we going to get a Santa Claus?

MR. BENSON (*Pointing to himself*): Right here! (*Opens the large box*)

KIM (*Dropping coat on sofa and running to him*): Oh, Dad, you're wonderful!

MR. BENSON: I've been a little slow-witted. But I don't intend to let my daughter recite that long poem without her own father there to hear her. (*Puts on the red jacket*)

AUNT VINNIE: Of course not.

MR. BENSON: Just wait till I ho-ho-ho!

MRS. BENSON: Why should an old meeting be important? I'm going, too!

KIM (*Gratefully*): Oh, Mother!

MRS. BENSON: Want to come, Aunt Vinnie?

AUNT VINNIE: That's what I've intended to do all along. (KIM *gives her a hug.*)

KIM: I'm so happy! (KIM *removes other parts of Santa costume from box.* MR. BENSON *struggles to get into the red trousers, helped by* KIM, *as* MRS. BENSON *tries to stuff a sofa pillow under jacket.*)

AUNT VINNIE (*Beaming*): This is what I call Christmas spirit! I'll get my coat. (*Goes out left*)

KIM (*Laughing at her father*): You can put those things on later. (*Recites as she helps him*)
"He sprang to his sleigh, to his team gave a whistle,
And away they all flew like the down of a thistle."
(AUNT VINNIE *comes in left wearing her coat. She picks up Santa's red hat, and* MRS. BENSON *takes black boots and her coat.* MR. BENSON *hooks the white beard over one ear and picks up his coat. Followed by* KIM, *they all hurry out right. Then,* KIM *dashes in again, turns off the tree lights, and picks up her coat. To audience*)
"But I heard him exclaim, ere they drove out of sight,
'Happy Christmas to all, and to all a good night.'"
(*Curtain*)

THE END

Christmas Comes to Hamelin

by Grace Evelyn Mills

Characters

THE STRANGER
MAYOR
THE TOYMAN
DOLLS, *who walk and dance*
MISS JENKINS
CITIZENS

ROSEMARY	ALICE	
ELSIE	SUE	
JOE	FRED	
IRMA	PEGGY	
BETTY	ALMA	
ANN	BOB	*children at*
ANGELINE	HUGHIE	*the Orphanage*
NANCY	PETE	
RUTH	JOHN	
DICK	ANDY	
RALPH		

SCENE 1

SETTING: *Town Hall of Hamelin.*

AT RISE: *People of Hamelin are sitting, or standing about the Town Hall. At the table sits* THE MAYOR, *with a large book open before him, in which he apparently makes notations with his pen. Everyone seems very serious; a couple of gentlemen look over his shoulder; a clerk, perhaps, hands him notes across the table.* A STRANGER *enters hesitantly.*

STRANGER: Pardon me, my good people. I trust I am not intruding. (*The people move back suspiciously, as if to make room for him.* THE MAYOR *lays down his pen.*) I am a stran-

137

ger in your village; I met no one, and came hither.   May I
ask why you are gathered here with such sad faces?

1ST CITIZEN: We are met because of a sad anniversary.

STRANGER (*Leans on his staff to listen. People eye him very suspiciously*): Anniversary?   Anniversary of what?   And what a
strange town it is, anyway; do you know, I have not seen a
child since I entered it.

2ND CITIZEN: *That* is the reason for our sad anniversary.

STRANGER: You speak in riddles.

3RD CITIZEN: Have you not heard what happened in Hamelin?

MAYOR: Methought all the world knew our tragedy.   Tell him;
make short work of the story; and then, Sir, we shall appreciate it if you do not tarry here.

STRANGER: Nay, do not tell me, my friends, if the telling is indeed so painful as I see by your countenances it is.   (*They
gather about; several start to speak at once — "Strange that
you have not heard"—"From what land do you come?" "Surely you are from a far country indeed—"*) Yes, I am from a far
country.   Never have I seen so many sad faces.

4TH CITIZEN: We have reason to be sad.   It is a long story, and
one we thought the whole world knew.   Once upon a time,
Hamelin was visited with a plague of rats.   There were rats
everywhere.   No one was safe from them.   They drove us, lit-
erally, out of house and home.   Rats threatened our peace, our
security, our very lives.   We knew that steps must be taken—

5TH CITIZEN (*Interrupting*): So we went to the Mayor. We told
him something must be done.   He was a well-meaning man,
but a weak one.   He did not know what to do, any more than
we did.   As the meeting was still in progress, in came the Piper.

STRANGER: The Piper?

6TH CITIZEN: Aye.   The Piper.   He made a bargain with us.
He said he would rid our town of rats, for a thousand guilders.

STRANGER: A fair offer, I should think, since the rats were so bad.

7TH CITIZEN: Aye, but he did the thing so easily.   He simply
stepped to the door, blew three notes on that outlandish horn
of his, and out came the rats—'twas no effort on his part, the
scoundrel!

8TH CITIZEN: They came out of every house, and barn and shed
in Hamelin.   An army of rats followed the Piper—followed as
he piped through our streets, straight to the river brink.   And

then, the stupid rats fell in, and were drowned in the swift Weser. It was all a part of the spell he'd put upon them.

STRANGER: And then, I suppose, you paid him?

1ST CITIZEN: Nay! Then we did not pay him anything; and bitterly must we regret it. (*Voice among the mothers, "Aye, bitterly."*) The thing had been so easily done; we needed the money for other things; it had been a bad year, and the rats had played havoc. We people of Hamelin pride ourselves on our thrift, and on our ability to drive a bargain.

9TH CITIZEN: But here was a fellow who would not be bargained with. It was a thousand guilders or nothing —

10TH CITIZEN: And we refused to listen to his threat. More fools we! He played again—(*Here he pauses, as if overcome; others bury their faces in their hands, or gaze stonily away.*) And our children, our dear, innocent children—followed just as the rats had done.

STRANGER: The same?

11TH CITIZEN: Nay — for they were not drowned. We feared they would be. We were rooted to our places. We could not move to help our little ones. But the villain turned aside at the river — they turned too. Up the mountainside they went, the Piper leading them forever from us—

12TH CITIZEN: And a door in the mountainside opened to receive them. He went in—our children followed; the door closed, and we have never seen them since. They are lost to us forever.

STRANGER: A terrible calamity, truly.

MAYOR: All joy went from us, along with the children. You can see, perhaps, Sir, why we like not strangers. Ever since that fatal day, we have been suspicious of strangers in our midst.

STRANGER: No need, good Sir, to feel at all suspicious about me. I am but a poor countryman, and my heart aches for you— since you say that joy has gone from you forever.

13TH CITIZEN: Every year, we meet several times to commemorate the occasion. They left on the twenty-second of July—

STRANGER: This then, is not the anniversary?

13TH CITIZEN: No, this is the half-yearly commemoration of the sad event. You see, we endeavor to keep things exactly as the children liked to have them—in case they should come back, you know.

ANOTHER: But they do not come! They do not come!

14TH CITIZEN: All is exactly as they would like it to be. Down by the stream, the grapevine swings are allowed to grow; the teeter-totters, the rope swings, the trapezes, the playhouse, are all kept in perfect condition. The toymaker keeps a fresh supply of toys always on hand.

3RD CITIZEN: And every year, he makes more marvelous toys!

4TH CITIZEN: At last, he has even achieved dolls that walk, dolls that talk, dolls that dance, and dolls that sing.

5TH CITIZEN: Nowhere in all the world are there such toys as ours.

7TH CITIZEN: He made them life-size—he thought if they looked like children, it might comfort the mothers.

8TH CITIZEN: But what is a mechanical doll, to one who has had a real child to love?

9TH CITIZEN: It is a comfort to our bereaved hearts to know that if they should come back, at any season of the year, they will find things as they most wish to have them; the finest berries are left unpicked, the nuts are left ungathered in the Fall; the cookie jars are always full; thick new mittens await their hands, skates are kept bright—all is in readiness for their return.

STRANGER: May I see those dolls that walk and talk and sing?

MAYOR: Stay and see them if you like; the toymaker will bring them in—he won't mind. Call him, will you, somebody? (*Someone goes out and returns immediately with a little bent man in spectacles and apron and whiskers.*)

TOYMAKER: Something's gone wrong with Belinda. (*He scratches his head in perplexity.*)

10TH CITIZEN: That's the talking doll, sir. This gentleman (*Turns to* TOYMAKER.) wants to see the dolls.

TOYMAN: Just a minute. If one of you gentlemen will help me, I'll be glad to bring them in. Sorry about Belinda. Something's wrong with her works. (*He goes off, followed by a couple of men who will assist him.*)

STRANGER: Who's that funny old lady over there? (*The "funny old lady" sits up straight and tall, all during this, with glasses and a bonnet on, a book on her lap, and a ruler or pointer held stiff and upright in her hand. She appears not to notice the others, but relaxes to watch the dolls presently*)

11TH CITIZEN: S-sh. That's the schoolmistress. She's not quite right here (*Touches head.*) since the children went away. We never knew how much she loved the children, until it happened. Every day she opens the schoolhouse door as usual—no one has the heart to tell her not to; we continue to pay her her salary just as if she were really teaching—(*A citizen near him lays a hand on his arm, saying, "Here's the Toyman." There is the whirr of toys being wound; it may be a loud mechanical toy, or a couple of eggbeaters beating rapidly offstage; the* WALKING DOLLS *walk across the stage, very stiffly. They enter from the direction the* TOYMAN *went in, walk across stage, where a citizen gently turns each in turn to the audience, and they stop, looking expressionlessly straight ahead; last of all comes the* TOYMAN *towing the* DANCING DOLL, *who is limp and graceless. The* TOYMAN *winds and the doll goes into her specialty dance —stiffly at first—then like a person, as of course, she is; at the end, she goes stiff and wobbly and collapses. The* TOYMAN *helps her off, winding her up just enough so she can make it; there is a whirr as each of the remaining dolls is wound up by a citizen; they go off, stiffly the way they came.*)

5TH CITIZEN: Do they not look real?

STRANGER: Indeed they do! What about the singing doll?

MAYOR: I'd rather not embarrass the toyman. He is very sensitive, and feels to blame for Belinda's trouble. It is a beautiful doll—a work of art—but some of her delicate mechanism has become broken, apparently.

TOYMAN (*Reappearing*): Here she is! Here's Belinda! (*Citizens cry "She works!"* BELINDA *is brought in; she is wound up; there is a different whirr—the kind of whirr a mechanical toy makes when the spring is released. The* TOYMAN *looks troubled. Shakes head, and produces from his apron pocket an oil can. He applies it, and winds again. This time* BELINDA *opens her mouth, and crumples up in a heap on the floor.*)

TOYMAN: Oh, my poor Belinda! Help me, someone. (*Two men support* BELINDA *between them and take her out. The* TOYMAN *follows, looking unhappy.*)

STRANGER: What a pity there are no children to enjoy them!

9TH CITIZEN: Do we not know it?

1ST CITIZEN: Would we not give our lives, if our children could see them?

STRANGER: If not your children—why not others?

MAYOR: Sir! You speak like a madman. No other children will ever be welcomed here! We will have no children but our own!

STRANGER: My friends, listen to me. As I passed through a town not far from here, I visited an orphanage; a cold, bleak, cheerless place, with a cold and cheerless woman in charge of it. I did a few tricks, told some old jokes, played a few games with those unfortunate children. My friends, you have no children; think, I beseech you, of the far more desolate state of those children who have no parents. Friends—do not nourish your own sorrow forever. Think of those more afflicted than you—

2ND CITIZEN: I knew it was a mistake to be cordial to you!

STRANGER: You are selfish—

3RD CITIZEN: Who are you to call us selfish?

ANOTHER: Aye—who indeed?

STRANGER: Who I am, makes no difference. I shall go, for I like not your dreary town. Through greed, you lost your children; through selfishness, you destroy your souls. You say yourselves, that joy has gone from you. Your hearts are hard. You are not willing to give these other little ones the joy that belongs to childhood. Until you think of others, you will never know peace.

4TH CITIZEN: Away with this rude stranger!

1ST CITIZEN: Soft! We dare not hurry him urgently away—we did that once—to our sorrow!

STRANGER: I go, of my own accord. Friends, yonder is the spire of a great cathedral. Go there to make your decision. Go there —and may the spirit of the Christmas season enter into your hearts. (*He goes.*)

11TH CITIZEN: What manner of man is this? (*They look strangely at one another.*)

12TH CITIZEN: Something about him awakens an old thought— old words I had almost forgotten—"I was a stranger, and ye took me not in—"

7TH CITIZEN: We need decide nothing rashly; but this I know. Another Christmas approaches. Too long it has been an empty day. Can we face another childless festival? (*Cries of "no" as curtain closes.*)

* * *

Scene 2

SETTING: *The Orphanage.*

AT RISE: *A group of children of all ages are grouped about a big girl,* ROSEMARY. *She is telling them a story.*

ROSEMARY:
"And I heard him exclaim, as he drove out of sight,
Merry Christmas to all, and to all a good night."

ELSIE: I never saw Santa Claus.

JOE: Nor I.

ROSEMARY: Some day, p'raps you will.

IRMA: Not here. Miss Jenkins doesn't approve of him.

BETTY: I guess he doesn't come to orphan asylums.

ANN: Tell us about when you were little, Rosemary, and had parents and a home and everything.

ANGELINE: What was it your mother called you?

ROSEMARY: She called me "Bunny." We lived in a little white house. And we did have the grandest time at Christmas.

NANCY: Tell us again about the Christmas cookies.

ROSEMARY: My mother had special cutters she used only at Christmas—

RUTH: I like to hear about the pink ones best. I had some once. A lady sent them to me. In a box.

ROSEMARY: My Daddy had made those cutters himself, so there weren't any like them in the whole world. There was a bird, and a squirrel and a fish and an elephant. They had red candy eyes—my mother let me put the eyes in. And we'd have gifts, all done up so beautiful; and we'd sing carols and have a tree—

DICK: So'll we have a tree. And sing carols. We always do.

ROSEMARY: Yes—I'm glad. You can look at the tree and imagine you're home. There'll be a good dinner, too—chicken maybe—and ice-cream. And toys. The rich children always send us the toys they don't want any more—

RALPH: Aw! I'd like a toy just for me!

ELSIE: Why, Rosemary, you're crying!

ROSEMARY: Oh, no. It's just a cold—and remembering. (*Wipes eyes.*) It isn't the tree and the lights and the cookies and the gifts that make Christmas—it's being loved by one's very own people.

RUTH: I had an aunt once.

JOE: I never had any.

ANOTHER: Nor I.

ANOTHER: Nor I.

ALICE: Oh, I had a doll once. I guess I was too little to appreciate it.

ROSEMARY: If you're very good, perhaps some day you'll be adopted like Ginny was.

SUE: But Ginny could sing and play the piano, and she had curls —I don't believe anyone would want just a plain child like me.

ELSIE: Well, there's Beth: She plays a violin.

FRED: It's the girls that get adopted, every time. I guess no one wants a boy. The only time I ever saw Miss Jenkins smile was the time she read somewhere that a small boy is a noise with dirt on it. Gosh, I can't remember all the things she thinks are important—table manners, and clean shoes, and scrubbed nails, and slick hair—

ROSEMARY: Mothers aren't cross about those things. Mine wasn't. If they scold, they don't really mean it. It's just that they want us to make a good impression on the neighbors.

IRMA: Say " 'Twas the night before Christmas," Rosemary. Won't you please?

ROSEMARY: " 'Twas the night before Christmas—"

MISS JENKINS (*Offstage*): Rosemary!

ROSEMARY: Yes'm — Here I am, Miss Jenkins. (*Children stand up.*)

MISS JENKINS (*Entering*): Rosemary! What are you doing?

ROSEMARY: N—nothing, Miss Jenkins. Just amusing the children. (*The children wiggle back from* MISS JENKINS *and are quiet.*)

MISS JENKINS: I should prefer to have you do something useful. I shall send the rest in, and you may practice for the Christmas exercises until supper time.

ROSEMARY: Yes, Miss Jenkins.

MISS JENKINS: I am particularly anxious for you to make a good impression on the trustees, and be a credit to my training. I hope you will be orderly, well-mannered, quiet, and intelligent. Otherwise, perhaps they will not provide such a good Christmas for you ever again. (*Other children enter; they creep past* Miss Jenkins *as she leaves the stage. As she goes, more than one child makes a face behind her retreating back.*)

Rosemary: Well—that's fun, practising for Christmas, I mean. First, let's hear your Scripture Verses. (*They repeat in concert, the part of Luke, beginning "And there were in the same country, shepherds, keeping watch over their flocks by night—"* Now let's hear Ann's solo. She doesn't really need to rehearse, but I do love to hear it.

Ann: All right. (*Sings "Silent Night."*)

Hughie: Bet Ann'll get adopted!

Rosemary: Let's sing a carol. What will it be?

Ruth: "Good King Wenceslas." (*They sing one stanza.*)

Peggy: I'd like to sit on someone's lap.

Rosemary: Come on.

Peggy (*Looks disparagingly at* Rosemary's *lap, but slides over*): I'd like a lady with a great big lap.

Alma: Once *I* sat on a lady's lap.

Bob: I'd like the kind of mother that could make cookies.

Betty: And sew doll clothes.

Hughie: I choose the kind that comes upstairs and tucks you in bed.

John: Fathers are nice, too.

Irma: You never did finish the story, Rosemary.

Rosemary: Where was I? 'Twas the night—

Miss Jenkins (*Entering*): Attention! (*They stand, the little ones tumbling off* Rosemary's *lap.*)

Miss Jenkins: I have news for you. (*Children steal wondering looks at one another.*) All the citizens of Hamelin will be here tomorrow. If they like you, there is a chance that you may be adopted. Watch your manners. Stay clean! Don't make any noise! Be seen and not heard! Remember, nobody ever adopts a naughty child. (*Exit.*)

Pete: Gosh!

John: All the people of Hamelin? That doesn't seem sensible to me. There's something wrong.

Rosemary: Why, that's the town that hasn't any children—

Andy: Aw, they'll never even look at a guy like me. They'll want the little cute kind. I know.

Sue: You can't tell. Somebody might even like a boy. Oh, Rosemary, isn't it exciting?

RUTH (*A tall, lanky child*) : I wish I was little and cuddly!

ROSEMARY: Don't you worry! If the whole town comes—who can tell what might happen. Perhaps lots of you will be adopted!

SEVERAL: Oh, goody! (*They join hands in a circle, and dance around the stage, singing.*)

CHILDREN:

We're going to be adop — ted
We're going to be adop — ted —

BETTY: I made up a poem, all by myself. It goes like this —

No more cereal in thick dishes,
No more lonely little wishes,
No Miss Jenkins — cross old thing!
We shall dance — and we shall sing.
(*They gallop about the stage, singing.*)
We want moth–ers
We want moth–ers
We want —

MISS JENKINS (*Heard offstage as curtain closes*) : Cease this unseemly noise!

* * *

SCENE 3

SETTING: *The Orphanage.*

AT RISE: *The orphans are seated very decorously about the same room, with hands folded. MISS JENKINS, showing signs that her composure is not what it might be, reads from a list. ROSEMARY, trying to conceal her excitement, answers sedately, but it is evident that she is bursting — and the orphans occasionally bounce in their chairs with suppressed happiness. They have hard work keeping sober faces, and when MISS JENKINS' eyes are on the list they nudge one another, and clap hands noiselessly.*

MISS JENKINS (*Consulting list*) : These people are most unreasonable — Here's one — wanted, one little girl with front teeth missing.

ROSEMARY: There's Sue — and May, too. P'raps we'd better send both of 'em to interview the lady.

MISS JENKINS: Sue! May! Go at once to the reception room. Do not loiter —´ (*Reads*) Three boys. Ages preferably five, seven, and nine. Boys with healthy appetites preferred. Hmf! (*Three boys arise as one: "That's us, Miss Jenkins." They go.* MISS JENKINS *continues to read*) Wanted: One small girl who likes kittens. One girl who likes to play with biscuit dough.

ROSEMARY: Oh — I know! Ruthie and Alma!

MISS JENKINS: Hurry along, you two. Let us get this silly matter over with. Mercy! "One small boy afraid of the dark"! Not one parent has asked for anything sensible! Dick, you may go. (*He runs out, looking gleefully back over his shoulder.*) One child who likes doll-clothes —

BETTY: O — oh! May I go try out for that one, Miss Jenkins?

MISS JENKINS: As well you as any other! I never heard of anything so preposterous! Not one person has asked for a *useful* child! (*Reads*) Two little girls who look like sisters. One should be plump.

ROSEMARY: That'd be Irma and Alice, Miss Jenkins. They're always together.

MISS JENKINS: Hush! (*The little girls sneak out fast.*) Two small children the size to cuddle. Cuddle, indeed! Nobody ever cuddled *me.*

ROSEMARY: P'raps that's what's the matter—

MISS JENKINS: Are you being impertinent?

ROSEMARY: Oh, no, Miss Jenkins! (*Hastily*) Don't you think Hugh and Peggy —

VOICE (*Offstage*): Are there any more, Miss Jenkins? We're so delighted so far — (*Kind motherly soul enters*)

MISS JENKINS: It certainly doesn't take much to please some people! (*The lady disregards the tone.*)

LADY: I think you're wonderful, Miss Jenkins, to pick exactly the child each of us most wanted — (MISS JENKINS *smiles and tries to look as if she'd done it herself.* ROSEMARY *opens her mouth in some amazement. The other parents come on, each with the child or children of their choice. They touch their new children hungrily, lovingly, and one or two wipe their eyes.*)

SUE: And you don't mind my front teeth?

NEW MOTHER: No, indeed! There's just one thing nicer than a little girl with no front teeth — and that's two of 'em! (*She squeezes both little girls to her.*)

PEGGY: Are you sure I'm not too big to be a lap-sitter.

MOTHER: No, indeed. You're exactly the right size.

PETE: To think anybody'd pick me up! Gosh!

JOHN: Where's Rosemary?

ALICE: Yes, where's Rosemary gone?

PEGGY: I want Rosemary!

IRMA: She mothered us when we hadn't any mothers —

ELSIE: I don't want any mother unless Rosemary has one too —

OTHERS: Nor I!

A MOTHER: There, there. Rosemary won't be forgotten. She may go exactly where she likes.

ROSEMARY (*Entering*): Oh, what do you think? The Toyman has given me a job! A real, sure-enough job! To tend the dolls, and take care of the toys, for always!

TOYMAN: I want to show my dolls.

A FATHER: Did — did you get Belinda to working? Does she sing?

TOYMAN: Yes, sirree! Nobody can beat me when it comes to tinkering. Just needed a bit of overhauling, that was all. (*Toys are brought in, same way as before. The orphans applaud. Last of all, BELINDA is brought in. Her song is "Santa Claus is Coming to Town" or some such classic. She starts — and goes over one note again and again, as a phonograph record does when it is cracked. More winding: another false start. THE TOYMAN is perturbed.*) Funny thing. Where's that oil can? (*Someone hands it to him. He works back of BELINDA; there is a whirr, we see his winding motion, and this time her song is sung to a successful conclusion. THE TOYMAN approves; the orphans applaud.*)

AN ORPHAN: I never was so happy in all my life!

ROSEMARY: Let's sing our carols! (*They stand and sing.*)

1ST CITIZEN: We have found Christmas.

2ND CITIZEN: We have found happiness.

3RD CITIZEN: We have found peace. (*They sing, "Joy to the World" as the curtain closes.*)

THE END

No Room at the Inn

by *Emma L. Patterson*

Characters

THE INNKEEPER
TWO TRAVELERS (*Men*)
THE BOY, *servant to Innkeeper, about ten years old*
JOSEPH
MARY
FOUR SHEPHERDS
SERVANT TO BALTHAZAR

BALTHAZAR, *a young man*
MELCHIOR, *a middle-aged man* }*The Three Wise Men*
CASPER, *an old man*
SERVANTS *and* GUESTS *at the Inn*

TIME: *Eve and early morning of the first Christmas.*

SCENE 1

SETTING: *A section of the inn yard at Bethlehem.*
AT RISE: *It is late afternoon. There is a red cast in the sky more intensified at left. People entering the courtyard from the highway are framed in a red glow. Throughout the scene there is activity—servants coming from the inn with pitchers or jars to draw water from the well, people walking between the stable and the inn. If the stage is shallow, this activity should be omitted in order not to cause confusion. The* INN-KEEPER *is seated on the bench beside the door.* TWO TRAV-

149

ELERS *enter through left gate. The* INNKEEPER *rises and advances toward them. They meet at center.*

FIRST TRAVELER: Are you the keeper of this inn?

INNKEEPER: I am, sirs. How may I serve you?

SECOND TRAVELER: We wish lodging for the night.

INNKEEPER (*Rubbing his hands*): How many are there of your party?

FIRST TRAVELER: We are traveling alone.

INNKEEPER (*Hesitantly*): Oh, I see. And you left your pack animals outside?

FIRST TRAVELER: We have no pack animals, no baggage.

SECOND TRAVELER: The very simplest accommodations will do for us. We are not wealthy.

INNKEEPER: Gentlemen, I am sorry, but I haven't a bed left. People have been pouring into town all day, registering to be taxed, you know.

SECOND TRAVELER: Yes, that is what brings us. We have come quite a distance.

INNKEEPER: Yes? Well, you will have to try somewhere else for lodging.

FIRST TRAVELER: Is there another inn here in Bethlehem?

INNKEEPER (*Walks back to bench*): No, but you will doubtless find some place. Perhaps you have friends who live near.

SECOND TRAVELER: No, we are strangers.

INNKEEPER: Oh, too bad. (*Sits on bench.*) Well, good evening, gentlemen, and good luck to you in finding a place. (*The* TRAVELERS *hesitate an instant, then turn and go out by left gate.* INNKEEPER *claps his hands and calls*) Boy, where are you? Come here, boy. (BOY *enters at center gate.*)

BOY: Yes, master?

INNKEEPER: Come here, you lazy oaf. Why do you loiter in the stables when there is so much work to do?

BOY: Why, master, you told me to feed the horse of the guest who just arrived.

INNKEEPER: Umph! You took too long about it.

BOY: I am finished now, master. What shall I do next?

INNKEEPER: Go stand outside the entrance gate. If any wayfarers come past and wish to enter, tell them there is no more room in the inn.

BOY: But, master, have you forgotten? There is still a room vacant, a fine large one, the best in the house.

INNKEEPER: Silence, fool! Of course I know that, but I am not so stupid as to rent that to any common traveler for a few farthings when if I but wait an hour some man of wealth is sure to come along and give me a good price for it.

BOY: Yes, master.

INNKEEPER: Go, now. Stand outside the gate and note the travelers carefully. If they come on foot or with only a pack mule, tell them there is no room. But if you see a man on horseback with a retinue of servants, send for me at once. We will have room for him.

BOY: Yes, master.

INNKEEPER: There! Someone approaches now, a couple of peasants. See, he is lifting her down from the donkey. Go and meet them. Tell them there is no room. (*The* BOY *runs off stage left. The* INNKEEPER *sits on the bench beside the door, folding his hands on his stomach.* JOSEPH *and* MARY *enter left. She is leaning heavily upon his arm. The* BOY *runs in after them and circling around in front of them, bars the way so that they are forced to halt.*)

BOY: I tell you, sir, it is no use to come in here. There is no room. (JOSEPH *leads* MARY *to the well-curb and she sits down, leaning back wearily. The* BOY *crosses to right.*) I told them what you said, master, but they would come in. The lady is very tired.

INNKEEPER: Humph! Lady, is it? Woman is good enough for her. Just a peasant woman. (JOSEPH *crosses to right and stands before* INNKEEPER.)

JOSEPH: Is there not some small place somewhere that you could give us for the night? My wife is too exhausted to go further.

INNKEEPER (*With an extravagant show of patience*): The boy told you there was no room. Why, then, must you persist in intruding? Do you expect *me* to move out and sleep in the mire of this courtyard in order to give you a place? Move on, now, and don't annoy me further. (JOSEPH *turns away reluctantly.*)

BOY (*To* INNKEEPER): There is a vacant cattle stall. Perhaps we could—

INNKEEPER: Be quiet, boy. We will need that for the horses of the late-comers.

JOSEPH: But you have no room for late-comers. So you have said.

BOY: Horses can be picketed anywhere, master.

INNKEEPER: But these people would not wish to be lodged with the beasts.

JOSEPH: Indeed we would be very glad even of such a place.

BOY: I will put down some fresh sweet hay for a bed.

INNKEEPER (*Reluctantly*): Very well. The price will be the same as for the stabling of a beast—of two beasts.

BOY (*Capering toward the exit*): This way, sir. I will make it ready for you. (JOSEPH *goes to the well-curb and helps* MARY *up. Exeunt* BOY, MARY *and* JOSEPH.)

INNKEEPER: See that you get back here promptly. I am going in to my supper. (*Exit* INNKEEPER *right.*)

CURTAIN

* * *

SCENE 2

TIME: *Six hours later. It is after midnight.*

AT RISE: *The* INNKEEPER *is seated on the bench. The* BOY *enters at rear.*

BOY: Oh, master, the most wonderful thing has happened. A baby has been born, a little boy.

INNKEEPER: A baby born! Where?

BOY: In the stable.

INNKEEPER: Umph! A wonderful thing indeed. One more added to the already too numerous population of the poor and ignorant.

BOY: But this baby seems different. When I look at him, it makes me feel—well, I can't describe it. You come and see him, master.

INNKEEPER: I? I go to look at a peasant child born in my stables? (*He gives a short, scornful laugh.*)

BOY: I can stay here in the courtyard and keep watch for travelers.

INNKEEPER: Travelers! There are none abroad tonight. Here it is past midnight and my best room still vacant. In all my life I never had such bad luck at this season.

BOY: Someone may stop even yet. It is a good night for traveling, starlit and mild.

INNKEEPER: Yes, I never knew it to be so light at midnight.

BOY: That one star seems to hang right over the stable. (*Enter* FOUR SHEPHERDS *left. They pause and look about them, then cross to center.*)

INNKEEPER (*Brusquely*): Well, what is your business, shepherds?

FIRST SHEPHERD: Sir, could you tell me. Has there been a child born at this inn tonight?

BOY (*Eagerly*) : Yes, there has, a wonderful baby! He is in a manger in our stable. Shall I show you—? (*He runs toward rear exit.*)

INNKEEPER: Stay here, boy. (*The* SHEPHERDS *draw together at center and talk among themselves.*)

SECOND SHEPHERD: This must be the place.

THIRD SHEPHERD: It is as they said—lying in a manger.

FOURTH SHEPHERD (*To* INNKEEPER) : May we go and see the child?

INNKEEPER: A fine lot of shepherds you are, leaving your sheep in the middle of the night to look at a baby. I manage my business day and night and even so can scarcely make a living.

THIRD SHEPHERD: There are more important things than business.

INNKEEPER: Well, move on. Don't clutter up the courtyard. (*Exeunt* SHEPHERDS.)

BOY: How do you suppose they knew about the baby?

INNKEEPER: They are probably relatives or friends of the couple. They are the same class of people. I don't like to have such common trash making free about the place. It gives people wrong ideas about the sort of guests I keep.

BOY: Why, master, shepherds are very fine people. I know one named—

INNKEEPER: On second thought, perhaps you had better go to the stables and keep an eye on those shepherds. See that they don't hide some lambs under their cloaks on the way out.

BOY: Yes, master! (*He turns and starts toward rear gate. Stops at center and gazes out through left gate.*) Master! Master! There is a camel caravan at the gate. (INNKEEPER *leaps up and stares through left gate.*)

INNKEEPER: Horses too! Arabian horses and servants galore. (*There is the sound of hoofs in the dust and of men calling.*) Ah, my chance has come. Now if I only had three or four vacant rooms. Oh, such wealth! Such magnificence!

BOY: They are stopping. Some are dismounting. Shall I go out and greet them?

INNKEEPER: No, I will attend to this. You go into the stables and send those shepherds away. (*Exit the* BOY. *Enter left the* SERVANT OF BALTHAZAR. *He stands very erect just inside the gate, bows, then folds his arms.* INNKEEPER *advances and bows.*) A good evening to you, sir. My humble dwelling is at your disposal.

SERVANT (*In a deliberate, expressionless tone as though speaking in a tongue foreign to him.*) : Is there a newborn babe in this place?

INNKEEPER: A newborn babe? Why—why—yes, there is— but—it is not—(SERVANT *bows and goes out left.* INNKEEPER *stares after him, puzzled. He paces across the courtyard muttering.*) Newborn babe! What do they want of a newborn babe? There must be some mistake. (*Enter* SERVANT OF BALTHAZAR *left. He takes up his previous stand by the gate. Enter the* THREE WISE MEN *each bearing a small coffer. They cross to center.* INNKEEPER *bows very low.*)

MELCHIOR: Where is the child?

INNKEEPER (*With many bows indicates rear gate*): This way, my lords. (*The* WISE MEN *walk out at rear.* SERVANT *crosses and takes up position beside rear gate, arms folded.* INNKEEPER *starts to follow* WISE MEN *but comes face to face with* SERVANT *who has the attitude of standing guard.* INNKEEPER *halts, crosses back to bench, turns and goes back to face* SERVANT.) This child is no person of importance. His parents are ordinary peasants. They came here begging a place to stay only this afternoon. If I had not taken pity on them and allowed them in, the child might have been born right by the roadside. Oh, no, your masters must have made a mistake.

SERVANT: My master is a prince of India. The other two are

Oriental nobles. Their wisdom is great and infallible. They do not make mistakes.

INNKEEPER: But what do they want of this child?

SERVANT: There is for him a great destiny. They have read it in the stars. They wish to do him homage. They bring him gifts.

INNKEEPER (*Shrugs his shoulders*): All this sounds foolish to me. But then I am not a sage, only a simple business man—and speaking of business, these gentlemen will wish to stay overnight here, won't they?

SERVANT: I will ask my master when he returns.

INNKEEPER: But surely they would not think of starting on at this hour. Shall I have beds prepared?

SERVANT: I will ask my master when he returns. (*Enter the* SHEPHERDS. *They start toward gate at left.*)

INNKEEPER: Well, my men, did you find the child for whom you were searching?

SECOND SHEPHERD: Yes.

INNKEEPER: Is he a very remarkable babe, unusual in any way? (*The* SHEPHERDS *look at each other. They speak a few words in an undertone.*)

FIRST SHEPHERD: He appears like any other child.

INNKEEPER (*To* SERVANT): You see? (*To* SHEPHERDS) And why did you wish to see the child? How did you hear about him? (*Again the* SHEPHERDS *confer with each other.*)

THIRD SHEPHERD: While we watched our flocks we were told of it.

INNKEEPER: Ah, by someone who had been here and seen him perhaps?

FOURTH SHEPHERD: Perhaps. (*Exeunt the* SHEPHERDS *left.*)

INNKEEPER: You see, it is just the ordinary story of a very ordinary birth. It is remarkable how rapidly news gets around among the lower classes. I'm afraid your masters will have to seek further—tomorrow. (*Enter the* THREE

WISE MEN *rear.* SERVANT *approaches* BALTHAZAR *and murmurs something in a foreign tongue.* BALTHAZAR *looks sharply at the* INNKEEPER.)

BALTHAZAR: Is it true that you have a vacant room in your inn?

INNKEEPER: Yes, my lord, it is at your service, a fine large room. I have held it for you at great expense and inconvenience.

BALTHAZAR: Then why must this family whom we have just left be lodged on a bed of straw in a cattle stall?

INNKEEPER: But—but—my lord, I did not realize—I would have gladly—a boy, one of my servants, took them there. I did not know—(*His stammerings fade off into silence.*)

MELCHIOR: Innkeeper, this night you are host to a king. Your finest room, if hung with the rarest of our tapestries, would have been but a poor setting for his glory. And you entertained him—in a manger. (INNKEEPER *falls to his knees.*)

CASPER: Friends, your words of reproof are useless and worse than useless. It were better to leave this man in his ignorance. Come, let us journey on. (*The* THREE WISE MEN *turn left to depart.*)

INNKEEPER: Masters! Masters! Stay but a few moments and I will even now show homage to this king. I will prepare the room with my own hands and myself lift him from the straw to a bed of down.

CASPER: Do not disturb the child. All has taken place as it was destined to do since the beginning of time.

INNKEEPER: But a king lying in a stable!

BALTHAZAR: That is of no consequence to him. Yours is the loss, not his. Had you shown kindness to these humble people last evening, you would have been lauded and revered through all the ages to the end of time. You chose otherwise.

INNKEEPER: But, my lords, I have none of your great learning. How was I to recognize royalty in such a guise?

MELCHIOR: It is not a question of learning. The shepherds

knew him and so did your little errand boy. Those who have saved room for him in their hearts shall see him and know him. The rest shall go blind to their graves.

BALTHAZAR: You had no room for him in your heart or in your house, no room for anything but yourself, comfort for yourself, money for yourself. Is it not true?

INNKEEPER (*With bowed head*): It is true. My heart is as empty as that vacant room.

CASPER: Do not despair, innkeeper. You were thoughtless and selfish, but it is not too late for you to do this king a service yet.

INNKEEPER: What is it, my lord? Only tell me and it shall be done.

CASPER: It is this. Say nothing to anyone of our visit. Help the parents to escape with the child in secrecy from the country. Herod is seeking him to kill him.

MELCHIOR: The shepherds are pledged to silence. If you say nothing, the child is safe.

INNKEEPER: I shall keep silence, my lords.

CASPER: It is well. Let us depart. (*Exeunt left* THREE WISE MEN *and* SERVANT.)

INNKEEPER (*Rises from his knees, goes to bench and sits lost in thought. Enter the* BOY *from rear*): Come here, lad. Those Oriental princes who were just here told me about the babe, who he is. I think I should like to see him.

BOY: Oh, master, I am so glad! Come, I will show you.

INNKEEPER: Just a minute, son. You started once to tell me how it made you feel to look upon this child, but I would not hear it. Now I am ready to listen.

BOY: Well, master, it is a hard thing to describe. I forget about myself and my heart seems to swell within me. And I feel that the only important thing in life is being friendly and kind.

INNKEEPER: I need that. Yes, I need to see him. But I have no gift to take him.

BOY: You need no gift, master.

INNKEEPER: But those Eastern princes carried in rich coffers.

BOY: Yes, and, master, one box was heaped with gleaming gold.

INNKEEPER: But out of their great wealth those gifts were nothing. Their real service to him was in finding him and in recognizing him as king.

BOY: That is true, and we can do that also.

INNKEEPER: It will be easier for you than for me. All my life I have assumed that kings could be recognized by their fine raiment.

BOY: I will help you, master.

INNKEEPER: Good! With your help I shall succeed. And my gift will be the empty room, the room that was too good for a king.

BOY: How do you mean, master?

INNKEEPER: I shall never rent that room again. Hereafter it will be free each night to the one who needs it most.

BOY: He will like that gift the best of any you could make.

INNKEEPER: Come, lad. Morning will soon break. Lead me to the king. (INNKEEPER *rises and takes the hand of the* BOY *who leads him to rear gate.*)

THE END

Of all the holidays of the year, Christmas perhaps comes the closest to being an international day of celebration. Whether it is called Christmas or *Kerst-Misse, Nöel, Il Natale, Weihnachten,* or *El Natal,* Christmas means generosity and hope. As a religious celebration, this "season of joy and giving" goes back about two thousand years, but the "spirit" of the day is even older than that. The ancient Romans, for example, observed the Saturnalia, honoring Saturn, the god of agriculture, many years before the coming of Christ, with feasting and gift-giving at about the same time of the year. And even after the coming of Christ, non-Christian peoples continued to celebrate such a season with no reference to the Christ story. Romans, for example, who were followers of Mithraism, celebrated their most important feast day, *Dies Solis Invicti Nati* (Birth of the Unconquered Sun) on December 25, many years before Pope Julius selected that date as the official day for the Christian feast.

The United States has been the rich heir to the thousands of customs and legends associated with Christmas: gift giving and the Magi, the Christmas tree and the Yule log, Nöel and St. Nicholas. This play attempts to remind young Americans of some of their legacy.

And Christmas Is Its Name

by Paul T. Nolan

Characters

DR. FISHER	MRS. SHEARER
MR. SHEARER	NURSE

JESSICA SHEARER

Christmas-in-England Episode

FATHER CHRISTMAS	TOM
SIR BELVEDERE	DICK

HARRY

Russian Episode

ST. SYLVESTER	FIRST WISEMAN
BABOUSCKA	SECOND WISEMAN

THIRD WISEMAN

Children-of-the-World Episode

MARCUS and OCTAVIA, *Romans*
GRETCHEN and FRITZ, *Germans*
MARIA and PABLO, *Spaniards*
CHRISTINA and SWEN, *Scandinavians*
PANCHO and NITA, *Mexicans*

TIME: *The day before Christmas.*
SETTING: *The corridor of a hospital, to be played before the curtain. On the center of the curtain hangs a sign*

*which reads "Children's Ward: Quiet Please." A small
table is next to the curtain.*

BEFORE RISE: DR. FISHER, MR. SHEARER, *and* MRS.
SHEARER *enter.* DR. FISHER *and* MRS. SHEARER *carry
boxes of Christmas tree ornaments, and* MR. SHEARER
carries a small, table-sized Christmas tree.

DR. FISHER: You can put it there on the table, Mr.
Shearer.

MR. SHEARER (*Carrying the tree to the table and setting
it up*): I'm afraid it's rather small.

MRS. SHEARER (*Putting boxes on table*): It's big enough,
Walter. She'll be able to see it, and it will be hers.
Maybe, next Christmas . . .

MR. SHEARER: Yes, Bertha, maybe next Christmas.

DR. FISHER (*Putting boxes on table*): Don't be so gloomy,
you two. Everything that medical science can do is being done for Jessica. Why, she'll be walking out of
the hospital before you know it.

MRS. SHEARER: Walking, Doctor?

DR. FISHER: Yes, I hope so.

MRS. SHEARER: But you don't know?

DR. FISHER: Nobody knows for sure. One of these days,
she'll take a step. Then she'll take another. The day
that she does will be the day she starts walking home
again.

MRS. SHEARER: Yes, but when will the day come that she
takes that first step? Doctor, how long will it be?

MR. SHEARER: Now, Bertha, Doctor Fisher has done all
he can, and he's told you all he knows. We simply have
to have faith.

DR. FISHER: Your husband's right, Mrs. Shearer. You have to have faith.

MRS. SHEARER: It's easier for me to have faith than it is for Jessica, Doctor. It's been three months now since the accident, and she hasn't walked a single step. (NURSE *enters.*)

MR. SHEARER: We have to keep hoping, Bertha.

NURSE: Dr. Fisher, Jessica saw you coming into the hospital with the tree. She wants to come out of her room to see it. Is it all right?

DOCTOR: She does? That's just fine, Miss Long. Wheel her out.

NURSE: Yes, Doctor. (*Turns and exits.*)

DR. FISHER: You see? Maybe that's a sign. She wants to come out. Do you realize that's the first time she's wanted to leave her room? (NURSE *reappears pushing* JESSICA *in wheel chair.*)

MRS. SHEARER: She looks so pale.

MR. SHEARER: Now, Bertha, you're here to give her courage and strength, not pity.

MRS. SHEARER (*Going to* JESSICA): Jessica, you're looking much better, dear.

JESSICA: I feel a little better, Mama.

MRS. SHEARER (*To* NURSE *as she takes chair*): I'll push her over, Miss Long. (*To* JESSICA) See what a beautiful tree Daddy brought you, darling.

JESSICA: It is beautiful, Daddy. May I stay and watch you trim it?

MR. SHEARER: Yes, dear, of course.

MRS. SHEARER: We don't have all the ornaments, Walter. We left some in the car.

MR. SHEARER: I'll go get them.

DR. FISHER: I'll help you.

JESSICA: Why don't you go with them, Mama? I'll be all right here. I'd just like to sit and watch the tree quietly for a while. I wish . . . I wish that I could trim it.

MRS. SHEARER: But dear, don't you . . . All right, dear, I'll go help your father. (DR. FISHER *and* MR. *and* MRS. SHEARER *exit.*)

NURSE: Do you want me to say with you, Jessica?

JESSICA: No, Miss Long, I'd just like to sit and look at the tree. I'll be all right.

NURSE: All right, Jessica. I'll be down the hall if you want me.

JESSICA: Would you get me that little box before you go? (*Points toward a small box on the table*)

NURSE (*Picking up box*): This one?

JESSICA: Yes, that, please. (NURSE *hands her the box.*) It's an angel from Czechoslovakia. My grandfather brought it with him as a young man when he came to the United States. It's a kind of Santa Claus.

NURSE: It looks very nice.

JESSICA: In Czechoslovakia, it is the *angel* who travels with St. Nicholas and gives presents. Maybe if I were there, the angel would bring me—would help me walk.

NURSE: You'll walk, Jessica. You'll walk. Just you wait and see. (*Pause*) Well, I'll be at the other end of the hall if you want me.

JESSICA: Yes, Miss Long. (NURSE *exits and the lights dim.*)

JESSICA (*Takes the angel out of the box and talks to it*): Little Angel, if I were a Czech girl, would you help me walk? (*Sighs*) I guess not. I guess even you couldn't do that. (*She leans back and closes her eyes. The lights go out and the curtain opens. A single spotlight picks out a large Christmas tree in the center of the stage. On stage left is a large log.* FATHER CHRISTMAS *stands in the middle of the stage, and* SIR BELVEDERE, TOM, DICK, *and* HARRY *lie sprawled around him.*)

FATHER CHRISTMAS (*Coming down and tapping* JESSICA *on the shoulder*): Jessica, are you asleep?

JESSICA (*Sitting up*): My goodness, who are you?

FATHER CHRISTMAS: It's plain to see, you're no English girl, or surely you'd know me. I'm Father Christmas from England and I'm here to bring you a gift, if you can tell me, in rhyme, that you've been good.

JESSICA: Well . . . I don't know if I've been good, but I've been sick.

FATHER CHRISTMAS: Oh, indeed, that's too bad, for little girls are surely sad on Christmas if they cannot tell that with goodness they do dwell. But since you're not an English girl, I'll give you a gift anyway. Look, a scene for you. (*He points to the upstage scene, and as he does, the characters get up and stretch.*)

TOM (*Nudging* DICK *with his toe*): All right, Dick, how about pulling Dun out of the mire?

DICK: If you want that yule log moved, do it yourself. I'm tired.

TOM: (*Goes to the yule log and ties his rope around it*): All right, I will. When old Dun is stuck in the mire, there's nothing to do but pull it out. (*He tries to pull, but the log doesn't move.*) Old Dun is stuck deep!

HARRY (*Getting up and going to* TOM): Oh, sit down, Tom, and let a man pull. (*He ties his rope around the log.* Tom *steps back to watch, with his hands on his hips.*) It's all in knowing how, my lad. (*He pulls, but the log doesn't move.*)

Tom (*Jeering*): And how's *how,* Harry?

Dick (*Gets up, goes to log and ties his rope around it*): I should have done it in the first place. Old England's not growing the lads she did in good King Alfred's time. (*He pulls unsuccessfully, then slips and falls.*) Ah, let the log stay where it is for all of me.

Tom: Yeah, let it stay.

Sir Belvedere: Now, wait a minute, lads. The yule log was never meant to be a lonely man's task. We'll do it together. (*He ties his rope around the front of the log, and the other three all pick up their ropes.*) All right, my lads, and as we pull with our arms, let's sing good old Herrick's song from our hearts.

Harry: We're with you, Sir Belvedere. Sing away.

All (*Singing as they pull the log into a position downstage right of the tree*):
>Come bring, with a noise,
>My merry, merry boys
>The Christmas Log to the firing;
>While my good dame, she
>Bids you all be free
>And drink to your heart's desiring.

Sir Belvedere (*Standing on the log*): Now let this yule log burn. It burns away old hatreds and misunderstandings. Let your fears and envies vanish, and let the spirit of good fellowship reign supreme for this season and through all the year. Merry Christmas! (*Curtain closes*)

Father Christmas: That's my gift to thee, Jessica, and this little yule log. (*He takes a small log from his pocket and places it on the table beside* Jessica's *tree.*)

I place this beneath your tree as a remembrance that the hardest tasks are easiest done when we pull together and sing a song—a song from the heart.

JESSICA: Thank you, Father Christmas, I'll try. (FATHER CHRISTMAS *exits right. Lights go out. Then the lights come up slowly.* JESSICA *is asleep in the chair.* NURSE *enters from left, calls* "Jessica" *softly, sees she is asleep, and withdraws. From off right, a voice is heard calling softly,* "Jessica, Jessica." JESSICA *sits up straight—and looks right.*)

JESSICA: Who is it? (SYLVESTER *enters.*)

SYLVESTER: It is I, Sylvester.

JESSICA: St. Sylvester of the Russians? Aren't you a long way from home?

SYLVESTER: No one with joy in his heart is a long way from home on Christmas Eve, but I must be back home in a week, for that is my night of the year, you know. The night before the New Year.

JESSICA: Oh yes, St. Sylvester. I don't know *how* I know, but I *do* know:

> St. Sylvester's evening hour,
> Calls the maidens round;
> Shoes to throw behind the door,
> Delve the snowy ground.
> Peep behind the window there,
> Burning wax to pour.

SYLVESTER (*Interrupting, taking a handful of grain from his feedbag and throwing it on the floor*):

> And the corn for chanticleer,
> Reckon three times o'er.
>> (*Takes a ring from his finger and puts it on* JESSICA's *finger*)
> Solemnly the golden ring

> Earrings, too, of gold;
> Kerchief white must cover them
> While we're chanting over them
> Magic songs of old.

JESSICA: But what are you doing here, St. Sylvester?

SYLVESTER: I saw my friend, Father Christmas, who said you were feeling blue. So I thought I'd just fly over and see what I could do.

JESSICA: I am feeling blue, but I'm afraid there's nothing you can do. Tomorrow's Christmas, and I have been wishing so hard for ever so long that I might be home to trim the tree, but see—my daddy had to bring a tree to me.

SYLVESTER: Why don't you trim this one?

JESSICA: I cannot even walk.

SYLVESTER: Oh? Dr. Fisher says you may one day if you will really try.

JESSICA: He doesn't know how hard it is for me even to move a hand. I'll never be able to walk. I can't even stand.

SYLVESTER: Sometimes the easiest thing to do is the thing that seems the hardest at the moment. You remember Babouscka, don't you?

JESSICA: Babouscka?

SYLVESTER: Yes. Babouscka is a kind of Santa Claus like your Czech angel. If you were a Russian child, Jessica, you would be waiting for her on this Eve, just as in other lands, children wait for Kris Kringle, St. Nicholas, or our friend, Father Christmas. Every Christmas Eve, Babouscka goes about peeping into every child's house and leaving small gifts. She moves quickly, and she weeps as she goes. When a Russian child hears the wind whistling and whining, he thinks, "It is Babouscka and she looks for me."

JESSICA: But what is she looking for? Tell me, and I shall ask my daddy to help her find it. (*The curtain opens. In addition to the tree and the yule log from the first scene, there is now the front of a little hut with a door and one lighted window.* BABOUSCKA *stands with a broom of rushes.*)

SYLVESTER: A great many yesterdays ago, Babouscka lived in a little hut. This is the coldest corner of cold Russia, but she had a very comfortable little hut and was happy spending her days just keeping herself comfortable. Then one night, three men came to her . . . (THREE WISEMEN *enter.*)

BABOUSCKA: Greetings, my lords. Have you lost your way?

FIRST WISEMAN: Indeed we have for these many, many years.

SECOND WISEMAN: But now we may have found it again.

THIRD WISEMAN: For we have seen a star.

BABOUSCKA: A star?

FIRST WISEMAN: A star! But what a star! It leads us to Him.

BABOUSCKA: To him? Is he a great king?

SECOND WISEMAN: The greatest of all.

THIRD WISEMAN: It is the star that leads to the Child.

BABOUSCKA: A child! I thought it was a king.

SECOND WISEMAN: You should come with us, Old Woman, to visit Him.

BABOUSCKA: Is he rich and powerful, this child?

THIRD WISEMAN: Rich in love, not in jewels.

FIRST WISEMAN: Powerful in goodness, not in armies.

BABOUSCKA: Well, then I don't think I'd better go. You

gentlemen are rich and may chase off after anything that pleases your heart, but I am a poor woman and must be practical and stay home by my hearth. I have to look out for myself.

FIRST WISEMAN: You will regret it, Old Woman.

BABOUSCKA: Not I. The night is dark and cheerless, and my little fire is my only comfort. I'll stay with it.

SECOND WISEMAN: Then we will go on. (*They start off.*)

BABOUSCKA (*Calling after them*): What is this child's name?

THIRD WISEMAN (*Turning back for a moment*): He is called the Christ. (WISEMEN *exit.*)

SYLVESTER: Babouscka did not go, Jessica, but she thought about the Wisemen and the Christ child, and the more she thought, the more miserable she became, until at last she could stand the sight of her home and comforting fire no longer. Then she went to look for him, and now almost two thousand years later, she is looking still. She lives on, looking in every child's face, always disappointed, always seeking. Will she find him one day? Who knows? (*Curtain closes and off-stage a chorus sings to the tune of "God Rest Ye Merry, Gentlemen."*)

> And so 'tis said on Christmas Eve
> When high the drifts are piled,
> With staff, with basket on her arm,
> Babouscka seeks the Child;

> *Refrain*
> Above each little face half-hid
> By pillows white as snow:

"And is He here?" she softly sighs, softly sighs,
"Then farther I must go."

At every door she looks for Him,
Her wistful face so mild,
Her gifts at every house she leaves,
And murmurs to each child

Refrain

Above each little face half-hid
By pillows white as snow:
"And is He here?" she softly sighs, softly sighs.
"Then farther I must go."

JESSICA: And is she still seeking?

SYLVESTER: So the children of Russia believe.

JESSICA: What a great deal of sadness there is in this world, even on Christmas Eve.

SYLVESTER: Yes. But there's a great deal of love, too. In fact, there is a great deal of a great many things in this world on Christmas Eve.

JESSICA: I have been feeling very sad because it was Christmas Eve, and I couldn't go home. But now, I think that if I could walk, I'd like to go all over the world and say, "Merry Christmas," to everyone.

SYLVESTER: Well, perhaps we can do better than that. Father Christmas, St. Nicholas, Santa Claus, and I were talking to some children earlier this evening, and we told them you were sad. They said they would like to come by for a moment and share part of their Christmas with you. Would you like that?

JESSICA: Oh, very much.

SYLVESTER: Then let's begin. (*The curtain opens.* MARCUS *and* OCTAVIA *come downstage.*)

MARCUS: From ancient times we come, from the Roman Empire in the days before Christ.

OCTAVIA: At this time of year, we gave gifts to those we loved.

MARCUS (*Holding up a jar*): So a jar of honey do I bring that your year may be sweeter, Jessica.

OCTAVIA (*Holding up a lamp*): And I a lamp of silver bring that light and wealth may attend you. (*They set their gifts before the large tree, and then stand together upstage left.* GRETCHEN *and* FRITZ *enter.*)

GRETCHEN: In our native Germany, Santa is a baker.

FRITZ: We have brought you cookies, the kind that German children like.

GRETCHEN (*Tying a gingerbread man onto the large tree*): Pfeffernusse. (*fef-er-nis-ee*)

FRITZ (*Tying his gingerbread man onto the tree*): And one from me. With these cookies, we bring our love.

GRETCHEN: For in our country, the word for Christmas cookies is *lebkuchen,* and that is also the word for love. (*They go upstage and stand next to the Romans.* MARIA *and* PABLO *enter.*)

MARIA: *Noche-buena,* Jessica.

PABLO: We are children of Spain, and a crêche we bring for you. (*He sets down the model of the stable before the large tree.*) As a reminder of the humble origin of Him for whom this day is named.

MARIA: I set the figures in order. (*Goes to stable and points with finger*) Joseph, Mary, and the baby Jesus.

(They sit before the crêche, and CHRISTINA *and* SWEN *enter.)*

SWEN *(Setting up a birds' tree—a pole with a sheaf of grain tied to it)*: In all the cold lands of Scandinavia— Sweden, Denmark, Norway—the Christmas snow brings woe to our friends, the birds.

CHRISTINA: So we set out a Christmas tree for birds, a sheaf of grain so that they may share the feast with us this day. *(Holding up an ornament of a bird)* For your tree, a bird we bring, that your spirit, too, may soar on Christmas Day, Jessica. *(She puts the bird on the large tree.* SWEN *and* CHRISTINA *stand upstage next to the others, as* NITA *and* PANCHO *enter.* PANCHO *sets a piñata in the middle of the stage. He then hands* NITA *a blindfold; she ties it on, and he leads her by the arm downstage.)*

PANCHO: In my country of Mexico, we do not have a Christmas tree.

NITA: We have a *piñata*.

PANCHO: Then we are blindfolded and given a stick.

NITA: But I shall use my feet.

PANCHO: If we break the *piñata,* all the goodies inside are ours. *(*PANCHO *leads* NITA *through a short simple Mexican dance; they stop, and she kicks the piñata, which breaks. It is full of Christmas tree ornaments— candy canes and tinsel rope. All the children rush down and pick them up to hang on the tree.)*

PANCHO: It is because of our love for you, Jessica, that we have all come to trim your tree.

NITA: Merry Christmas, Jessica. *(Curtain closes)*

JESSICA: Oh, thank you, thank you, thank you. It's been so

wonderful, Sylvester, but I wish . . . I still wish that I could trim my own tree.

SYLVESTER: That is what your mother and daddy wish for you, too. But I must go now, Jessica. Merry Christmas. (*Lights go out. When the lights come up,* MR. *and* MRS. SHEARER *and* DR. FISHER *enter from left carrying boxes which they place on table.*)

MRS. SHEARER: There, Jessica, dear, we weren't gone long, were we? (*Pauses and looks at* JESSICA) She's fallen asleep.

MR. SHEARER: I guess the day has been too much of a strain on her.

MRS. SHEARER: I shouldn't have left her alone.

MR. SHEARER: What shall we do now?

DR. FISHER: Wake her, of course. Jessica's body is now much stronger than her will, but she needs to use her strength if she is ever to be well. (*To* JESSICA) Come on, Jessica, wake up. It's time to trim the tree.

JESSICA (*Sitting up with a start*): Trim the tree? But I thought all the children of the world were going to trim it for me, Sylvester.

DR. FISHER: Sylvester? Are you awake or still asleep, Jessica?

JESSICA: Oh, I'm awake. But I had the most wonderful dream.

MR. SHEARER: What shall I put on the tree first, darling?

JESSICA: I want to put my angel from Czechoslovakia on . the tree.

MRS. SHEARER: All right, dear, hand it to me.

JESSICA: No, I want to put it on myself.

MR. SHEARER: All right, dear, I'll push you over.

JESSICA: No, Daddy, I'm going to . . . I'm going to walk over by myself.

MRS. SHEARER: But, you can't.

DR. FISHER: (*Touching* MRS. SHEARER'S *arm*): Let her try. Let her try.

JESSICA (*Struggling to get up*): I know I can if I can just get up.

MR. SHEARER: Would you like to take Daddy's arm—just to steady you?

JESSICA: Yes, Daddy, after I get up. I might be a little woozy. I've been in bed so long, you know. (*She struggles out of the chair and finally stands for a moment alone; then she grabs* MR. SHEARER'S *arm and leans on it.*)

JESSICA (*Almost to herself*): I did it. I stood. All alone. I stood. (*To* MR. SHEARER) Now, Daddy, if you would help me to the tree, I want to put my angel up. (MR. SHEARER *helps her to the tree on the table, and she places the angel on a branch.*)

MRS. SHEARER: She's walking. It's a miracle. For a time, I thought I would never see it.

DR. FISHER (*To* JESSICA): Now, little lady, I'd suggest you get back to bed. Christmas is tomorrow, and you should get up bright and early to see what Santa has brought you.

JESSICA: I've already gotten my Christmas present, Dr. Fisher.

DR. FISHER: That's your hospital present. But maybe he left you something more at home.

MRS. SHEARER: You mean she can come home tomorrow?

DR. FISHER: All she needs now is sleep, rest, and exercise

—especially exercise and she'll get that more at home than here. Hospitals are for sick people, aren't they, Jessica?

JESSICA: Yes, Dr. Fisher. But could I be a sick person just for a few minutes longer and ride back to my room? I'm so tired.

DR. FISHER: Certainly, Jessica. (MR. SHEARER *helps* JESSICA *into the wheel chair.*)

JESSICA: It was so nice of Father Christmas and St. Sylvester and all the children of the world to come and visit me on Christmas Eve and bring me gifts. I do believe they helped me walk—knowing that so many people in so many places love me makes me feel stronger. (*She leans back and closes her eyes.*)

MRS. SHEARER: Father Christmas? Sylvester? I don't understand, dear.

DR. FISHER (*Nudging her*): She's been dreaming.

MRS. SHEARER: Oh, yes, of course. Well, Walter, I guess you'd better take all the Christmas tree ornaments back downstairs to the car. We'll need them at home this year. I'll take Jessica back to her room. It's been such a wonderful Christmas Eve! (*She wheels* JESSICA *off left.*)

MR. SHEARER (*Stacking the boxes to carry off*): It's a funny thing—these are much lighter to carry back than they were to carry in.

DR. FISHER (*Taking the angel off the tree*): Well, Jessica trimmed her tree.

MR. SHEARER: Just a single ornament, but that's the big one.

DR. FISHER (*Picking up the little yule log*): This is a clever ornament.

MR. SHEARER: What's that?

DR. FISHER: This little yule log.

MR. SHEARER: I've never seen that before. It's not ours, I'm sure.

DR. FISHER (*Laughing*): Perhaps Jessica's friend, Sylvester, brought it to her.

MR. SHEARER: Or Father Christmas. Didn't she say he had been here, too? (*They both laugh and exit right, carrying boxes. Lights go off. The curtain opens, and the stage is now lighted by the large Christmas tree. All the characters in the play are grouped in a semi-circle. FATHER CHRISTMAS and SYLVESTER come onstage from rear, wheeling JESSICA down to the curtain line.*)

JESSICA: And now, Father Christmas and Sylvester, my parents, Dr. Fisher, Nurse Long, Sir Belvedere, and all my friends—and all of you out there—join me in the singing of that famous Austrian hymn, "Silent Night." (*All sing. Curtain.*)

THE END

Santa Claus for President

by Jane McGowan

Characters

PROLOGUE

SANTA CLAUS

MRS. SANTA

JINGLE ⎫
JANGLE ⎭ *elves*

THREE REPORTERS

ENGLISH CHILD

PERUVIAN CHILD

DUTCH CHILD

MEXICAN CHILD

FRENCH CHILD

DANISH CHILD

ITALIAN CHILD

THREE AMERICAN CHILDREN

PROLOGUE (*Before the curtain*):
  My Daddy says that politics
  Present a serious question.
  And that is why at Christmas time,
  We have a good suggestion.

  If you would have a President
  Who's great in every way
  Just leave it to the boys and girls
  Throughout the U.S.A.

  We now present our candidate,
  A gentleman of note:

We know that Mr. Santa Claus
Is sure to get your vote.

*   *   *

SETTING: *Santa's workshop.*

AT RISE: MRS. SANTA *is listing telegrams as the two elves,*
JINGLE *and* JANGLE, *call them off to her.* SANTA CLAUS,
his hands behind his back, is pacing up and down.

JINGLE: Pottstown, Pennsylvania.

JANGLE: Albany, New York.

JINGLE: Kansas City, Kansas.

JANGLE: Portland, Maine.

JINGLE: Hollywood, California.

JANGLE: Dallas, Texas.

JINGLE: And here's the last one—Richmond, Virginia.

MRS. SANTA: The last one! Good! That makes five million
telegrams asking Santa Claus to be President of the
United States. (*Shakes head and makes disapproving
sounds*) And I don't approve of it one bit! Not a single
bit!

JINGLE: But, Mrs. Santa, the children want him.

JANGLE: Five million of them. We counted them.

MRS. SANTA: But do children always know what's best?

SANTA: Of course they do. We wouldn't have toy trains,
or dolls, or lollypops, or ice cream, if it weren't for the
children. The little dears always know what's best.

MRS. SANTA: That's where you're wrong. If children always knew what's best, we wouldn't have stomach-aches
from eating too much candy and green apples.

SANTA: Nevertheless, if the children want me to be President, I think it is my duty to please them.

MRS. SANTA: Fiddlededee! It's your duty to stay right here and make hobby horses and candy canes and doll babies and sleds and roller skates.

JINGLE *and* JANGLE: Besides, Santa, it wouldn't be any fun.

SANTA: FUN? Who's talking about fun?

JINGLE *and* JANGLE: We are. We think fun is important.

SANTA: Don't you think the President has any fun? (JINGLE *and* JANGLE *shake their heads "No."*)

JINGLE: If you were President, you couldn't live at the North Pole.

JANGLE: You'd have to live in Washington.

JINGLE: And you couldn't keep your reindeer in the White House.

JANGLE: And you couldn't ride in your sleigh.

JINGLE: And you couldn't come down chimneys.

BOTH: It wouldn't be proper.

SANTA: I never thought of that.

MRS. SANTA: There's plenty you never thought about.

SANTA: Still, if the children want me . . . (*Sound of sleighbells*)

MRS. SANTA: There's someone at the door. Jingle and Jangle, you may answer it. (*Exit* JINGLE *and* JANGLE) Please, Santa, take my advice. Don't run for President. You won't be happy.

SANTA: But if I could make *the children* happy. . . . (JINGLE *and* JANGLE *enter with three* REPORTERS. *Each wears a "Press" sign in his hat and carries a big red notebook, oversized green pencil.*)

JINGLE *and* JANGLE (*Announcing*): The Gentlemen of the Press!

REPORTERS (*Bowing*): Good evening, Santa. Good evening, Mrs. Santa.

SANTA *and* MRS. SANTA: Good evening, gentlemen.

FIRST REPORTER: Is it true that you are going to run for President, sir?

SECOND REPORTER: We'd like to get the whole story.

THIRD REPORTER: And we'd also like a few pictures.

SANTA: I'm afraid you are too early, gentlemen. I have not yet decided.

FIRST REPORTER: But, sir, the whole world is waiting for your answer.

SANTA: If I were only sure that all the children want me.

SECOND REPORTER: Oh, but they do, sir.

THIRD REPORTER: Think what it would mean to them.

FIRST REPORTER: Free toys for all.

SECOND REPORTER: Christmas every day.

THIRD REPORTER: The children of the United States would be the happiest, luckiest boys and girls in the world.

SANTA: In that case, my answer must be *yes*.

REPORTERS: May we print that, Santa?

MRS. SANTA: Oh dear, oh dear, oh dear! (*Goes over to* JINGLE *and* JANGLE *who try to comfort her.*)

FIRST REPORTER: This is the best news of the year.

SECOND REPORTER: The biggest Big Story in the world!

THIRD REPORTER: Santa Claus for President! What a headline!

FIRST REPORTER: Please, Sir, may we have some pictures?

SECOND REPORTER: You and Mrs. Santa and perhaps a few of your elves?

SANTA: Of course. (*To* MRS. SANTA) Come, my dear. They want to take your picture as the future Madame President. (*Sleighbells jingle violently.*)

FIRST REPORTER: May we keep your company waiting until after the pictures? (JINGLE *and* JANGLE *run to the door.*)

JINGLE *and* JANGLE: There are children to see Mr. Santa.

SANTA: In that case, we cannot keep them waiting. Santa Claus is never too busy to see children. Tell them to come in. (*Exit* JINGLE *and* JANGLE)

SECOND REPORTER: I suppose these are more children who want you to run for President.

THIRD REPORTER: They'll be glad to know it's all settled. (JINGLE *and* JANGLE *enter, heading a parade of children from foreign countries. Each child bears a banner with the name of his country. They march in and salute* SANTA CLAUS.)

SANTA: Welcome! Welcome, boys and girls! I am always glad to see my little friends, and I can guess why you have come to see me. You want me to be President. Am I right?

ALL: NO!

SANTA: What? You don't want me to be President of the United States?

ALL: No, indeed!

SANTA: But why? Tell me why.

ENGLAND: We represent the boys and girls,
From far across the sea.
If you become a President,
Where will *our* children be?

PERU: If you are strictly U.S.A.
Then what about Peru?
How will we spend our Christmas
If we do not have you?

HOLLAND: And who will fill our wooden shoes
With candy and with toys?
If you stay here in U.S.A.
We'll have no Christmas joys.

MEXICO: You'll be so tired with taxes

And all affairs of state,
That Christmas treats in other lands,
Will simply have to wait.

FRANCE: Dear Santa, you're a friend of all,
The whole wide world around.
You make all children happy
Wherever you are found.

DENMARK: No single country has the right
To claim you for its own,
To shed your blessings on one land
And leave the rest alone!

ITALY: So please, dear Santa, don't you see
You *can't* accept this post,
For in one land you'd have to stay
And serve that country most.

ALL (*Kneeling*):
We beg you, Santa, on our knees
Before we have to go,
Oh, Santa, Santa, won't you please
Tell them your answer's *no!*

SANTA: Why bless my soul! I had no idea the rest of the children in the world would feel like this.

ALL: We won't give you up. You belong to us. You belong to every child in every land!

MRS. SANTA: The children are right. You yourself said that children know best.

SANTA: But what about the children of the United States? I belong to them too, you know. How will they feel if I refuse to be their President?

MRS. SANTA: Let's ask them and find out. (*To audience*) Dear children of America, you've heard the voices of your little friends across the sea. They too love our Santa Claus. They depend on him to fill their stockings and put up their Christmas trees and bring them toys. Do you still want him to be your President and leave the rest of the world without a Santa?

CHILDREN IN AUDIENCE: No! Christmas is for everybody. (*Three children come to the stage with American flags.*)

FIRST AMERICAN: The children of the U.S.A.
Can understand your plight.
If we kept Santa for ourselves
We'd not be doing right.

SECOND AMERICAN: And Christmas is the time of year
To love and help each other,
For everyone throughout the world
To be a friend and brother.

THIRD AMERICAN: It's better to be right, they say,
Than to be President.
And Santa's international—
A world-wide resident.

SANTA: Gentlemen of the Press, you've heard the children. I've changed my mind. My answer is *no.*

ALL: Hurrah! Hurrah! Hurrah! (*Cast and audience join in closing song, to the tune of "Up on the House Top."*)

Santa belongs to the whole wide world,
Matters not what flag's unfurled.
Over the ocean with lots of toys
All for the good little girls and boys.
Chorus:
Ho, ho, ho, there he will go,
Ho, ho, ho, there he will go.
All 'round the world he'll click, click, click
Down ev'ry chimney comes good Saint Nick!

THE END

Piccola

A French Christmas story

Adapted by *Rowena Bennett*

Characters

SNOW, *a young girl*
WIND, *a young boy*
FISHERMAN
WIFE OF FISHERMAN
PICCOLA, *their daughter*

TIME: *Christmas Eve.*
SETTING: *In front of a fisherman's hut in Brittany.*
BEFORE RISE: SNOW *enters from right, wearing a glittering, white dress and carrying a small, artificial bird in her hand.*

SNOW (*Stroking the bird's feathers*): Poor little fellow! Did the naughty wind scare him? Such a bad, bad wind to chase a little birdie on a cold winter night. There, there! Snow will warm him. Mustn't make any noise, or—

WIND (*Offstage right*): Come here, you stupid bird! Come and feel my whip. (*Crack of whip is heard offstage.*)

SNOW: Sh-h-h! Here he comes! (*She cups her free hand over the bird.*)

WIND (*Running in and lashing his whip*): Come here, you bunch of foolish feathers! Don't you know I am your master? (*He stops suddenly as he sees* SNOW.)

185

WIND (*To* SNOW): Hello, Queen Snow. Out for a dance tonight?

SNOW (*Haughtily*): Not with you.

WIND: Why not? You know you like to dance with me. (*He moves toward her.*) Come on, just one little waltz.

SNOW (*Backing away*): Not tonight.

WIND: But I'll drive everyone else indoors—all the people into their houses, all the wild things into their holes. Then we'll have the whole wide world to ourselves— just to dance in.

SNOW: You are cruel and selfish! You do nothing but chase poor, harmless creatures.

WIND (*With bravado*): But I am master of the winter night. Don't forget that. Everyone must know I'm master. (*He cracks his whip, and the sound of a bird peeping is heard.* WIND *stops suddenly and listens.*) What was that? Sounded like a bird. Must be the one I was chasing.

SNOW: Nonsense! (*She holds the bird closer to her, and moves a step away from* WIND.)

WIND (*Sternly*): What's that you have in your hands?

SNOW (*Coquettishly*): Don't you wish you knew?

WIND: Tell me, or I'll— (*He raises his whip.*)

SNOW (*Laughing*): Perhaps it's a nice cold snowball for you to eat.

WIND (*Brightening*): Is it really?

SNOW: I said, "Perhaps." Now, open your mouth and shut your eyes . . .

WIND (*Obeying*): I like snowballs better than ice-cream cones.

SNOW (*Backing toward left on tiptoe*): . . . and I'll give you something (*She disappears off left, but her voice is still heard.*) . . . to make you wise.

WIND: Well, hurry up about it. (*He opens his eyes.*) I'll be blown! The little minx! She's tricked me! Snow! Snow! Where are you? (WIND *runs out left, after her.*)

* * *

Scene 1

SETTING: *The main room of the Fisherman's hut in Brittany.*

AT RISE: *A dim fire is burning in the fireplace.* FISHERMAN *and his* WIFE *sit at either side of the hearth, mending a long fishnet stretched between them.*

FISHERMAN: Isn't it time for Piccola to come in?

WIFE: I told her she might go down to the village.

FISHERMAN: And why did you let her do that?

WIFE: She needed a change, poor child—shut in with the snow so long.

FISHERMAN: But have you forgotten what night this is?

WIFE (*Throwing up her hands in despair*): Goodness! It's Christmas Eve! I meant to keep the little one from knowing.

FISHERMAN: She would never have guessed at home. All days are the same by the sea.

WIFE: But down in the village, the shops will be filled with chocolate and toys . . .

FISHERMAN: And Piccola will see them.

WIFE: If only we could buy her some little thing.

FISHERMAN (*Shaking his head*): There's not a sou in the house. If it weren't for the fish we'd starve.

WIFE (*Wistfully*): She's never had a toy.

FISHERMAN: Perhaps next year . . .

WIFE (*Bitterly*): Every year we say, "Perhaps next year . . ."

FISHERMAN: Hush! Here she comes! (PICCOLA *enters right, gay and smiling, breathless with excitement.*)

PICCOLA (*Crossing to them*): Oh, Mother! Oh, Father! What do you think? This is Christmas Eve!

WIFE (*Weakly*): Are you sure?

FISHERMAN: How do you know, Piccola?

PICCOLA: I heard the children talking about it in the village. And the shop windows are full of toys—dolls and boats and little wooden animals!

FISHERMAN (*Trying to be cheerful*): That's the fun of Christmas—looking in at the shop windows.

WIFE (*Cheerfully*): Yes, toys are pretty to *look* at. That's mostly what they're for.

PICCOLA: Oh, but they're meant to play with, too! St. Nicholas rides around the world in his jingling sleigh and leaves a toy in every wooden shoe. That's why the boys and girls put their shoes by the chimney. See! I'm going to put mine there. (*She takes off one of her wooden shoes.*)

WIFE: No, no, Piccola! St. Nicholas won't come to this house. It's too small, and too far from the village. He won't even see it.

FISHERMAN: You don't understand, little daughter. Christmas gifts are for the rich, not for the poor—

PICCOLA: That's not what the children said. They know all about it. Some of them have *seen* him. They say he goes to *every* house, rich and poor. (*She sets her shoe in the chimney corner.*)

WIFE (*To her husband*): It's no use. She can't understand.

FISHERMAN: Put your other shoe by the fire, too, Piccola. And warm them for tomorrow.

PICCOLA: No, I couldn't leave *both* shoes. St. Nicholas would think I'm greedy. I'll put the other under my bed.

FISHERMAN: What? Are you going to bed so soon?

PICCOLA: The sooner I go, the sooner the good saint will come. (*She runs to her mother and throws her arms about her.*) Good night, Mother dear.

WIFE (*Kissing her*): Good night, Piccola. (*She takes a candle from the mantel.*)

PICCOLA: Good night, Father (*She kisses him.*)

FISHERMAN (*Sadly*): Good night, little one.

PICCOLA (*Taking candle from her mother*): Oh, I'm so happy! I can hardly wait till tomorrow. (PICCOLA *goes out right, with her candle. The* FISHERMAN *and his* WIFE *look after her sadly. There is a long pause.*)

WIFE (*Going to the hearth and picking up the little wooden shoe*): What will she do when she finds it empty? Poor little shoe. (*She shakes her head sadly*) You will never go dancing so lightly again.

FISHERMAN: Come, come. We'd better go to bed ourselves. It'll save the coals.

WIFE (*Astonished*): We've forgotten to eat supper! (*She replaces the shoe.*)

FISHERMAN: No matter. There'll be all the more for tomorrow. (*He takes another candle from the mantel.*)

WIFE: Yes. We'll make a bigger fire tomorrow, and have a second bowl of soup. Perhaps it will help Piccola forget.

FISHERMAN (*Doubtfully, sighing*): Perhaps, yes, perhaps . . . (*The* FISHERMAN, *carrying candle, leads the way out, and his* WIFE *follows. Gradually, the stage grows darker. A storm howls outside. The fire flickers.* SNOW *tiptoes in, right, and shuts door softly behind her. She is breathless and nervous.*)

SNOW (*In a hoarse whisper*): Are you all right, little bird? (*She takes the bird from inside her dress and smoothes its ruffled feathers. The sound of the bird peeping is heard.*) There! Were you frightened? Poor little fellow! Snow will find a place to hide you from the wicked Wind. (*She walks around the room looking in all the corners.*) Not here, nor here, nor here. Did you ever see such a house! It's so bare there's not a hiding-place in it. If only they had something besides wooden stools. You can see right over and under everything. There isn't even a clock on the mantel.

WIND (*Offstage*): Who-oo-oo-oo.

SNOW (*Clasping the bird to her*): Oh, dear! He's after us again. What shall we do? (*She runs frantically about.*) If there were only a place to hide you! (*She trips over* PICCOLA's *wooden shoe.*) What's this? (*She picks up shoe.*) A shoe! A wooden shoe! Just the thing! Whoever heard of a bird in a shoe?

WIND (*Offstage*): Who-oo-oo-oo! (SNOW *hastily tucks the bird into the wooden shoe and puts the shoe back in the chimney corner.* WIND *bursts noisily through the door at right.*)

WIND (*Seeing* SNOW): Oh-ho! So here you are!

SNOW (*Coldly*): Yes—here I am.

WIND: Thought you'd given me the slip, eh? Where's that bird?

SNOW: What bird?

WIND: I know you're hiding a bird. That's what you had in your hands. And you tried to make me think it was a snowball. Pooh! Give me that bird!

SNOW: Well, search me. (*She holds out her hands.*)

WIND (*Pushing her aside*): No! You've hidden him somewhere in this room. (WIND *rushes about, looking under the stools and the table. He starts to explore the chimney corner, and* SNOW *cries out.*)

SNOW (*Trying to divert his attention*): Look, Wind! (*She runs to the window and rattles the latch.*) See how these windows rattle!

WIND: What of it?

SNOW: Think what wonderful castanets they would make!

WIND (*Excitedly*): You mean you will dance with me?

SNOW: That's just what I mean! (WIND *rushes over to* SNOW, *grabs her arms and they whirl about gaily, at times dangerously close to wooden shoe, as they dance with increasing animation, as curtain falls.*)

*   *   *

Scene 2

Time: *Christmas morning.*
Setting: *The same as Scene 1.*
At Rise: *The sun is streaming in through window. There are mounds of snow (cotton batting) around the room and the stools are turned over. The fire has gone out. The* Fisherman *and his* Wife *enter right.*

Wife (*Rubbing her hands*): Oh, what a cold, bitter world!
Fisherman (*With an effort at cheerfulness*): Things will be better when the fire is lighted. The wind must have blown it out.
Wife (*Crossing to the window*): See how the snow has come in at the cracks.
Fisherman: We'll soon melt that. (*He lights the fire; the* Wife *puts on the kettle, and then picks up a broom from corner of the room, and starts sweeping snow.*)
Wife: I thought the wind would pull the house down last night.
Fisherman: Ah, but look how the sun comes in at the window! The day's making up for the night.
Wife (*Mournfully*): But there'll be nothing in Piccola's shoe.
Fisherman (*Sighing*): No—nothing.
Piccola (*Offstage*): Merry Christmas! Merry Christmas!
Wife (*In despair*): She's coming.
Fisherman: Poor child! (Piccola *enters, right.*)
Piccola (*Running to the window*): Oh, what a beautiful day! St. Nicholas has sent us the sun.
Fisherman (*Hopefully*): The sun is gift enough for one day.

PICCOLA: But he's left something in my shoe, too. (PICCOLA *runs to the wooden shoe. The* WIFE *covers her face with her hands. The* FISHERMAN *turns away sadly.* PICCOLA *takes the bird from shoe.*) Oh, see! See what good St. Nicholas has left me!

WIFE (*Looking up, startled*): What is it?

FISHERMAN (*Coming forward*): It's a bird!

WIFE: A bird!

PICCOLA (*Carefully holding the bird and smoothing its feathers*): It's much nicer than a wooden toy.

WIFE (*Aside, to her husband*): It must have flown down the chimney in the storm.

FISHERMAN: No—it seems as though it had been sent, especially for Piccola.

PICCOLA: Oh, how happy I am! (*She sets the bird on the mantel.*) Listen! He's going to sing! (*The bird bursts into song—a record may be played offstage for the bird's song, or a mechanical "singing bird" may be used. They all listen in happy amazement, as the curtain falls.*)

THE END

The Santa Claus Twins

by Jane McGowan

Characters

MISS JINGLE	CLOWN
CHRISTMAS FAIRY	COWBOY
JACK-IN-THE-BOX	WEIGHER
TOY SOLDIER	MEASURER
NED	TEDDY BEAR
FRED	MESSENGER
RAG DOLL	SOLDIERS
FRENCH DOLL	CHILDREN

SETTING: *Classroom stage with no decoration except a Christmas tree.*

AT RISE: MISS JINGLE, *the teacher, is ready to rehearse her Christmas play.*

MISS JINGLE:
I'm putting on a Christmas play!
And it's a lot of trouble!
Sometimes I get so tired that
I think I'm seeing double!
The children are as good as gold.
They learned their parts with ease.
And now, the cast! I'll call your names.

Assemble, if you please. (*Enter* CHRISTMAS FAIRY, JACK-IN-THE-BOX *and* TOY SOLDIER)
Now, little Christmas Fairy,
Why do you wear a frown?
I see you have your silver wand,
And lovely, sparkly crown.

FAIRY: I'm just as nervous as can be!
Suppose I should forget!

MISS JINGLE:
Oh, nonsense! You know every word!
On that it's safe to bet. (CHRISTMAS FAIRY *moves to one side of stage.*)

MISS JINGLE:
Now, let me see! Oh yes, it's Jack!
But where on earth's your box?

JACK: Too heavy, Teacher! And it feels
As if it's filled with rocks!
But Dad will make another
Especially for the play.

MISS JINGLE:
All right! I guess we'll do without,
And make believe today!
Toy Soldier next! Come let me see
Your shiny sword and gun.

TOY SOLDIER:
My mother's finished with the suit,
But gee! . . . the hat's not done!

MISS JINGLE:
Oh, never mind. You look first-rate,
So stand up straight and tall.
Remember, you're the captain bold,
Commander of them all!

Toy Soldier (*Saluting*): 'Ten shun! Forward march!
(*Other toy soldiers enter and drill.*)

Miss Jingle:

Bravo! Bravo! (*Applauds the drill*)
I'm proud of you. You marched without a pause.
And now it's time we take a look
At Mr. Santa Claus! (*Two boys enter, one from each
side of the stage, dressed exactly alike in Santa Claus
suits.*)

All: Two Santa Clauses!

Miss Jingle: What's this? What's this? I told you yester-
day
That only *one* could take the part
Of Santa in our play.

Ned:

I got here first! I know my lines!
And I can say them too!

Fred: But I have talent! I can act!
I'm better far than you!

Ned: You're not!

Fred: I am! My mother says so!

Miss Jingle:

Boys! Boys! Behave yourselves!
Now listen, both, to me.
We need *one* Santa Claus . . . no more
Beside our Christmas tree!
It may be Ned; it may be Fred.
We'll put you to the test,
And let the children help decide
Which one of you is best. (*Clapping hands as a sum-
mons*)
Come, children! Quickly gather round. (*Children enter*)

Now you must cast your vote
For Fred or Ned, and which should wear
The Santa pants and coat. (*Children assemble in groups on the stage.*)
RAG DOLL: Oh, please, Miss Jingle, please explain
How we can pick and choose.
I do not know how we can tell
Which is the best to use.
MISS JINGLE: Well, well! I guess we'll have to think
Of what he needs to do,
And choose the one who is the best
At picking up his cue.
RAG DOLL: A Santa must be merry,
And speak up loud and strong,
And shout a "Merry Christmas"
Or even sing a song!
FRED: Anything you can shout, I can shout louder! I can shout anything louder than you!
NED: No, you can't!
FRED: Yes, I can!
NED: No, you can't!
FRED: Yes, I can!
BOTH (*At the top of their lungs*): MERRY CHRIST-MAS!
FRENCH DOLL (*Hands over ears*): We have to cover up our ears!
TOY SOLDIER: That must have been a tie!
RAG DOLL: But what about a Christmas song?
MISS JINGLE: We'll give each one a try. (*Each contestant sings one verse of a Christmas song.*)
COWBOY:
You boys know how to rope a song!

You really know your staff!
But Santa must be jolly—
I'd like to hear you laugh. (*There is a loud chorus of Ho-Ho-Ho's and Ha-Ha-Ha's, each Santa trying to out-laugh the other. All children begin to laugh.*)

MISS JINGLE:
Enough! Enough! Now call a halt!
We're getting indigestion!
Attention, children. Quiet, please!
We must decide this question. (*Children quiet down.*)

FRED:
My mother's coming to the play
And all my aunts and cousins.

NED: My relatives are coming, too,
And I have simply dozens!

FRED:
They want to see me on the stage
With Santa's bulging pack.

NED: And if *I* don't play Santa Claus,
They'll want their money back!

MISS JINGLE:
Well, children, it is up to you,
And I would know your pleasure.

CLOWN: I guess we'll have to take their weight
And also take their measure.

MISS JINGLE: Go get the tape, go get the scales. (*Children bring in tape measure and scales.*)
We'll judge on pounds and inches.

FRED (*Stepping on scales*): You'll find I am a heavyweight!

NED (*As child pulls tape around his chest*): Ouch! Ouch!
That tape line pinches. (NED *and* FRED *are weighed and measured.*)

THE WEIGHER:
    Alack! Alas! They weigh the same!
    No difference by the pound!
THE MEASURER:
    They're just as tall, and just as broad,
    And just as big around!
TEDDY BEAR:
    Oh dear, oh dear! It's getting worse.
    I can't make up my mind.
    But one big thing we 'most forgot,
    A Santa's always kind.
MISS JINGLE:
    Then who can speak for Ned or Fred
    And name a kindly deed?
    Step forward quickly, if you will,
    And testify with speed.
CLOWN:
    Fred helps his mother every day,
    Runs errands to the store.
COWBOY: Ned mows the lawn and rakes the leaves
    And scrubs the cellar floor.
RAG DOLL:
    Fred never never picks a fight
    Or teases little girls!
FRENCH DOLL:
    Ned helps his little sister out
    And never pulls her curls.
TOY SOLDIER:
    Fred always feeds a dog or cat
    That has a hungry look.
JACK-IN-THE-BOX:
    Ned shares with others all the time—

A game, or toy or book.

MISS JINGLE:

We'll have to put it to a vote,
Raise hands, if you're for Fred.
(*Half the group votes for* FRED)
And you who do not raise your hands
Are casting votes for Ned. (*Naturally the vote is a tie*)

MISS JINGLE:

Oh, goodness gracious, it's a tie!
Whatever shall we do? (*Enter* MESSENGER BOY *with telegram*)

MESSENGER BOY: Telegram for Miss Jingle! Telegram for Miss Jingle!

MISS JINGLE: I'm Miss Jingle, boy.

MESSENGER BOY: Then here's a wire for you!

ALL: A telegram! A telegram!

MISS JINGLE: Dear me! It's from the North Pole!

ALL: From the North Pole!

MISS JINGLE: Why, it's from Santa Claus. The *real* Santa Claus.

ALL: What does it say?

MISS JINGLE: Oh, dear, I'm so excited. It says: Dear Miss Jingle:

ALL: Dear Miss Jingle!

MISS JINGLE (*Reading*):

The Christmas Fairy in your play
Has told me you're in trouble.
Instead of *one* boy Santa Claus,
You're really seeing double.
I understand that both these boys
Are fully qualified,
And when you put it to a vote,
You found the vote was tied.

I hear you're in a dither now
Deciding what to do.
The answer's very simple for
You'd better use the *two*.

ALL: Two Santa Clauses! Who ever heard of such a thing?

MISS JINGLE (*Continuing reading*):
Experience has taught me that
Two hands are not enough.
You need at least an extra pair
To handle Christmas stuff.
For every year at Christmas when
The holiday begins . . .
I have a very solemn wish:
I wish that I were twins!

ALL (*Laughing*): The Santa Claus Twins! Hurrah for the Santa Claus Twins.

MISS JINGLE (*Continuing reading*):
I hope this solves your problem
Of putting on your play.
And now, to all your players . . .
A merry Christmas Day!

> Signed
> Santa Claus
> St. Nicholas
> Kris Kringle Incorporated

FRED: Now tell me, Christmas Fairy,
How did you do this trick?

NED: Did you write to Mr. Santa,
Or telephone St. Nick?

CHRISTMAS FAIRY:
Oh, no. I used my magic wand
And wished with all my heart
That Santa Claus himself would choose

The best boy for the part.

Toy Soldier:

And now the matter's settled—
The best man always wins,
And here you see the only pair
Of Father Christmas twins.

All (*Singing the following song to the tune of "Up on the Housetop"*):

Up on the housetop the job begins
Out jump both our Santa Twins;
Down through the chimney with
    lots of toys,
Doubling all your Christmas joys!
(*Chorus*) Ho, ho, ho! Who wouldn't go!
Ho, ho, ho! Who wouldn't go!
Up on the roof with merry grins,
Down through the chimney with Santa Twins!

First comes the stocking of little Nell,
Oh, dear Santas, fill it well.
She wants a dolly that laughs and cries,
Let it be twins as a big surprise!
                    (*Chorus*)
Next is the stocking of little Bill.
Both of you must work to fill.
He wants a train and a mile of track,
Lucky for him there's an extra pack!

                    (*Chorus*)

THE END

CREATIVE DRAMATICS

The Christmas holiday is an ideal opportunity for schools and drama groups to put on an improvised play or program, since the traditions of Christmas are better known to children than those of any other holiday. Children may want to make up their own programs, based on a popular song, a traditional carol, or holiday game, or they may decide to use a familiar story, such as the following tale by the Brothers Grimm, as the basis for a pantomime or improvised drama.

* * * * *

The Elves and the Shoemaker

by Sylvia Chermak

Once upon a time, there was a Shoemaker who was so poor that he had only enough leather for one pair of shoes, and no money to buy more. When evening came, he cut out the leather ready to sew the next day, and went to bed. In the morning when he went to his workbench, to his astonishment, he found a beautiful pair of shoes where he had left the cut-out leather. Soon a customer appeared and liked the shoes so much that he gave the Shoemaker enough money to pay for leather for two pairs of shoes. That evening the Shoemaker cut out the leather for two pairs of shoes and left it on his table, ready to be made the next morning, but again, when he awoke, and went to his workbench, the two pairs were there, all ready. Before long, two customers came into his shop and paid him enough money for the shoes to buy leather for four pairs of shoes.

That night before he went to bed, the Shoemaker again cut out the leather and went to bed, and in the morning found the four pairs of shoes finished. And so it continued day after day: no matter how many pairs of shoes the Shoemaker cut out in the evening, he found them finished on his workbench in the morning. Soon he was prosperous and no longer in need.

The night before Christmas, the Shoemaker said to his wife, "Let us stay up tonight and see who has been helping us so generously." His wife agreed. They lit a candle and hid in the corner to watch.

When the clock struck midnight, two tiny, shabbily dressed elves appeared, sat down at the Shoemaker's bench, took the cut-out leather and started to bore holes, to sew, and to hammer so nimbly and quickly that the Shoemaker couldn't believe his eyes. They didn't stop working until all the shoes were finished. Then they quickly dashed away.

The next morning was Christmas Day and the Shoemaker's wife said, "The elves have made us rich — we should do something for them in return. Their clothes are so ragged, I am going to make them little shirts, coats, vests, and trousers, and I'll knit each of them a pair of socks. You can make each of them a pair of little shoes."

The Shoemaker said it was a fine idea, so they set to work, the wife knitting and sewing, he making tiny shoes busily. At night, when everything was ready, they put their presents on the Shoemaker's bench and hid again to see what the elves would do.

At midnight, the elves came skipping in and went to the workbench, ready to begin work, but instead of the leather they found the handsome clothes and shoes. They were astonished and delighted, and put on their new clothes as quickly as possible, then skipped and danced and jumped over the chairs and tables, singing:

"We're such well-dressed little men
Why should we make shoes again?"

After a time, they danced out the door and never came back again. The Shoemaker remained a wealthy man for the rest of his life and succeeded in everything he did.

* * * * *

The procedure to follow in helping children to improvise a Christmas play based on "The Elves and the Shoemaker" is first to read the story aloud to the class. Then the class should list all the movements that take place in the story by the various characters. Such a list might read as follows:

1. Shoemaker and elves: cutting leather for shoes; boring holes in leather with awl; threading large needles with heavy thread or leather thongs; sewing with long needles; hammering nails into shoe soles; lacing up shoes.

2. Customers and shoemaker: trying on shoes; taking money from pocket or purse; counting out coins; wrapping up the shoes in a paper parcel and tying the parcel.

3. Shoemaker's wife: sewing clothes for the elves, including cutting out fabric with scissors; sewing fine stitches with a small needle; sewing on buttons; knitting.

4. Elves: Putting on clothing — getting into shirts and coats; buttoning vests; stepping into trousers; pulling on socks; putting on shoes and tying them; showing off new clothes; skipping, dancing, leaping, jumping; mirror image movements.

5. Shoemaker and wife: Hiding behind a drape and peering out; lying down to sleep; lighting a candle; walking more slowly in imitation of adult movement.

Everyone in the class may practice these movements and any other movements which seem appropriate to the story. The children can pair off to practice mirror image movement as the elves.

When the movements have all been practiced, the teacher or narrator can assign the parts in the story to the children. Many children can take the parts of customers, and it would also be possible for more than two children to be elves — either a whole group of elves could come in and sew the shoes, or two different ones could come each night. Other children can be property men or stagehands, and musicians, providing the sound effect of the clock striking twelve on a xylophone or gong. The musicians can play appropriate musical background accompaniment on recorders, triangles, xylophone, tambourine or wood blocks, etc. If there are enough children and instruments, a rhythm band could be formed to accompany the entire play.

The play can be put on informally, with one child as narrator telling or reading the story while the others act it out in pantomime. Or, there could be a speaking presentation, with no narrator required, for which the children can make up dialogue appropriate to the story and then act it out, speaking these lines. The children should be encouraged to use their own words rather than repeating those of the story, and to pay particular attention to making their lines responsive to those spoken by other characters. In this way, the dialogue will sound natural.

The children should be free to change the story in a variety of ways, expanding it with additional dialogue and action for the Shoemaker, the wife, the elves and the customers, and even possibly introducing more plot complications than in the original story. As an alternate or suggested ending, the play might end in a tableau of all the characters and musicians singing and playing a simple Christmas song, and having the audience join in the singing.

* * * * *

MOVEMENT

There are a number of activities associated with the Christmas season which lend themselves to dramatic interpretation through creative dramatics, improvised body movement, pantomime, and related techniques of the stage. Here are a few, quickly recognized and identifiable, which young performers may work out in any of these dramatic methods or styles, or a combination of them:

1. Buying the Christmas tree or chopping one down in the woods; carrying it home and setting it up; making ornaments, such as stringing cranberries and popcorn and making paper chains; trimming the tree; hanging stockings.

2. Christmas presents: making gifts (sewing, knitting, hammering, sawing, painting, etc.); wrapping boxes; tying bows; hiding secret packages; shaking and poking packages to try to guess the contents.

3. Christmas foods: stirring cookie batter; cracking nuts; chopping fruits; rolling out cookie dough, cutting dough with cookie cutters; baking cookies in oven; stuffing the turkey.

4. Outdoor Christmas events: putting on boots, heavy coats, mufflers, hats, mittens; trudging through the snow; pulling sleds up hills and sliding down hill; walking on ice; ice skating; sleighrides; Christmas caroling.

Here are several ways to use these Christmas activities as the theme for creative dramatics exercises and improvisations:

Movement: Children may act out these Christmas activities, or any others they think of, as a classroom movement exercise.

Pantomime: One child or a group may act out several of the Christmas activities in sequence, telling a story through pantomime.

Charades: As a variation of pantomime, children can play a game of Christmas charades, using the Christmas activities. The class divides into two teams, and the first team goes into a huddle and decides which activity to pantomime. Then he pantomimes the activity for the second group, who try to guess what it is. If they guess correctly, they have a chance to pantomime a Christmas activity themselves. If they can't guess correctly, the first team gets another turn.

Improvisation: As the children pantomime a sequence of Christmas activities, they may want to invent speeches and conversation to explain their actions and to respond to one another, in a kind of skit. This can be an end in itself, or the group may want to expand the pantomime and dialogue into a brief playlet.

* * *

CHRISTMAS SONGS AND CAROLS

The following Christmas carols and songs suggest a wide variety of movement and dramatic actions which can be used in different types of dramatic activity in the classroom, assembly or for a Christmas party: *Up on the Housetops; Jolly Old St. Nicholas; Deck the Halls with Boughs of Holly; The Twelve Days of Christmas; Jingle Bells; Christmas Is Coming (Please Put a Penny in the Old Man's Hat); Good King Wenceslaus; We Three Kings of Orient Are; Bring a Torch, Jeanette, Isabella; The First Noel; The Friendly Beasts; Away in a Manger.*

Movement and Pantomime: These are songs which describe varied activities and lend themselves to movement practice — for example, children may take one song or carol, and list the movements in it, then practice them individually or as a group. They then may pantomime the words of the entire song or carol, while it is played on the piano or sung.

Charades: Children can play Christmas charades using titles, first lines or choruses of songs or carols. The class divides into two teams and each team takes a turn at pantomiming the song selected for the second group. If the second group guesses the song, they take a turn; otherwise, the first group takes another turn.

Dance: Children may create a dance to the music of the songs or carols.

* * *

CREATING A CHRISTMAS PROGRAM

All of the elements of creative dramatics — movement, pantomime, dance, dialogue, improvisation — can be combined to create a Christmas program based on the activities and songs already outlined here. For example, the first part of the program might be called "Getting Ready for Christmas," and a sequence of several Christmas activities, with improvised dialogue, could be presented by some children. They could act out the story of cutting down the tree, bringing it home, setting it up and trimming it, while singing, "Deck the Halls," then baking cookies, and eating them while hanging their stockings. Then the class could present "The Story of the First Christmas," with a chorus singing "We Three Kings of Orient Are," and three children pantomiming the progression of the Magi to the stable. Then a tableau of the Holy Family could be shown while "The First Noel" or "Away in a Manger" is sung. Finally, the chorus can sing, "Up on the Housetops," and Santa Claus can enter, to conclude the program with the distribution of presents, or the traditional Christmas grab-bag, to all the children.

Mr. Scrooge Finds Christmas

From "A Christmas Carol," by Charles Dickens

Adapted by *Aileen Fisher*

Characters

MARLEY'S GHOST
GHOST OF CHRISTMAS PAST
GHOST OF CHRISTMAS PRESENT } *three spirits*
GHOST OF CHRISTMAS YET TO COME
EBENEZER SCROOGE
BOB CRATCHIT, *his clerk*
FRED, *Scrooge's nephew*
A SOLICITOR
BOY CAROLERS
BELINDA
PETER
BOY
GIRL } *the Cratchit family*
MRS. CRATCHIT
MARTHA
TINY TIM
TWO MEN, *from the Stock Exchange*
POULTRYMAN
(*A number of parts may be doubled up.*)

SCENE 1

TIME: *Afternoon of Christmas Eve.*
SETTING: *A darkened stage, with spotlight on one side;*

or the meeting between MARLEY'S GHOST *and the* THREE SPIRITS *may be acted in front of the curtain. Behind the curtain the stage is set for the office of "Scrooge and Marley."*

AT RISE: MARLEY'S GHOST *and* THREE SPIRITS *are in spotlight (or walk in front of the curtain).*

MARLEY: Thank you for coming, friends. I am in dire need of your help. There is a soul to be saved! My name is Marley—Jacob Marley. Rather, I should say, that was my name on earth. And you . . . which is which?

1ST SPIRIT (*Stepping forward*): I am the Ghost of Christmas Past.

2ND SPIRIT (*Stepping forward*): I am the Ghost of Christmas Present.

3RD SPIRIT (*Stepping forward*): I am the Ghost of Christmas Yet to Come.

1ST SPIRIT: We hurried right off to this London street, as soon as your message came, Mr. Marley. We hope we can help you. Have you been over on our side of the world long, sir?

MARLEY: Seven years, this very night. (*Points toward wings*) And, look, my partner never had my name painted out! See, there above the warehouse door— SCROOGE AND MARLEY.

1ST SPIRIT: Brokers?

MARLEY: Connected with the London Exchange. You see, he's not entirely bad, my friends. Just blind, so to speak. Going around with his eyes closed to the things that really matter . . . the way I used to. Thinking that money is everything. (*Rattles chain*) He's forging himself a chain as heavy as mine.

2ND SPIRIT: Who, sir?

MARLEY: Ebenezer Scrooge. Poor fellow.

3RD SPIRIT: And what do you want us to do?

MARLEY: Help me get him to see the light. It's just a case of reaching through to him. And what better time than Christmas Eve?

1ST SPIRIT: Scrooge, you say?

MARLEY (*Nodding*): My former partner, executor, and heir—Ebenezer Scrooge. (*Sighs*) He has the reputation of being a squeezing, wrenching, grasping, scraping, clutching, covetous old sinner. But don't take my word for it. Come along, step inside the countinghouse with me for a few minutes and see for yourselves what kind of man he is—to outward appearances, at least. This way, my friends. No one will see us. (*They go out. If the scene has been acted in front of the curtain, curtain rises; if on stage, lights go on.*)

*   *   *

SCENE 2

SETTING: *The office of Scrooge and Marley.*

AT RISE: *On a stool, hunched over a high bookkeeper's desk, sits* BOB CRATCHIT. *He has a long white muffler around his neck.* SCROOGE *sits at his desk at the other side of the room. There is a meager fire in the grate on each side of the room.* BOB *shivers, rubs his hands. Then, with a furtive glance at* SCROOGE, *gets off his stool, takes the coal shovel and carefully approaches the coal-box.*

SCROOGE (*Looking up, angrily*): At three o'clock in the afternoon, Cratchit? Wasting coal, so close to closing time?

BOB: It's cold and foggy, sir. Penetrating . . .

SCROOGE: Cold, nonsense! Haven't you a candle there on your desk?

BOB: Yes, sir. But the figures suffer when my hand shakes.

SCROOGE: Warm your hands over the candle, then. How many times do I have to tell you? If you persist in being so extravagant with the coal, we shall have to part company, you and I. I can get another clerk, you know. More easily than you can get another position, I warrant.

BOB (*Going back to stool*): Yes, sir. (*Rubs hands over candle. Huddles in muffler. After a moment of silence,* FRED *bursts into the room.*)

FRED (*Cheerfully*): A Merry Christmas, uncle! God save you!

SCROOGE (*Without looking up*): Bah! Humbug!

FRED: Christmas a humbug, uncle? You don't mean that, I am sure!

SCROOGE: I do. Merry Christmas! What reason have you to be merry? You're poor enough.

FRED: Come, then, what reason have you to be dismal? You're rich enough.

SCROOGE (*Banging down ruler*): Bah! Humbug!

FRED: Don't be cross, uncle.

SCROOGE: What else can I be when I live in such a world of fools as this? What's Christmas-time to you but a time for paying bills without money; a time for finding yourself a year older, and not an hour richer? If I could work my will, every idiot who goes about with "Merry Christmas" on his lips should be boiled with his own pudding, and buried with a stake of holly through his heart.

FRED: Uncle!

SCROOGE: Keep Christmas in your own way, and let me keep it in mine. Much good it has ever done you!

FRED: I have always thought of Christmas-time as a good time . . . a kind, forgiving, charitable, pleasant time; the only time I know of when men and women seem by one consent to open their shut-up hearts freely . . . I say, God bless it! (BOB *claps his hands, then, embarrassed at his impulse, huddles over his work.*)

SCROOGE (*To* BOB): Let me hear another sound from *you,* and you'll keep your Christmas by losing your position.

FRED: Don't be angry, uncle. Come, dine with us tomorrow.

SCROOGE: Good afternoon!

FRED: I want nothing from you. I ask nothing of you. Why cannot we be friends?

SCROOGE: Good afternoon!

FRED (*Shrugging, cheerfully*): Well, Merry Christmas, uncle! And a happy New Year!

SCROOGE: Good *afternoon!* (FRED *stops at* BOB's *desk, and they exchange smiles and greetings.* BOB *goes with him to the door. As* FRED *exits, a* SOLICITOR *comes in with books and papers.* BOB *gestures him toward* SCROOGE, *then goes back to his work.*)

SOLICITOR: Scrooge and Marley's, I believe? Have I the pleasure of addressing Mr. Scrooge or Mr. Marley?

SCROOGE: Mr. Marley has been dead these seven years

SOLICITOR (*Presenting credentials*): At this festive season of the year, Mr. Scrooge, it is more than usually desirable that we should make some slight provision for the poor and destitute . . .

SCROOGE: Are there no prisons? No workhouses?

SOLICITOR: There are. But, under the impression that they scarcely furnish Christian cheer, a few of us are endeavoring to raise a fund to buy the poor some meat and drink, and means of warmth. What shall I put you down for?

SCROOGE: Nothing!

SOLICITOR: You wish to be anonymous—is that it?

SCROOGE: I wish to be left alone. I don't make merry myself at Christmas, and I can't afford to make idle people merry. Good afternoon, sir.

SOLICITOR: *Good afternoon!* (SOLICITOR *goes out, shaking his head.* BOB *opens door for him, then hurries back to his stool.*)

SCROOGE (*Glaring at* BOB): *You'll* want all day tomorrow, I suppose?

BOB: If quite convenient, sir.

SCROOGE: It's not convenient, and it's not fair.

BOB: It's only once a year, sir.

SCROOGE (*Bangs down ruler*): A poor excuse for picking a man's pocket every twenty-fifth of December!

Curtain

*   *   *

SCENE 3

BEFORE RISE: MARLEY'S GHOST *and* THREE SPIRITS *appear in spotlight on darkened stage* (*or enter before curtain*).

MARLEY: There!

1ST SPIRIT: I see what you mean, Mr. Marley. Ebenezer Scrooge is a bad case.

2ND SPIRIT: No wonder you need help, if you want to try to reform *him.*

3RD SPIRIT: He's been this way so long, I'm afraid it's a bad habit.

MARLEY: Surely we must try to save him, my friends. We can at least warn him, at least give him a chance to escape my fate. (*Clanks chain*) Poor man, he has no idea what lies ahead of him if he doesn't change his ways.

1ST SPIRIT: What is your plan? How can we warn him? When?

MARLEY: This very night of Christmas Eve! After closing the office, he will take his dinner in the usual tavern, read the papers, go over his accounts, and then home to bed. I know his lodgings well. Fact is, they used to belong to me. He will be quite alone in the house. I will appear before him as he gets drowsy.

2ND SPIRIT: Won't it be rather a shock to him—to see you?

MARLEY: He needs a shock to open his eyes, poor fellow.

3RD SPIRIT: And what about us? Where do we come in?

MARLEY: You wait in the shadows until I call you. First I must lay the groundwork. When I stand before Ebenezer in my usual waistcoat, tights, and boots, I will clank this infernal chain about my middle—this chain made of cash-boxes, keys, padlocks, ledgers, deeds, and heavy purses wrought in steel!

1ST SPIRIT: He will be scared out of his wits!

MARLEY: He needs to be. I will tell him that he is forging a chain just like mine, that I have no rest, no peace, because in life my spirit never roved beyond the narrow limits of our countinghouse. It is no way to live.

2ND SPIRIT: Can a man of business understand such talk, Mr. Marley?

MARLEY: We must *make* him understand, my friends. We must get him to see that mankind, not money, is his business. That common welfare is his business. Charity, mercy, forbearance, and benevolence are all his business! And you are to impress it upon him.

SPIRITS: How?

MARLEY: I will warn Ebenezer that he will be haunted by three Spirits in his sleep tonight. (*Points to* 1ST SPIRIT) As Ghost of Christmas Past, you will take him back to his life as a schoolboy and as an apprentice, and show him that Christmas meant something to him then. That he shouted "Merry Christmas" with the rest of them, in good spirit. (*Points to* 2ND SPIRIT) As Ghost of Christmas Present, you will show him how joyously his clerk Bob Cratchit will celebrate Christmas with his family tomorrow, for all Bob's meager salary. (*Points to* 3RD SPIRIT) And you, as Ghost of Christmas Yet to Come, will show him what will happen if he dies as he is—if he does not change.

1st SPIRIT: And all this to be done tonight?

MARLEY: Tonight, while Ebenezer Scrooge lies abed. Otherwise, we shall be too late for Christmas tomorrow.

SPIRITS: Lead on! We're with you! (*In a moment* BOY CAROLERS *come in singing,* "God Rest You Merry, Gentlemen." *After a stanza or two, they move on. A brief pause . . . then* SCROOGE *and* GHOST OF CHRISTMAS PAST *enter before curtain.*)

SCROOGE: Where now, Spirit?

1st SPIRIT: You'll see.

SCROOGE: You've whisked me back to Christmas of my childhood and my school days. I'd forgotten how my heart used to beat with the excitement of the occasion. (*Hardens*) But what's Christmas to me now? Out with it! What good is it?

1st SPIRIT: One more place, Mr. Scrooge. Do you recognize the thoroughfares of this city? (*Stops, points toward wings*) Do you know that warehouse door?

SCROOGE: Know it? I served my apprenticeship here.

1st SPIRIT: Look in the window. (*They step closer, peering toward wings.*)

SCROOGE (*Pleased*): Why, it's old Fezziwig! Bless his heart! It's Fezziwig alive again.

1st SPIRIT: He's laying down his pen, looking at the clock, laughing all over himself as he calls out, "Ebenezer! Dick!"

SCROOGE: He's calling me and Dick Wilkins, his two apprentices.

1st SPIRIT: He's saying, "No more work tonight. Christmas Eve, Dick. Christmas, Ebenezer! Hilli-ho! Clear away, my lads, and let's have lots of room here for the party."

SCROOGE (*Excited, as he watches*): The floor swept . . .

the lamps trimmed . . . fuel heaped upon the fire. There comes the fiddler with his music book. Here comes Mrs. Fezziwig, with her substantial smile. And the three Miss Fezziwigs . . . and all the young men and women employed in the business, one after another . . .

1ST SPIRIT (*As if calling out a dance*): Hands half round and back again the other way . . . down the middle and up again . . . round and round . . .

SCROOGE: Look, cold roast beef and cold boiled beef! And mince pies. And ale. Dear old Fezziwig, giving us a Christmas party like that!

1ST SPIRIT (*Imitating the unregenerate* SCROOGE): A small matter, to make these silly folks so full of gratitude.

SCROOGE (*Turning on him*): Small!

1ST SPIRIT: Is it not? He has spent but a few pounds of your mortal money.

SCROOGE (*With heat*): It isn't that. The happiness he gives is quite as great as if it cost a fortune. (*Hesitates*) I . . .

1ST SPIRIT: What's the matter?

SCROOGE: Nothing particular.

1ST SPIRIT: Something, I think?

SCROOGE (*Meekly*): No. I should like to be able to say a word or two to my clerk Bob Cratchit just now. That's all. (*They go out.* CAROLERS *come in again, sing another stanza or two of "God Rest You Merry, Gentlemen," then move on. Shortly* SCROOGE *comes in with* GHOST OF CHRISTMAS PRESENT.)

SCROOGE: As Ghost of Christmas Present, you are to show me Christmas as it is here and now, I take it. Conduct me where you will. If you have anything to teach me, let me profit by it.

2ND SPIRIT: Are you familiar with this section of the city, Mr. Scrooge?

SCROOGE: Can't say that I am.

2ND SPIRIT: Hard-working, respectable people live here, doing their best to make ends meet on meager salaries.

SCROOGE: I don't doubt it.

2ND SPIRIT (*Stopping, pointing*): In that four-room house lives a kind and honest man with a large family to support . . . on fifteen bob a week.

SCROOGE: Fifteen bob? Why, that's what I pay my clerk Bob Cratchit.

2ND SPIRIT: I know. And do you ever wonder how the family manages to live on it? I'll tell you. The oldest girl, though she's still young, goodness knows, has to work out, apprentice to a milliner. That's Martha. Bob's wife has to keep making over clothes. She's turned her best dress twice, investing sixpence in ribbons. Belinda, the second girl, also depends upon a few brave ribbons. Master Peter Cratchit swims in one of his father's shirt collars. Tiny Tim . . . they can't afford the proper care for him. One wonders where they got money for a crutch and iron braces for his thin little legs. Then there are the two young Cratchits . . . Stand back! Here they come now. . . . (2ND SPIRIT *pushes* SCROOGE *back to wings.*)

*   *   *

SCENE 4

SETTING: *Kitchen-dining room of* CRATCHIT *house.*

AT RISE: PETER *is trying to keep the fire burning.* BELINDA *is setting the table. The two young Cratchits dash in.*

BOY: We smelled the goose!

GIRL: We were outside the baker's and smelled the goose!

PETER (*Blowing on fire*): How do you know it was ours?

BOTH: Sage and onion, Peter!

PETER: The goose won't do much good if I can't keep the fire burning under the potatoes.

BELINDA: Did you see Martha coming? Or Father and Tiny Tim coming home from church?

BOY: We only smelled the goose.

GIRL: Maybe it isn't very big, Belinda. But it *smells* big. (MRS. CRATCHIT *comes from other room, and bustles around as she talks.*)

MRS. CRATCHIT: What has ever kept your precious father? And your brother, Tiny Tim? And Martha wasn't as late last Christmas Day.

MARTHA (*Opening door*): Here's Martha, Mother!

BOY: Here's Martha!

MRS. CRATCHIT (*Kissing* MARTHA): Why, bless your heart alive, my dear, how late you are!

MARTHA: We'd a deal of work to finish up last night, and had to clear away this morning. (*Sighs, takes off coat*) I'm tired.

MRS. CRATCHIT: Sit before the fire, my dear, and warm yourself, Lord bless you.

PETER: Sit here, Martha. (*Makes a place for her.*)

BOY (*At window*): Father's coming.

GIRL: Hide, Martha, hide! (MARTHA *hides behind the closet door.* BOB CRATCHIT, *his long muffler dangling, comes in with* TINY TIM. BOB *stoops to rub* TIM'S *hands to warm them; then he looks around.*)

BOB: Why, where's our Martha?

MRS. CRATCHIT: Not coming.

BOB: Not coming! Not coming upon Christmas Day!

MARTHA (*Running out from hiding place to her father's arms*): Not coming, because I'm *here.*

BOY *and* GIRL (*Jumping around*): Merry Christmas, Merry Christmas! (*They take* TINY TIM *with them into other room.*)

MRS. CRATCHIT: And how did little Tim behave?

BOB: As good as gold, and better. He told me, coming home, that he hoped the people saw him in church, because he was a cripple, and it might be pleasant for them to remember, upon Christmas Day, who made lame beggars walk and blind men see. (*Turns to* BE-LINDA) And now, where's the saucepan, Belinda? Time for me to mix up something hot for us to toast with on Christmas Day. And the lemons? (BOB *and* BELINDA *work merrily at kitchen table.* BOB *puts saucepan on hob.* PETER *continues to blow on the fire.*)

MRS. CRATCHIT: Peter, you mash the potatoes before go-ing with the two young 'uns to fetch the goose. Belinda, you sweeten up the applesauce. Martha, can you find glassware for drinking the toast?

MARTHA (*At cupboard*): Two tumblers and a custard-cup without a handle.

BOB: They'll hold the hot stuff as well as golden goblets. Here we are! (*Takes pan from hob, pours into glasses. Hands a glass to* MRS. CRATCHIT *and* MARTHA *and takes one himself. Holds it high.*) A Merry Christmas to us all, my dears. God bless us!

OTHERS: A Merry Christmas to us all!

TINY TIM (*Standing with crutch at door*): God bless us, every one! (*The glasses make the rounds. When* BOB *gets his back, he raises it again.*)

BOB: To Mr. Scrooge! I'll give you Mr. Scrooge, the founder of the feast!

MRS. CRATCHIT: The founder of the feast, indeed! I wish I had him here. I'd give him a piece of my mind to feast upon, and hope he'd have a good appetite for it.

BOB: My dear, the children! Christmas Day.

MRS. CRATCHIT: I'll drink his health for your sake, and the Day's, not for his. (*Raises her glass*) Long life to him! A

Merry Christmas and a Happy New Year! (*Curtain falls, as* BOB *drains his glass.*)

*   *   *

SCENE 5

SETTING: *In front of curtain.*

BEFORE RISE: SCROOGE *and* GHOST OF CHRISTMAS PRESENT *come in.*

SCROOGE: Spirit, tell me, will Tiny Tim live?

2ND SPIRIT: I see a vacant seat in the poor chimney corner, and a crutch without an owner, carefully preserved. If these shadows remain unaltered by the Future, the child will die.

SCROOGE: No, no! Oh, no, kind Spirit! Say he will be spared.

2ND SPIRIT: If these shadows remain unaltered by the Future, he will die.

SCROOGE (*As they go out*): No . . . no. (BOY CAROLERS *come in again, sing another stanza or two of "God Rest You Merry, Gentlemen." They move on. After a slight pause,* SCROOGE *and* GHOST OF CHRISTMAS YET TO COME *appear before curtain or in spotlight on darkened stage.*) You are about to show me shadows of the things that will happen in the time before us. Is that so, Ghost of Christmas Yet to Come? (3RD SPIRIT *does not answer.*) I fear you more than any specter I have seen. But as I know your purpose is to do me good, and as I hope to live to be another man than what I was, I am prepared to bear you company. Oh, are you taking me to the Stock Exchange? I shall be among friends there. (3RD SPIRIT *draws him to one side as* TWO MEN *from the Exchange enter.*)

1ST MAN: I don't know much about it either way, and I don't care. I only know he's dead.

2ND MAN: When did he die? His partner went years ago. I thought he'd never die. What was the matter with him?

1ST MAN: God knows. (*Shrugs*) It's likely to be a very cheap funeral, for, upon my life, I don't know of anybody to go to it. That tight-fisted old sinner! (*They exit.*)

SCROOGE (*With a shiver*): They couldn't be talking about me, could they? Could they? (*Looks imploringly at* SPIRIT, *gets no answer.*) Where now, Spirit? (*They take a few steps back and forth;* SPIRIT *does not speak.*) Oh, Bob Cratchit's house again? This looks like the street. Yes, there's his little house. . . . (*They walk off.*)

*   *   *

SCENE 6

SETTING: *The same room in Cratchit's house.*

AT RISE: MRS. CRATCHIT *and* BELINDA *sit at table, sewing.* PETER *is near the grate, reading aloud from the Bible. The two* YOUNG CRATCHITS, *quiet and subdued, listen intently.*

PETER (*Reading*): "And he took a little child, and set him in the midst of them."

MRS. CRATCHIT (*With muffled sob, laying work on table, putting hand to eyes*): The color hurts my eyes. (*After a pause*) I wouldn't show red eyes to your father when he comes home, for the world. It must be nearly time for him.

PETER (*Closing book*): Past it, rather. But I think he has walked a little slower than he used to, these few last evenings, Mother.

MRS. CRATCHIT: I have known him walk with—I have known him walk with Tiny Tim upon his shoulder very fast indeed.

PETER: And so have I. Often.

BELINDA: And so have I.

MRS. CRATCHIT: But he was very light to carry, and his father loved him so that it was no trouble—no trouble. (*There is a noise at the door.*) And there is your father at the door! (BOB CRATCHIT *enters, quietly takes off his long muffler.*)

BOB: Good evening, my dears. (*Sits near the others*)

MRS. CRATCHIT: Let me pour you a cup of tea. (MRS. CRATCHIT *brings tea, the two* YOUNG CRATCHITS *kneel beside* BOB.)

BOY: Don't mind it, Father.

GIRL. Don't be so grieved.

BOB: No. No. (*Suddenly brightens*) You can't imagine the extraordinary kindness of Mr. Scrooge's nephew today. I'd scarcely seen him but once or twice before. He's the pleasantest-spoken gentleman you ever heard. Met me on the street today and said—said he thought I looked a little—just a little down, you know. So I told him about Tiny Tim.

MRS. CRATCHIT: I'm sure he's a good soul.

BOB: He gave me his card and said, "That's where I live. Pray come to me if I can be of service to you in any way." It really seemed as if he had known our Tiny Tim, and felt with us. (*Pause*) I shouldn't be at all surprised if he got Peter a better position.

MRS. CRATCHIT: Only hear that, Peter!

BOB (*After a pause*): I am sure we shall none of us forget our poor Tiny Tim—shall we?

OTHERS: Never! Never! (SCROOGE *and* 3RD SPIRIT *enter darkened stage in spotlight, or come before curtain.* SCROOGE *is much shaken.*)

SCROOGE (*Falling to his knees before* 3RD SPIRIT): Good Spirit, assure me that I may yet change these shadows you have shown me by living a different life! (3RD

SPIRIT *kindly helps him to his feet.*) I will honor Christmas in my heart, and try to keep it all the year. I will live in the past, present, and the future. The Spirits of all three shall strive within me. I will not shut out the lessons that they teach. Good Spirit, assure me . . . (3RD SPIRIT *takes his arm, and they go out.* BOY CAROLERS *come by again, singing; exit.*)

Curtain

*   *   *

SCENE 7

SETTING: *In front of curtain.*

BEFORE RISE: MARLEY'S GHOST *and the* THREE SPIRITS *enter.*

MARLEY: Well done, my friends.

1ST SPIRIT: How well done remains to be seen.

2ND SPIRIT: Do you think we have opened his eyes?

3RD SPIRIT: Will he *really* change, or was his repentance only a passing whim?

MARLEY: If I know Ebenezer Scrooge, what he has gone through will make a different man of him from now on.

1ST SPIRIT: It's Christmas morning. We shall soon see. (*Bells ring and* CAROLERS *enter.*)

2ND SPIRIT: Christmas morning in good old London.

3RD SPIRIT: Look, Mr. Scrooge is coming . . . (*They stand aside, watching.* SCROOGE *hurries in, calling* . . .)

SCROOGE: Boy, boy! You there, boy! (*One of* CAROLERS *comes forward.*) What's today, my fine fellow?

BOY: Today! Why, *Christmas Day.*

SCROOGE: Do you know the poulterer's in the next street, at the corner?

BOY: Of course, I do.

SCROOGE: Do you know whether they've sold the prize turkey that was hanging there?

BOY: The one as big as me? It's hanging there now.

SCROOGE: Is it? Go tell them I want to buy it. Come back with the man and I'll give you a shilling. (BOY *runs out.* SCROOGE *begins to cross stage. The* SOLICITOR *approaches.*) Wait . . . don't I know this gentleman? (*Stops* SOLICITOR) Merry Christmas, sir. I hope you succeeded in raising a big fund for the poor and needy. It was very kind of you.

SOLICITOR: Mr. Scrooge?

SCROOGE: Yes, that's my name, and I fear it may not be pleasant to you. Allow me to ask your pardon. And will you have the goodness . . . (*He whispers something in* SOLICITOR'S *ear.*)

SOLICITOR: Lord bless me! My dear Mr. Scrooge, are you serious?

SCROOGE: If you please, not a farthing less. A great many back payments are included in it, I assure you. Will you do me that favor?

SOLICITOR: My dear sir, I don't know what to say to such munifi . . .

SCROOGE: Don't say anything, please. Bless you! (SOLICITOR, *still unbelieving, goes out.* POULTRYMAN *returns with* BOY. POULTRYMAN *carries large turkey in bundle under his arm.*) Ah, here we are. (*Gives* BOY *a coin*)

BOY: Thank you, sir. (*Merrily*) Merry Christmas!

SCROOGE: That *is* a turkey. Impossible to carry a bird as big as that to Camden Town where my clerk Bob Cratchit lives. You must take a cab, my dear fellow. Here . . . (*Scribbles address*) . . . this is the address. (*Gives him money*) And here's more than enough for the turkey and the cab and your trouble. Merry Christmas to you!

POULTRYMAN (*Much pleased*): And to you, sir. Thank

you, sir. (*Hurries out. Several passers-by cross stage.* SCROOGE, *beaming, smiles "Merry Christmas" to them. Then* FRED *enters.*)

SCROOGE: Fred!

FRED: Why, bless my soul, if it isn't my Uncle Scrooge! What are you doing out on Christmas morning, sir? Going to church? You don't mean . . .

SCROOGE: What are *you* doing out on Christmas morning?

FRED (*Laughing*): Last minute errand for my wife. Forgot the lemons for the punch!

SCROOGE: I was planning to go to your house for Christmas dinner, Fred. If you'll let me come . . .

FRED: If I'll let you! Why, uncle, we'll be delighted, my wife and I. Come along. I always said there was nothing like a family dinner on Christmas Day. (*They go out arm in arm.* MARLEY'S GHOST *and* THREE SPIRITS *come forward.* MARLEY'S GHOST *no longer wears a heavy chain, but merely a large watchchain holding his waistcoat together.*)

MARLEY: He sees! He really sees. He won't slip back now. I'd bet my bottom dollar on it . . . if I had a dollar. Spirit of Christmas Yet to Come, tell us what you see *now* in the future.

1ST *and* 2ND SPIRITS: Yes, tell us!

3RD SPIRIT: He will be better than his word. He will do more, infinitely more. He will raise Bob Cratchit's salary first of all. And Tiny Tim will *not* die, for Scrooge will get the best doctors in London for him. He'll be a second father to him. Scrooge will become as good a friend, as good a master, and as good a man as the good old City ever knew, or any other good old city, town, or borough in the good old world.

MARLEY: Thank you! Thank you again, my friends. If we lived in a world where toasts were in order, I would propose a toast to you. (*Raises hand in mock toast*) To Christmas—past, present, and future. (*Suddenly*) My chain! What has happened to my chain?

1ST SPIRIT: It's gone, Mr. Marley. Most of it is gone!

2ND SPIRIT: Only a few links left—just enough to hold your waistcoat in place!

3RD SPIRIT: It's because Christmas came to your heart, too, sir. (*Holds up hand in mock toast*) As Tiny Tim would say, "God Bless Us, Every One!"

ALL: Every one! Everywhere! (*Curtain*)

THE END

The Birds' Christmas Carol

by Kate Douglas Wiggin

Adapted by *Helen Louise Miller*

Characters

THE CAROLERS
NARRATOR
GRANDMA BIRD
DONALD ⎫
HUGH   ⎬ *the Bird children*
PAUL   ⎪
CAROL ⎭
NURSE PARKER
UNCLE JACK
MRS. RUGGLES
NINE RUGGLES CHILDREN
MRS. BIRD

BEFORE RISE: CAROLERS *enter on apron of stage.*

1ST CAROLER: Is this our last stop? My feet are nearly frozen!

LEADER: Yes, this is the last one. Then home to my house for plenty of hot chocolate.

2ND CAROLER: Someone must be up late in that big house

across the street. All of the windows on the second floor are lighted.

3RD CAROLER: Maybe they'll invite us in to get warm.

LEADER: Think about the music instead of your feet, and you won't be so cold. Now, this is our last performance, so let's do our very best. (CAROLERS *sing several selections*.) That was truly beautiful. I'm sure anyone who was listening would feel the real spirit of Christmas in your music.

2ND CAROLER: I wonder if they were listening in that big house. The lights are still on, but no one is opening the door.

3RD CAROLER: I wonder how many people have heard our carols tonight, and what they thought of them.

LEADER: That's something we'll never know. But I have an idea that our Christmas caroling affects people more than we imagine. Who knows but what Christmas will take on a deeper meaning to some folks, just because of the carols we sang tonight. (CAROLERS *exit, all but one who serves as* NARRATOR.)

NARRATOR: And even our leader would have been surprised at the results of our carol-singing in the big, brownstone house. The family's name was Bird, and the reason why the Birds' Nest was all lighted up in the small hours of Christmas morning was that a new little fledgling, a very precious Baby Bird, had come into the world shortly after midnight. As the other children gather in the living room after breakfast, their Christmas gifts are almost forgotten in the excitement of hearing about their baby sister. (*Exits*)

*   *   *

Scene 1

SETTING: *A living room decorated for Christmas.*
AT RISE: *Three small boys are gathered about their grandmother.*

HUGH: What's the baby's name, Grandma? What are they going to call her?

GRANDMA: I can't say for sure, dear, but I think your mother's going to call her *Lucy*. Would you like that?

HUGH: Oh, yes, well enough. It will do . . . for a *girl!* If it had been a boy, I think *Texas* would be a good name.

DONALD *(In disgust)*: Aw, Texas isn't a real boy's name. It's the name of a state.

HUGH: It can also be a boy's name. Lots of boys are named *Texas!*

DONALD: Only in stories. Not for real! Anyhow, the baby's not a boy, it's a girl, so what are we arguing about?

PAUL: I think Luella's a pretty name.

HUGH: Yeah! Ever since you had that pretty nurse in the hospital named Luella, that's your favorite name. You even wanted to name our puppy Luella.

DONALD: Dorothy's a good name, too.

HUGH: Especially when it belongs to Dorothy Hagen, the girl who sits across the aisle from you.

DONALD: Now listen, you. . . .

GRANDMA: Children! Children! Not so loud! We don't want to disturb your mother or wake the baby! Anyhow, we can't be absolutely sure what the baby's name is until we hear from your mother.

PAUL: Maybe Dad will have a good idea for a name.

HUGH: Nope. Dad named all three of us boys. He says it's Mother's turn this time.

DONALD: Uncle Jack says a first girl baby should always be named for its mother.

GRANDMA: Well, one thing you can be sure of. Your mother will never allow her baby to go overnight without a name. In fact, I wouldn't be surprised if the matter has already been settled.

PAUL: When are we going to see the baby?

GRANDMA: As soon as the nurse says you may go up.

DONALD: Aw, I don't want to see it. I'd rather ride my new tricycle around the block.

GRANDMA: Donald Bird! What a dreadful thing to say! Of course, you want to see your little sister. (*Enter* NURSE)

NURSE (*To* GRANDMA): Excuse me, ma'am, but Mrs. Bird would like you to bring the boys upstairs now to see the baby.

GRANDMA: That's wonderful, Nurse. We'll be right up.

PAUL: What's the baby's name, Miss Parker? Has Mother decided yet?

NURSE: Indeed, she has, and I think she has selected the most perfect name in the world for a Christmas baby. *Carol.* Isn't that a sweet name?

ALL: Carol?

GRANDMA: Is it short for Caroline?

NURSE: No, indeed. It means just what it says. . . . *Carol* —a song of joy for Christmastide.

GRANDMA: Strange, she never even mentioned that name before.

NURSE: No, the idea came to her early this morning. Right after the baby was born, Mrs. Bird heard the carolers singing on the corner, and said the music was so sweet, it sounded as if the angels were bidding the baby welcome. "Carol" . . . she said . . . "She's Mother's little Christmas Carol," and that's how she decided on the name. A lovely thought if you ask me, ma'am.

PAUL: Gee Willikers! I guess if she had been born on the Fourth of July, they'd have named her *Independence!*

HUGH: If it had been February twenty-second, they might have called her *Georgiana* or maybe even *Cherry!*

DONALD: Carol! I think that's a pretty name. What are we waiting for? Let's go and see her. (*Starts for door*)

GRANDMA: Not so fast, young man! I thought you didn't want to see the new baby at all.

DONALD: Well, I've changed my mind since I know her name is *Carol.* I think it will be fun to have a little Christmas Carol around the house 365 days in the year.

CURTAIN

* * *

NARRATOR (*Entering*): And it *was* fun to have Carol around the house 365 days in the year. Perhaps because she was born at holiday time, Carol was a very happy baby, and also a very beautiful baby. Her cheeks and lips were red as holly berries; her hair was for all the world the color of a Christmas candle flame; her eyes were bright as stars; her laugh like a chime of Christmas bells, and her tiny hands were forever outstretched in giving.

But by the time ten Christmases had come and gone, a sad change had come over the Birds' Nest; for the little child who once brought such an added blessing to the day, lay month after month a patient, helpless invalid. A famous doctor had warned the family that someday soon Carol would slip quietly away from those who loved her so dearly. But in spite of their sorrow, the Birds determined to make Carol's tenth birthday the very best Christmas ever. Carol herself had planned the day down to the last detail, and she could hardly wait to describe her plans to her beloved Uncle Jack, just home from England in time for the holidays. (*Exits*)

*   *   *

SCENE 2

SETTING: *A corner of* CAROL'S *bedroom.*
AT RISE: CAROL *is in bed, propped up on pillows.* UNCLE JACK *is seated near her.*

CAROL: I want to tell you about my plans for Christmas, Uncle Jack, because it will be the loveliest one I've ever had. You know, ever since I discovered how wonderful it is to be born on Christmas Day, I've tried to make someone extra happy on my birthday, and this year it's to be the Ruggleses.

UNCLE JACK: That large brood of children in the little house at the end of the back garden?

CAROL: Yes. Isn't it nice to see so many together? Uncle Jack, why do *big* families always live in small houses and the small families in big houses?

UNCLE JACK: That's pretty hard to explain, Carol.

CAROL: Well, don't bother. I'm sure the Ruggleses have a good time in their little house. Ever since they moved in, I've watched them play in their back yard. One day when they were extra noisy, and I had a headache, Donald asked them not to scream quite so loud, and what do you think they did?

UNCLE JACK: I hope they listened to Donald.

CAROL: Oh, they did. They played Deaf and Dumb Asylum all afternoon so they wouldn't disturb me.

UNCLE JACK (*Laughing*): Quite an obliging family, I must say.

CAROL: Now, Sarah Maud, she's the oldest, stops every day to see how I am before they start their games. Then she and Peter tell the others what to play.

UNCLE JACK: Which is the pretty, little red-haired girl?

CAROL: That's Kitty.

UNCLE JACK: And the fat one?

CAROL: Little Larry. He's the youngest.

UNCLE JACK: And the most freckled one?

CAROL: Now, don't laugh! That's Peoria.

UNCLE JACK: Carol, you're joking.

CAROL: No, really, Uncle Jack, she was born in Peoria, Illinois.

UNCLE JACK: And is there a Chicago and Cincinnati?

CAROL: No. The others are Susan and Clement and Eily and Cornelius and Peter.

UNCLE JACK: How did you ever learn their names?

CAROL: I have a window-school. When the weather is warm, I sit on the balcony, and the Ruggleses climb up and walk along our garden fence, and sit on the roof of our carriage house, and I tell them stories.

UNCLE JACK: And how do these children fit into your Christmas plans?

CAROL: I want to give the nine Ruggles children a grand Christmas dinner, and afterwards a tree, just blooming with presents. Here, I've written the invitation. Please read it and tell me if it's all right.

UNCLE JACK (*Reading*): "Birds' Nest, December 17th: Dear Mrs. Ruggles: I am going to have a dinner party on Christmas Day, and I would like to have all your children come. I want them every one, please, from Sarah Maud to little Larry. Mamma says dinner will be at half-past five, and the Christmas tree at seven; so you may expect them home at nine o'clock. Wishing you a Merry Christmas and a Happy New Year, I am

Yours truly,

Carol Bird."

CURTAIN

* * *

NARRATOR (*Entering*): That invitation caused a tumult of excitement in the Ruggles household. Poor Mrs. Ruggles was almost beside herself with preparations. Such a washing and scrubbing and mending of clothes you never saw. Larry had a new suit made out of his mother's old plaid shawl. Sarah Maud trimmed her skirt with a row of brass buttons off her uncle's policeman's uniform, and Peoria gave half her candy to the next-door neighbor in exchange for a pair of stockings that matched. Finally the great day came, and after an extra tubbing and scrubbing, Mrs. Ruggles lined them up on a row of chairs in the kitchen for final inspection and a lesson in manners. (*Exits*)

* * *

SCENE 3

SETTING: *The Ruggles home.*

AT RISE: *The nine Ruggles children are lined up on kitchen chairs, a wood box and a coal hod.* MRS. RUGGLES *inspects them.*

MRS. RUGGLES: Well, if I do say so, I've never seen a cleaner, more stylish mess of children in my life! I do wish your father could look at you for a minute. (*Crossly*) Larry Ruggles, how many times have I told you not to keep pulling at your sash! Haven't I told you if it comes untied, your waist and trousers'll part company in the middle . . . and then where'll you be? (*Severely*) Now look me in the eye, all of you! I've often told you what kind of family the McGrills was. I've reason to be proud, goodness knows! Your uncle is on the police force of New York City, and I can't have my children fetched up common, like some folks. When my children go out, they've got to have clothes and learn to act decent. Now, I want to see how you're going to behave when you get there tonight! Isn't as easy as you think. Let's start in at the beginning and act out the whole business. Pile into the bedroom there, every last one of you, and show me how you're going to go into the parlor. This'll be the parlor, and I'll be Mrs. Bird. (*Children go off stage and* MRS. RUGGLES *assumes exaggerated pose of a society woman. On signal from their mother, the children straggle in,* SARAH MAUD *in the lead.* LARRY *is at the tail end, but suddenly he makes a mad dash, slips and slides into home base.*)

MRS. RUGGLES (*In complete disgust*): There! I knew you'd do it some such fool way. Now, go in there and try it again, and if Larry can't come in on two legs, he can stay at home, do you hear? (*Children exit again and re-enter in lock step, single file*) No! No! No! That's worse yet! You look for all the world like a gang of prisoners! There isn't any style to that! Spread out more, can't you, and act kind of careless-like! Nobody's going to kill you! That isn't what a dinner party is.

(*Children try again, do better, and seat themselves once more on the chairs.*) Now you know there aren't enough decent hats to go around, and if there were, I don't know as I'd let you wear 'em, for the boys would never think to take them off when they got inside. Now, look me in the eye! You're only goin' just around the corner. You needn't wear hats, any of you! When you get into the parlor, and Mrs. Bird asks you to take off your hats, Sara Maud must speak up and say it was such a pleasant evening, and such a short walk, that you left your hats at home. Now can you remember?

ALL: Yes, ma'am.

MRS. RUGGLES: What have *you* got to do with it? Wasn't I talking to your sister, Sarah Maud?

ALL (*Meekly*): Yes, ma'am.

MRS. RUGGLES: Now we won't leave anything to chance. Get up, all of you, and try it. (*Children rise.*) Speak up, Sarah Maud. (SARAH MAUD *swallows again and again in stage fright.*) Quick! Speak up!

SARAH MAUD (*In desperation*): Ma thought that it was such a pleasant hat, that we'd better leave our short walk at home. (*Roars of laughter from the children*)

MRS. RUGGLES: Oh, whatever shall I do with you? I suppose I've got to teach it to you word by word. Now try it again. The rest of you, sit down!

SARAH MAUD: Ma thought it was such a pleasant evening and such a short walk that we left our hats at home.

MRS. RUGGLES: Again! (SARAH MAUD *repeats phrase.*) There! I guess you've got it! Now, Cornelius, what are *you* gonna say to make yourself good company?

CORNELIUS (*Startled*): Who? Me? I dunno!

MRS. RUGGLES: Well, you aren't going to sit there like a bump on a log, without saying a word to pay for your vittles, are you? Ask Mrs. Bird how she feels this evening or if Mr. Bird's having a busy season or how this weather agrees with him, or something like that. Now, we'll make believe we're having dinner. That won't be hard, cause you'll have something to do. If they have napkins, Sarah Maud down to Peory, may put 'em in their laps, and the rest of you, tuck 'em in your necks. Don't eat with your fingers! Don't grab anything off one another's plates! Don't reach out for anything! Wait till you're asked! And if you never get asked, don't get up and grab it! Don't spill anything on the tablecloth, or like as not, Mrs. Bird'll send you away from the table. Susan, keep your handkerchief in your lap where Peory can borrow it if she needs it! And I hope she knows when she does need it, though I don't expect it! Now, we'll try a few things to see how they go. (*Adopting society pose*) Mr. Clement, do you eat cranberry sauce?

CLEMENT: You bet your life!

MRS. RUGGLES: Clement McGrill Ruggles! Do you mean to tell me you'd say that at a dinner party? I'll give you one more chance. Mr. Clement, will you take some of the cranberry?

CLEMENT (*Meekly*): Yes, ma'am, thank you kindly, if you happen to have any handy.

MRS. RUGGLES: Very good indeed! But they won't give you two tries tonight. Miss Peory, do you speak for white or dark meat?

PEORIA: I'm not particular as to color. Anything nobody else wants will suit me!

MRS. RUGGLES: First-rate! Nobody could speak more genteel than that! Miss Kitty, will you have hard or soft sauce on your pudding?

KITTY: Hard or soft? Oh, a little of both, please, and I'm much obliged.

PETER: What a pig!

ALL: Piggy! Piggy! (*They make grunting noises.*)

MRS. RUGGLES: None of that, and stop your grunting, Peter Ruggles. That wasn't greedy. That was all right! It's not so much *what* you say, as the way you say it. And don't keep staring cross-eyed at your necktie pin, or I'll take it off and sew it on Clem or Cornelius. Sarah Maud'll keep her eye on it, and if it turns broken side out, she'll tell you. Gracious! You'd think you'd never worn jewelry in your whole life!

Eily and Larry are too little to train, so you two just look at the rest and do as they do! Lord have mercy on you and help you to act decent! Now, is there anything more you'd like to practice?

PETER: If you tell me one thing more, I can't sit up and eat! I'm so cram full of manners now, I'm ready to bust without any dinner at all!

CORNELIUS: Me, too!

MRS. RUGGLES (*With sarcasm*): Well, I'm sorry for you both! Now, Sarah Maud, after dinner, every once in a while, you must get up and say: "I guess we'd better be going." Then, if they say: "Oh, no, stay a while longer," you can sit down. But if they don't say anything, you've got to get up and go! Now, have you got that into your head?

SARAH MAUD (*Mournfully*) It seems as if this whole dinner party sets right square on top of me! Maybe I could manage my own manners, but to manage nine manners is worse than staying at home.

MRS. RUGGLES (*Cheerfully*): Oh, don't fret! I guess you'll get along. Well, it's a quarter past five, and you can go now. (*Children line up to depart.* MRS. RUGGLES *follows them off stage, giving directions till the last child is out of sight and the curtains close.*) Remember about the hats! Don't all talk at once! Susan, lend your handkerchief to Peory! Cornelius, hold your head up! Sarah Maud, don't take your eyes off Larry! Larry, you keep tight hold of Sarah Maud and do just as she says! And whatever you do, all of you . . . never forget for one second. . . . (*Shouting*) THAT YOUR MOTHER WAS A McGRILL!

CURTAIN

* * *

NARRATOR (*Entering*): There never was such a party! There were turkey and chicken, with delicious gravy and stuffing, and there were half a dozen vegetables, with cranberry jelly, and celery and pickles; and after these delicacies were served, there were plum pudding, mince pie and ice cream; and there were more nuts and raisins and oranges than anyone could possibly eat. Then there was the tree with the presents! By nine o'clock the Ruggleses could hardly stagger home with their boxes, bags, bundles and packages. All in all, it was a Christmas the children would never, never forget. (*Ruggles children come across the stage, each one laden with gifts.*)

SARAH MAUD (*Carries a large paper bag in one hand, and holds onto* LARRY *with the other*): This is a bag of oranges Mrs. Bird sent along home to Ma. It's so heavy I can hardly carry it!

LARRY: I have a Noah's Ark with all the animals!

CORNELIUS: Would you believe it . . . every fellow had his own particular butter and there were pictures stuck right fast on to the dishes!

PETER: Wait a minute, everybody! I have to see what time it is on my new watch!

CLEMENT: You'll wear that watch out taking it in and out of your pocket. Be careful you don't break it before Ma sees it!

CORNELIUS: If he does break it, I can fix it with my new set of tools.

PEORIA: I can hardly wait to wear my beautiful new dress!

SUSAN: Me, too! And I bet my new coat is warm as toast!

KITTY: I love my doll baby! She has the most beautiful clothes in the world!

EILY: No, no! Mine are the prettiest! Aren't mine the prettiest, Sarah Maud?

SARAH MAUD: Everything's just lovely, Eily. Now come along while we can still walk! Ma'll be worried about us. And remember, not any of you is to tell her that Larry got stuck in the hall rack behind all those canes and umbrellas.

ALL: We won't! We won't!

KITTY: I wish Ma could have had some of that wonderful dinner and tasted that plum pudding!

PETER: Don't worry. She did! Mr. Bird told me they sent a whole dinner over to our house with ice cream and everything.

PEORIA: I'm glad! I hope she got a drumstick like mine.

LARRY: And I got the wishbone! (*Making a chant of it as the children exit*) I got the wishbone! I got the wishbone!

NARRATOR (*As children exit*): And if the Ruggleses had a
wonderful time, Carol Bird, their little hostess, enjoyed
it even more. She and her mother talked it all over
when Mrs. Bird came in to say goodnight. (*Exits*)

*   *   *

SCENE 4

SETTING: *A corner of Carol's bedroom.*
AT RISE: CAROL *is propped up on pillows, ready for the
night. Her* MOTHER *sits on the edge of the bed.*

CAROL: Oh, wasn't it a lovely, lovely time, Mother?
MOTHER: It certainly was, darling, but I'm afraid you've
had enough excitement for one day.
CAROL: From first to last, everything was just exactly
right! I'll never forget little Larry's face when he saw
the turkey, nor Peter's when he looked at his watch!
And, Mother, did you see Kitty's smile when she kissed
her dolly, and Sarah Maud's eyes when she saw her new
books!
MOTHER: We mustn't talk any longer about it tonight,
dear. You're far too tired.
CAROL: I'm not so tired. In fact, I've felt fine all day, not
a pain anywhere. Perhaps this has done me good.
MOTHER: I hope so. There was no noise or confusion, just
a happy, happy time. Now, I'm going to close the door
for a little while so you can get some rest. There's a
little surprise for you later on.
CAROL: Surprise?
MOTHER: Yes, dear. The Carolers did not come this way
last night, and so they're paying us a special visit this

evening just so you may hear your favorite carol. Isn't that nice of them?

CAROL: Wonderful, Mother, wonderful! I will stay awake to hear them.

MOTHER: Oh, they'll be here early. We asked them to come before ten o'clock because after that, you might be asleep.

CAROL: I'll listen to every word. And please, will you raise the shades. This morning, I woke ever so early, and one bright, beautiful star shone in the eastern window. I never noticed it before, and I thought of the Star in the East that guided the Wise Men to Bethlehem. Good night, Mother. Such a happy, happy day!

MOTHER: Good night, my precious Christmas Carol. Goodnight.

CAROL (*Calling her mother back*): And, Mother dear, I do think we have kept Christmas this time just as *He* would like it. Don't you?

MRS. BIRD: I'm sure of it, my darling. I'm sure of it. (*Curtains close as* MOTHER *leans over to kiss* CAROL *good night. On apron of the stage, the* CAROLERS *quietly assemble.*)

LEADER: We are here, as you know, by special invitation to sing for little Carol Bird. Eleven Christmases ago, the music of one of our caroling groups inspired Mrs. Bird to name her baby daughter *Carol*. So tonight, we'll sing the same carols that were sung on the little girl's birth day. (*Announces same carols used in prologue and* CAROLERS *sing them*)

1ST CAROLER: It's after ten o'clock. I do hope she heard us.

2ND CAROLER: Oh, dear! I hope she wasn't asleep! (*To* LEADER) Do you think Carol heard the music? Do you think she is still awake?

LEADER (*Looking up in the direction of* CAROL'S *window*): I can't be sure, child. Perhaps she *has* fallen asleep! But somehow, even if she did, I feel quite sure she heard the music, after all! (CAROLERS *leave stage softly humming the last carol as stage lights darken and house lights come on.*)

THE END

Christmas Every Day

by William Dean Howells
adapted by Adele Thane

Characters

KINDHEART, *the Christmas Fairy*
TINSEL ⎱ *two Christmas Elves*
TASSEL ⎰
MRS. PHILLIPS
MR. PHILLIPS
ABIGAIL ⎱ *their children*
ROBIN ⎰
JENNY
JIM

SCENE 1

TIME: *Christmas Eve.*

SETTING: *The living room of Abigail's home, decorated for Christmas and flooded with "winter moonlight." There is a fireplace, center in the rear wall, with four stockings hanging from the mantelpiece.*

AT RISE: *After a moment, the French windows at left open, and* KINDHEART *and her helpers,* TINSEL *and* TASSEL, *tiptoe into room. The Elves dance about, giggling as they turn on the lamps.*

KINDHEART: Sh-h-h!

TINSEL: Is this where she lives?

KINDHEART: Yes, Tinsel. Now be quiet, both of you, or you'll wake her up.

TASSEL: Wake up *who*, Kindheart?

KINDHEART: The little girl who wants it to be Christmas every day.

TASSEL: Every day in the year?

KINDHEART: Yes, Tassel. She began sending me post cards right after Thanksgiving asking if she might have it that way.

TASSEL: What's her name?

KINDHEART: Abigail.

TINSEL: Did you answer her?

KINDHEART: You know how fussy I am about my mail. I never answer post cards—only letters.

TASSEL (*Relieved*): So you haven't written her.

KINDHEART: Oh, yes, I have. About a week ago, she sent me a real letter.

TINSEL: I guess you couldn't ignore *that*.

KINDHEART: I should say not. (*Taking letter from pocket of cape*) I have the answer right here.

TASSEL: Christmas every day! What a horrible idea!

TINSEL: You couldn't just—*lose* your answer, and forget the letter, could you?

KINDHEART: No, my conscience would bother me. I really think I should grant her wish.

TASSEL: Not for always, Kindheart. Please, *please*—not for always!

KINDHEART: No, not for always. Just for one year. She'll want it stopped long before then.

TASSEL: How greedy she is!

KINDHEART: I think we'll change that. (*Holds up letter and looks around*) Now, where shall I put this so she'll be sure to find it first thing tomorrow morning?

TINSEL: Read it to us first!

KINDHEART: All right. (*She removes the letter from the envelope and reads.*) "Dear Abigail. After careful consideration, I have decided to grant your request for Christmas every day. Beginning December 25th, every one of the next three hundred and sixty-five days shall be Christmas. With sincere holiday greetings, Signed, Kindheart, the Christmas Fairy." (*She returns letter to envelope.*)

TASSEL (*Going to the fireplace*): Why don't you put the letter in her stocking? She's bound to find it there.

KINDHEART: Good idea! (*She tucks letter in top of ABIGAIL's stocking.*) There! Now, turn out the lights, my dears, and we'll be off. (*The Elves skip about, snapping off lamps, and then they follow KINDHEART through French windows, closing them without a sound.*)

CURTAIN

*   *   *

SCENE 2

TIME: *Christmas morning.*

SETTING: *Same as Scene 1.*

AT RISE: ABIGAIL *runs through the archway in her nightgown, and goes to the fireplace. She is followed immediately by* ROBIN *in his pajamas.*

ROBIN: Merry Christmas, Abigail!

ABIGAIL (*Turning to him*): Oh, Robin, I wanted to say it first!

ROBIN: You can say it now.

ABIGAIL (*Hugging him*): Merry Christmas! (*She turns back to the stockings.*) Everything's here.

ROBIN: I told you it would be. Which is mine? This is yours.

ABIGAIL: Here's yours. (*In the excitement of exchanging stockings,* KINDHEART's *letter falls unnoticed to hearth of the fireplace.* ABIGAIL *and* ROBIN *sit on floor and start emptying their stockings.*)

ROBIN: Hurray! A jackknife!

ABIGAIL: I want a jackknife, too.

ROBIN: You're a girl. You can't whittle.

ABIGAIL (*Reaching for knife*): I'll show you!

ROBIN (*Pushing her hand away good-naturedly*): No you don't! Look in your own stocking. (ABIGAIL *unwraps a fruitcake, baked in the shape of Santa Claus.*)

ABIGAIL: A Santa· fruitcake!

ROBIN (*Snatching at it*): Give me a piece!

ABIGAIL: Wait! I'll break it in half. (*She divides cake and hands* ROBIN *his portion.* MR. *and* MRS. PHILLIPS *enter right, in dressing gowns.* MR. PHILLIPS *yawns and stretches.*)

MRS. PHILLIPS: Merry Christmas, children! (ABIGAIL *and* ROBIN *leap to their feet.*)

BOTH: Merry Christmas, Mamma!

ABIGAIL (*Crossing to* MR. PHILLIPS *and shaking him*): Wake up, Papa! It's Christmas morning!

MR. PHILLIPS: It can't be morning. I just went to bed.

ABIGAIL: Yes, it is! Look in your stocking. (*She pushes him toward fireplace, and together they take down his stocking.* MRS. PHILLIPS *digs down into hers, with* ROBIN *helping.*)

ROBIN (*As* MRS. PHILLIPS *takes out a small parcel wrapped in tissue paper*): I know what it is!

MRS. PHILLIPS (*Unwrapping it and laughing*): A potato!

MR. PHILLIPS (*Pulling a lumpy parcel from his stocking and unwrapping it*): Lumps of coal!

ABIGAIL (*Laughing*): You always get coal for Christmas, don't you, Papa?

ROBIN: And Mamma always gets a potato.

MRS. PHILLIPS: Now, run along to the playroom, my dar-
lings, and look at the Christmas tree. But remember, we
don't open our presents till after we're dressed.

ABIGAIL: I know what they'll be! Books, and games, and
parasols, and dolls' houses—

MRS. PHILLIPS:—and boxes of handkerchiefs—

ROBIN:—and skates, and sleds, and sets of water colors—

MR. PHILLIPS:—and little easels and raincoats—

ABIGAIL and ROBIN (*Together*):—and *dozens* of ties for
Papa! (*General laughter as* ABIGAIL *and* ROBIN *run off
right.*)

CURTAIN

*   *   *

SCENE 3

TIME: *The day after Christmas.*

SETTING: *Same as Scene 1.*

AT RISE: ROBIN *is leading* ABIGAIL *through archway right.
She is wearing a blindfold over her eyes. Both are wearing their nightclothes. The four stockings are filled and
hanging from the fireplace mantel as in Scene 1.*

ABIGAIL: What is it? What's the matter?

ROBIN: Nothing's the matter. It's Christmas Day!

ABIGAIL: You can't fool me, smarty.

ROBIN: Who's a smarty? You just take off this blindfold
and look. (*He helps her undo the blindfold, and she
stares in amazement at bulging stockings.*) You see, it
really *is* Christmas.

ABIGAIL (*Crossing to the fireplace*): But how can it be?
Yesterday was Christmas. Don't you remember? (*She
feels stockings.*) You got a jackknife, and I got a Santa
fruitcake.

ROBIN: I can't help that. I have a jackknife and you have

a Santa fruitcake again—today. See? (*He shows her jackknife he has taken out of his stocking.*)

ABIGAIL (*Unwrapping fruitcake*): Oh, dear! Do you think I'll get a stomach ache again, too?

ROBIN: That depends. If you eat too much of it, you will.

ABIGAIL (*Nibbling fruitcake*): I won't. (MR. *and* MRS. PHILLIPS, *looking baffled, enter in their dressing gowns. They are carrying neatly wrapped presents.*)

MR. PHILLIPS: What's the meaning of this? The Christmas tree is blazing away in the playroom—with presents piled up a mile high!

MRS. PHILLIPS: Not a single one of them is unwrapped, either.

MR. PHILLIPS: It seems to me we had something like this yesterday—or did I dream it?

ABIGAIL (*Laughing*): Oh, Papa!

MRS. PHILLIPS: Where are we going to put everything? The house is crammed to the rafters, as it is.

MR. PHILLIPS (*Exasperated*): And what about the expense? Now I'll have to pay for everything all over again. I'll be bankrupt if this keeps up. (*He starts out right.*)

MRS. PHILLIPS (*Alarmed, following him*): If it keeps up! Are we going to have Christmas every day? (*They exit.*)

ABIGAIL (*Suddenly remembering*): Christmas every day! (ROBIN *catches sight of* KINDHEART'S *letter lying on hearth. He picks it up and looks at the inscription on envelope.*)

ROBIN: Here's a card or something, Abigail, with your name on it. It must have fallen out of your stocking.

ABIGAIL (*Taking it*): I wonder who sent it.

ROBIN: Why don't you open it and find out? I'm going to look at the Christmas tree. (*He exits right.* ABIGAIL *opens letter.*)

ABIGAIL (*Reading*): "Dear Abigail. After careful consideration . . . (*Her eyes skim over letter; she resumes read-*

ing) Beginning December 25th, every one of the next three hundred and sixty-five days shall be Christmas." (*She looks up with shining eyes.*) Oh, my goodness gracious! It's from the Christmas Fairy! I won't tell anyone—not even Mamma. I'll just keep this a secret. I'll have the greatest fun! (*She throws herself on divan, hugging herself in glee.*)

CURTAIN

* * *

Scene 4

Time: *The Fourth of July.*

Setting: *Same as Scene 1. The stockings and Christmas decorations are still up. The French windows are open.*

At Rise: Mrs. Phillips *is seated on the divan, checking her shopping list.* Mr. Phillips *is standing center, looking over a sheaf of bills.*

Mrs. Phillips: Fred, it's simply terrible! Mr. Giles is charging two thousand dollars apiece for turkeys.

Mr. Phillips: Great Scott! I'm sure I saw some at the delicatessen yesterday for *one* thousand.

Mrs. Phillips: That was yesterday. Anyway, Mr. Giles says we'd better be careful about buying cheap poultry.

Mr. Phillips (*Noticing an item on one of the bills, with a start*): What the dickens! Cranberries—a diamond each? It's highway robbery!

Mrs. Phillips: I know, dear. But I bought only one cranberry—for you. You do so love your cranberry sauce.

Mr. Phillips: Not at that price, I don't! I'll be satisfied with plain potatoes from now on.

Mrs. Phillips: That's another thing, Fred. These past six months, we've used so many potatoes to stuff the toes of our stockings that I can hardly get enough to make salads for Sunday suppers. And it's the same with coal. All the mines are cleaned out.

MR. PHILLIPS (*Exploding*): How are people going to *live*, Dora? On roots? There's no fruit to be had for love or money. All the orchards and woods are cut down for Christmas trees!

MRS. PHILLIPS: That reminds me. (*She goes to French windows and looks off.*) Mrs. Dawson is sending Jenny over with a Christmas-tree pattern.

MR. PHILLIPS: A *pattern?*

MRS. PHILLIPS: Yes. You cut the shape of the tree out of rags and stuff it with sawdust, like an old-fashioned doll.

MR. PHILLIPS: Rags! That's a wonderful idea! There's no scarcity of rags nowadays. What with people buying presents for each other all the time, they can't afford any new clothes, so they just wear their old clothes to tatters. (MRS. PHILLIPS *glances through French windows and waves.*)

MRS. PHILLIPS (*Calling off*): In here, Jenny! (*She turns back into room.*) Here comes Jenny now. I can't wait to start making that Christmas tree. (JENNY *enters through French windows. She crosses to* MRS. PHILLIPS *and gives her a folded newspaper pattern.*)

JENNY: Mom sent over this pattern, Mrs. Phillips. She says if you have any trouble figuring it out, she'll be glad to help you. We have three of them at our house.

MRS. PHILLIPS (*Studying pattern*): I don't think I'll have any trouble, Jenny. It looks simple enough.

JENNY (*Sitting down on divan with a sigh*): My, but it's peaceful here! Over at our house, everybody's getting crosser and crosser, losing their tempers and that sort of thing.

MR. PHILLIPS (*Laughing*): Well, we have our lost tempers here, too, Jenny. And what's more, we've nearly lost our voices saying "Merry Christmas" so much.

MRS. PHILLIPS (*Sighing*): Yes. I simply don't say it any more. Whoever would have thought that we'd be saying "Merry Christmas" every day of the year, even on Valentine's Day, Washington's Birthday, April Fools' Day, and now the Fourth of July?

JENNY: At least all the presents were fake on April Fools' Day. That certainly was a relief. (*A voice is heard off left calling "Jenny." She rises.*) That's Mom. I have to recite the Declaration of Independence at Soldier's Monument this afternoon, and Mom wants me to get ready. (*She walks slowly toward the French windows, reciting as she goes.*) "When in the course of human events it becomes necessary for one people to—" (*Without pausing, she breaks into a carol and sings*) "Deck the halls with boughs of holly, Tra-la-la-la-la, la-la, la, la! 'Tis the season to be jolly, Tra-la-la-la-la, la-la, la, la!" (*She exits left.*)

MRS. PHILLIPS (*Shaking her head sadly*): Isn't it perfectly awful?

MR. PHILLIPS: I have to go and shovel the presents off the sidewalk. If I don't, Constable Duggan says he'll have me hauled into court for obstructing a public way.

MRS. PHILLIPS: But where are we going to put them, Fred? There's not an *inch* of space left in the barn.

MR. PHILLIPS (*Shrugging*): Your guess is as good as mine, Dora.

MRS. PHILLIPS: If only we could find out who's responsible for all this Christmas! (MR. PHILLIPS *starts right and collides with* JIM, *who runs through archway, carrying a paper bag.*)

MR. PHILLIPS: Whoa there, Jim!

JIM: Excuse me, Mr. Phillips. Where's Rob?

MRS. PHILLIPS (*Looking off left*): He was on the porch, getting his fireworks together. There he is.

JIM (*Calling*): Hey, Rob! (*He waves the paper bag.*) I have them!

ROBIN (*Appearing in the French windows*): Have what?

JIM: Torpedoes!

MRS. PHILLIPS: Now, don't burn your fingers off. (*She exits right with* MR. PHILLIPS.)

JIM: No'm. (ROBIN *comes into room with two boxes of fireworks.*)

ROBIN (*Holding them up*): Look, Jim, Roman candles.

JIM (*Rummaging in his paper bag*): You'd better stuff your ears with cotton. I'm going to crash this torpedo right down on these bricks. (*He indicates hearth.* ROBIN *quickly sets his fireworks on divan and covers his ears with his hands.* JIM *hurls torpedo to hearth. There is a dull thud.*)

ROBIN (*Taking his hands away from his ears*): I didn't hear anything. Did you?

JIM (*Puzzled*): No. It must have been a dud.

ROBIN: Let me try one. (JIM *hands him bag.*) All right. Stand back, or you'll be *sorr-eeeee!* (*There is another dull thud as the torpedo hits bricks.* ROBIN *looks into bag*) What's the matter with these things? They make about as much noise as a wad of chewing gum.

JIM (*Snatching bag away*): Let me see them. (*He examines torpedoes.*) For Pete's sake!

ROBIN: Something wrong?

JIM: I'll say. These are no more torpedoes than the man in the moon!

ROBIN: What are they?

JIM: *Big—fat—raisins!*

ROBIN: *Raisins?* (*He takes handful of raisins out of bag.*)

JIM: Yes, raisins! Right out of a Christmas plum pudding, I'll bet! Isn't that something? Raisins instead of fireworks on the Fourth of July!

ROBIN: I wonder if my Roman candles—(*He opens a box.*) Oh, *no!*

JIM (*Nodding grimly*): Oh, *yes!*

ROBIN: They're candy canes! And I paid two dollars for them.

JIM: Doesn't it beat everything? *Another* Christmas Day! (*He sinks onto divan, disgusted, and* ROBIN *collapses beside him with a groan.* ABIGAIL *enters right, dangling a doll in one hand and a toy gun in the other. She throws toy gun at* ROBIN.)

ABIGAIL: Here, take it, you horrid old thing!

ROBIN (*Jumps to his feet, surprised*): What is it?

ABIGAIL (*Sullenly*): Your Christmas present.

ROBIN: Aren't you going to wrap it? (*He picks it up.*)

ABIGAIL (*Furiously*): I'm never going to wrap another Christmas present as long as I live!

JIM (*Rising*): But you just can't go around throwing 'em at people. You have to leave them at the front door, with little cards, saying—

ABIGAIL (*Interrupting; sarcastically*): "For dear Jim" or "Dear Jenny." Well, I *won't!* I'll *slam* them against the front door, or over the fence, or through the window! I hate the *sight* of presents! (*She begins to shake her doll, throwing it on the floor and sitting on it, sobbing hysterically.* MRS. PHILLIPS *hurries in right, and goes to her, worried.*)

MRS. PHILLIPS: Abbie! Abbie! Little sister! There, there. (*She puts her arms around* ABIGAIL *and leads her to divan.*) Run along, boys. Robin, you can help your father clear away the presents in front of the house. (*Boys exit left.* MRS. PHILLIPS *and* ABIGAIL *sit on divan.*)

ABIGAIL (*Bursting into sobs*): Oh, Mamma! It's all my fault!

MRS. PHILLIPS: What's all your fault, dear?

ABIGAIL: That we're having Christmas every day.

Mrs. Phillips (*Aghast*): What are you *saying*, Abbie?

Abigail: *I'm* to blame, Mamma. I wrote to the Christmas Fairy, and begged her to make it happen.

Mrs. Phillips: Whatever made you *do* such a thing, Abbie?

Abigail: I don't know. I was just greedy, I guess. Just a Christmas *pig!*

Mrs. Phillips: Why don't you write again, and ask the Fairy to stop it?

Abigail: I have. I write every day. I've even sent telegrams, but it doesn't do any good.

Mrs. Phillips: You might try calling at her house.

Abigail: I've done that, too, but the Elf who comes to the door always says, "Not at home," or "Engaged," or "At dinner." Oh, Mamma, what am I going to do?

Mrs. Phillips: I wish I knew, Abbie.

Abigail (*Panic-stricken*): What if the Fairy should forget to stop it when the year is up?

Mrs. Phillips: Did she say it would end in a year?

Abigail: Yes—see? Here's her letter. (Abigail *takes letter from her pocket and points to a sentence.*)

Mrs. Phillips (*Reading aloud*): "—three hundred and sixty-five days shall be Christmas." This is July fourth—six months to go. Well, Abbie, all we can do is to get through the rest of the days somehow.

CURTAIN

*   *   *

Scene 5

Time: *The day after Christmas.*

Setting: *Same as Scene 1.*

At Rise: *No one is in room, but apparently a celebration is taking place outside the house. Bells are ringing, whistles are blowing, people are shouting and cheering. After a moment, Robin gallops through archway right, shaking a noisemaker.*

ROBIN: Yippee! It's over! It's positively over! No more Christmas! Hurray! (*He goes about room, tearing down decorations.*)

ABIGAIL (*Running in right*): Robin, what's happening? Why are the whistles blowing?

ROBIN: It's the end of Christmas, Abbie!

ABIGAIL: Really? You mean I won't have to look at those lumpy old stockings another single solitary minute? Oh, joy! (*She yanks stockings off mantel and throws them into fireplace.*)

ROBIN: Don't throw those there!

ABIGAIL: Why not?

ROBIN: Up on Derry Hill they're making a huge bonfire of all the stockings and presents and decorations that people don't want. Let's take everything up there and burn it.

ABIGAIL: Candy and nuts and raisins, too?

ROBIN: No—the city carts are going around, picking up that junk.

ABIGAIL: What for?

ROBIN: They're going to dump it in the river.

ABIGAIL: But won't it give the fish a stomach ache?

ROBIN: Sure, but they'll survive—just as we did! Take down the rest of the decorations, will you? I'll meet you out front with my express wagon and we'll load it up. (*He exits right.* ABIGAIL *gets a chair and stands on it to take down wreath over fireplace, when French windows open softly, and* TINSEL *and* TASSEL *tiptoe into room, followed by Christmas Fairy,* KINDHEART. ABIGAIL *turns and sees them.*)

ABIGAIL (*Startled*): Oh! Who are you?

TINSEL: I'm Tinsel.

TASSEL: I'm Tassel.

BOTH: And this is Kindheart, the Christmas Fairy. (*They*

bow to KINDHEART, *who comes forward to center.* ABI-
GAIL *jumps off chair with a delighted cry.*)

KINDHEART: Merry Chr—I mean, good morning, Abigail.

ABIGAIL (*With a quick curtsy*): Good morning, ma'am.

KINDHEART: How did you like it?

ABIGAIL: Christmas every day? It was awful! I'm so glad
you stopped it. I was dreadfully afraid you wouldn't.

KINDHEART: I figured you'd had enough.

ABIGAIL: *More* than enough! It was such a relief to wake
up this morning and find out it wasn't Christmas at last.
I hope it never will be again.

TINSEL (*Plaintively*): No more Christmases?

TASSEL: Not ever?

KINDHEART: Is that what you want, Abbie?

ABIGAIL: Uh-huh. I'm tired of Christmas. I really am.

KINDHEART: Stop and think, Abbie. We can't settle this
matter right off—like *that*. (*She snaps her fingers.*)

ABIGAIL: We can't?

KINDHEART: Of course not. We have to consider it very
carefully.

ABIGAIL: Why?

KINDHEART: Because it's not only you and I who are concerned, Abbie—it's the whole United States—the whole
world. Christmas belongs to everybody.

ABIGAIL (*Deliberating*): Mm-m-m-m, I see. Well, in that
case, maybe we could have Christmas once in a thousand
years.

TASSEL (*To* KINDHEART): She's being selfish again, Kindheart—only the other way around.

ABIGAIL (*With spirit*): I am *not!*

KINDHEART (*Gently*): I'm afraid you are, Abbie.

ABIGAIL (*Ashamed*): Yes, I suppose I am. Well, how about
once every hundred years?

TINSEL (*Shaking her head*): There wouldn't be enough

work to keep Santa Claus busy. He'd be terribly un-happy.

ABIGAIL: Oh, I wouldn't want that! Let's make it once every ten years.

TASSEL: Ten years is a long time to wait for another look at a Christmas tree.

TINSEL: Or to go caroling with your friends or exchange Christmas gifts.

KINDHEART: And most important of all, what if you had to wait ten years to hear the Christmas story again? People might then forget the real meaning of Christmas—the feeling of peace on earth and good will to men.

ABIGAIL: Oh, dear, that mustn't happen!

KINDHEART: Indeed it must *not!* So how about going back to the old-fashioned way?

ABIGAIL: You mean Christmas once a year?

KINDHEART (*Nodding*): Isn't that the *best* way?

ABIGAIL: I *guess* it is—(*Suddenly she makes up her mind.*) I'm *sure* it is!

KINDHEART: Shall we make it a bargain?

ABIGAIL: Yes!

KINDHEART: What are your shoes made of?

ABIGAIL: Leather.

KINDHEART: Bargain's done forever.

ABIGAIL (*Hugging the Fairy*): Forever and ever and ever! (KINDHEART *starts to sing, and is joined by* ABIGAIL *and the Elves.*)

ALL:
Christmas is here, Christmas is here,
All sing with joy, all sing with joy,
It's the merry season, it's the merry season,
Good will to men, good will to men.
(*They sing together loudly and joyously, as the curtain falls.*)

THE END

Little Women

by Louisa May Alcott
adapted by Olive J. Morley

Characters

MEG ⎱
JO ⎰
BETH ⎱ sisters
AMY ⎰

MRS. MARCH, *their mother*
AUNT MARCH, *their aunt*
HANNAH, *the family servant*
THE HUMMELS, *two German children*

TIME: *A few days before Christmas, 1862.*
SETTING: *The living room of the March home in New England.*
AT RISE: *The March sisters are grouped around the fire. MEG, a sweet-faced, very womanly "little woman" of sixteen, sits upstage, busy sewing. Gentle BETH, aged thirteen, is at her feet on a low stool, knitting. Fifteen-year-old JO, tall, colt-like and boyish in manner, lies on the hearth-rug, with some knitting beside her. Fair-haired, self-important little AMY, aged twelve, sits in the center, sketching.*

JO: Christmas won't be Christmas without any presents.
MEG (*Sighing*): It's so dreadful to be poor! (*She looks at her frock distastefully.*)

AMY (*With an injured sniff*): I don't think it's fair for some girls to have lots of pretty things, and other girls nothing at all.

BETH: We've got Father and Mother and each other, anyhow.

JO: We haven't got Father here, and we shan't have him for a long time. (*There is a little sniff from* AMY, *and* BETH *wipes away a tear.*)

MEG: Now, girls, you know the reason Mother proposed not having any presents this Christmas was because it's going to be a hard winter for everyone; and she thinks we ought not to spend money for pleasure when our men are suffering so in the Army. We can't do much, but we can make our little sacrifices, and ought to do it gladly. But it's awfully hard. (*She sighs.*)

JO: Still, I don't see how the little we can spend would do any good. Anyway, we've each got a dollar, and the Army wouldn't be much helped by our giving that. I agree not to expect anything from Mother or you, but I do want to buy *Undine and Sintram* for myself; I've wanted it *so* long.

BETH: I planned to spend my dollar for new music. (*She sighs.*)

AMY: I shall get a new box of Faber's Drawing Pencils. I really need them.

JO: Mother didn't say anything about *our* money, and she won't wish us to give up everything. Let's each buy what we want, and have a little fun. I'm sure we work hard enough to earn it.

MEG: I know *I* do—teaching those dreadful King children nearly all day, when I'm longing to enjoy myself at home.

JO: You don't have half as hard a time as I do. How would you like to be shut up for hours with a nervous, fussy old lady, who keeps you trotting, is never satisfied, and worries you till you're ready to cry?

BETH: It's naughty to fret—but I do think washing dishes and keeping things tidy is the worst work in the world. It makes me cross, and my hands get so stiff, I can't practice well at all! (*She looks at her hands, gives an audible sigh.*)

AMY: I don't believe any of you suffer as I do, for you don't have to go to school with impertinent girls, who plague you if you don't know your lessons, and laugh at your dresses, and label your father if he isn't rich, and insult you when your nose isn't nice.

Jo (*Laughing*): If you mean *libel,* say so, and don't talk about *labels* as if Papa were a pickle bottle.

AMY (*With offended dignity*): I know what I mean, and you needn't be *statirical* about it. It's proper to use good words, and improve your *vocabilary.*

MEG: Don't peck at one another, children. Don't you wish we had the money Papa lost when we were little, Jo! Dear me, how happy and good we'd be, if we had no worries.

BETH: You said, the other day, you thought we were a great deal happier than the King children, for they were fighting and fretting all the time, in spite of their money.

MEG: So I did, Beth. Well, I think we are; for, though we do have to work, we have lots of fun, and are a "pretty jolly set," as Jo would say.

AMY: Jo does use such slang words. (Jo *immediately sits up, puts her hands in her pockets, and begins to whistle.*) Don't, Jo, it's so boyish.

Jo: That's why I do it.

AMY: I detest rude, unladylike girls.

Jo: I hate affected, niminy-piminy chits.

BETH (*Sweetly*): Birds in their little nests agree. (*Everyone laughs.*)

MEG: Really, girls, you are both to be blamed. You're old enough to leave off boyish tricks, and behave better, Josephine. It didn't matter so much when you were a little girl; but now that you are so tall, and turn up your hair, you should remember that you're a young lady.

JO: I'm not! And if turning up my hair makes me one, I'll wear it in two tails till I'm twenty! (*She pulls off her hair net, and shakes down her long hair.*) I hate to think I've got to grow up and be Miss March, and wear long gowns, and look like a China aster. It's bad enough to be a girl, anyway, when I like boys' games, and work, and manners. I just can't get over my disappointment in not being a boy, and it's worse than ever now, for I'm dying to go and fight with Papa, and instead I have to stay at home and knit like a poky old woman. (*She shakes her knitting till the needles rattle and the ball bounds across the room.*)

BETH: Poor Jo! It's too bad! But it can't be helped; so you must try to be contented with making your name boyish, and playing brother to us girls. (*She strokes Jo's hair.*)

MEG: As for you, Amy, you are altogether too particular and prim. Your airs are funny now, but you'll grow up an affected little goose if you don't take care.

BETH: If Jo is a tomboy, and Amy a goose, what am I, please?

MEG: You're a dear, and nothing else. (*Hugs* BETH) But look, girls, it's six o'clock. Marmee will be here any minute now. (*She rises and lights the lamp on the bookcase.* AMY *shakes up the cushions in the easy chair* MEG *has vacated.* BETH *sweeps the hearth and* JO *holds up an old pair of slippers to the fire.*)

Jo: These are quite worn out. Marmee must have a new pair.

Beth: I thought I'd get her some with my dollar.

Amy: No, I shall!

Meg: I'm the oldest!

Jo: But I'm the man of the family now that Papa is away, and *I* shall provide the slippers, for he told me to take special care of Mother while he was gone.

Beth: I'll tell you what we'll do. Let's each get her something for Christmas, and not get anything for ourselves.

Jo: That's like you, dear! What will we get?

Meg: I shall get her a nice pair of gloves.

Jo: Comfortable slippers, best to be had.

Beth: Some handkerchiefs, all hemmed.

Amy: I'll get a little bottle of cologne; she likes it, and it won't cost much, so I'll have some left to buy my pencils.

Meg: How shall we give the things?

Jo: Put them on the table, and bring her in and see her open the bundles. Don't you remember how we used to do on our birthdays?

Beth: I used to be *so* frightened when it was my turn to sit in the big chair, with the crown on, and see you all come marching round to give the presents, with a kiss.

Jo: We'll let Marmee think we are getting things for ourselves and then surprise her. We must go shopping soon, Meg. There's hardly any time left, with all we have to do about getting the play ready for Christmas night.

Meg: Oh, we'll have time to go tomorrow afternoon. And, anyway, I don't mean to act any more after this time. I'm getting too old for such things.

Jo: You won't stop, I know, as long as you can trail around in a white gown with your hair down, and wear gold-paper jewelry. You are the best actress we've got, and there'll be an end of everything if you quit the boards.

We ought to rehearse tonight. Maybe we could go over a few scenes before Marmee gets home. (*The girls move the table back, leaving a space in the center of the stage where the acting will take place. All exits and entrances refer to this area, so that none of the girls actually leaves the stage during the rehearsal.*) Come here, Amy, and do the fainting scene. You're as stiff as a poker in that.

AMY: I don't care. I never saw anyone faint, and I don't choose to make myself all black and blue, tumbling flat like you do. If I can go down easily, I'll drop; if I can't, I shall fall into a chair and be graceful. (*Arranges chair at back*)

JO: Do it this way; clasp your hands like this. (*She demonstrates.*) Then, stagger across the room, crying frantically, "Roderigo! Save me! Save me!" (*Jo screams melodramatically and does a beautiful stage fall.*)

AMY (*Feebly imitating, with her hands stretched out stiffly like a doll*): Roderigo! Save me! Save me! (*She moves across the stage jerkily, falls into the chair awkwardly, slides off it and falls on to the floor with a squeaky "Ow!"*)

JO: It's no use! Do the best you can when the time comes, and if the audience laughs don't blame me. Come on, Meg. We'll do the caldron scene. (BETH *hurriedly places a coal scuttle in the center.* MEG *seizes a witch's hat from the corner, and a cloak which has been hung up on the door. Jo pulls off the tablecloth and drapes it around herself in the form of a cloak, puts on a broad-brimmed hat with a feather, and proceeds to hitch up her skirts. She then puts on a pair of riding boots which have been hidden between the bookcase and the door.*) Ready, Meg? (*In a theatrical voice*) What ho, witch! I need thee! (*Claps her hands*) Fetch me the potions whereby I may win the fair Zara's love and kill my enemy Roderigo.

MEG (*Comes forward and stirs the "caldron" while she chants*):
Hither, hither, from thy home,
Airy sprite, I bid thee come!
Born of roses, fed on dew,
Charms and potions canst thou brew?
Bring me here, with elfin speed,
The fragrant philter that I need;
Make it sweet, and swift and strong;
Spirit, answer now my song! (AMY *dances daintily forward from the back. She has twined leaves in her hair, and carries a poker with wandlike effect in one hand, and a pepper shaker in the other.*)

AMY (*In a sing-song voice*) :
Hither I come,
From my airy home,
Afar in the silvery moon;
Take the magic spell,
Oh, use it well!
Or its power will vanish soon! (*She hops gracefully out, then, suddenly remembering the philter, she runs back and places the pepper shaker before the coal scuttle.*)
Oh, I forgot! (*She exits hastily.*)

Jo: *Amy!*

MEG: Now come hither, naughty sprite! Bring the draught that shall quench light! (BETH *enters, rather shyly, and places a salt shaker before the caldron.* MEG *and* BETH *both exit.*)

Jo: Well, not *bad*, I suppose. Now, we'll do the death of Hugo. Beth, you must be the servant. (*Enter* MEG, *smiling craftily. She waves her wand, an umbrella; then, hearing* Jo *make stamping noises at the back, she hides behind chair.*)

Jo (*Entering*): Ah ha, my handsome Roderigo, soon you will be dying at Zara's feet, and she will be mine! (*She gets three cups and a tray from the mantelpiece and places them on the table. She then takes the two philters, the pepper shaker and the salt shaker, from her boots. She pretends to empty the contents of the salt shaker into one cup and places the cup on the tray, muttering)* Death to Roderigo. *(She then takes the pepper shaker.)* And now for the love potion. Half for Zara and half for myself. *(She pretends to empty the pepper shaker into the other two cups. She places one of these cups on the tray and the other on the table within easy reach. She claps her hands.)* Minion! Minion! *(BETH enters, holding the toasting fork absentmindedly.)* Put that down, you dear little goose. *(Evilly)* I have evening refreshment prepared for the prisoners. Bear these two cups to them—the one on the left to Roderigo, the one on the right to Zara, and take care not to make any mistakes.

BETH: But—but, sire.

JO: Now you beckon me downstage. *(BETH does so.)* That's right. *(As JO and BETH stand whispering, downstage. MEG comes out of hiding, and quietly switches the cups —putting both love potions on the tray which BETH will carry to the prisoners and leaving the death potion for JO to drink. She then hastily hides.)*

BETH: The one on the left to Roderigo, the one on the right to Zara. *(She goes to the table and picks up the tray.)*

JO: Begone, I say, begone! *(BETH exits, taking tray. JO sits down at table and picks up poisoned cup.)* Ah ha— Ah ha! Love potion do your work! *(She drinks and then gasps.)* I have been tricked! *(She dies in horrid agony, rolling on the floor. All shriek with laughter. JO sits up and rubs her elbows.)*

MEG *(Removing her hat and smoothing her hair)*: It's the best we've had yet.

BETH: I don't see how you can write and act such splendid

things, Jo. You're a regular Shakespeare. (*She abstractedly picks up the toasting fork with a slipper at the end of it.*)

JO: Well, I do think *The Witch's Curse* is rather a nice thing. But I'd like to do *Macbeth.*

"Is that a dagger that I see before me?" (*She makes passes at the toasting fork.*)

MEG: No, it's the toasting fork with Marmee's slipper at the end of it instead of the bread. Beth's stage struck! (*All go into peals of laughter. Enter* MRS. MARCH, *carrying a shopping bag. She is a motherly looking woman with a can-I-help-you look about her.*)

MRS. MARCH: Glad to find you so merry, my girls.

GIRLS: Marmee!

MRS. MARCH (*During the following speeches the girls are helping* MRS. MARCH *off with her cloak and bonnet, and ensconcing her by the fire, where* BETH *and* AMY *divest her of her shoes and put on the warm slippers.*): Well, dearies, how have you got on today? There was so much to do for the soldiers, getting the boxes ready to go tomorrow, that I didn't come home to dinner. Has anyone called, Beth?

BETH: No one, Marmee.

MRS. MARCH: How is your headache, Meg?

MEG: Oh, it's worn off, thank you, Mother.

MRS. MARCH: Jo, you look tired to death. (*To* AMY) Come and kiss me, baby. (AMY *runs to her and sits on her knee. After a brief hug, she joins the other girls, who are now getting tea.* MEG *is arranging the table, and* AMY *removes some of the paper bags from* MRS. MARCH's *shopping bag, which she has put on a chair or on a corner of the table.* BETH *quietly goes back and forth from living room to kitchen, left, bringing in bread, milk, etc.* JO *goes out for wood, and overturns everything she touches with a great clatter.*)

AMY (*Peeping into one of the bags*): Ooh! Muffins!

MEG: Now, Amy, don't be greedy.

AMY: Can't I have just a taste?

MEG: They have to be toasted. You shall help Beth do them. (AMY *and* BETH *get busy at the fire, toasting and buttering muffins.*)

JO: And don't lick the butter, you disgusting child! (*As she sees* AMY *licking already greasy fingers.* AMY *quietly sticks out her tongue.*)

MRS. MARCH (*Reprovingly*): Amy! (AMY *looks shamefacedly down.*) Now, come, girls, be happy together. Remember, it's Christmas time. Besides, I have another treat for those who are good. (*She looks at* AMY, *and then draws a letter out of her bag.*)

JO: A letter!

OTHERS: A letter!

ALL: Three cheers for Father! (*All run to their mother.* JO *leans over the back of her chair,* MEG *sits on the arm,* AMY *on her knee, and* BETH *at her feet.*)

MRS. MARCH: Yes, a nice long letter. He is well, and thinks he will get through the cold season better than we feared. He sends all sorts of loving wishes for Christmas, and an especial message to you girls. (*Reading*) "Give them all my dear love and a kiss. A year seems very long to wait before I see them again, but remind them that while we wait we may all work, so that these hard days may not be wasted. I know they will remember all I said to them, and conquer themselves so beautifully, that when I come back I may be fonder and prouder than ever of my little women." (*There is a moment's serious pause.*)

AMY (*Hiding her face in her mother's shoulder*): I *am* a selfish girl, but I'll truly try to be better, so he mayn't be disappointed in me by and by.

MEG: We all will. I think too much of my looks, and hate to work, but won't any more, if I can help it.

JO: I'll try to be what he loves to call me, "a little woman." (BETH *wipes her tears.*)

MRS. MARCH: And now, dears, what about tea? Is the kettle ready, Beth?

BETH: It's just on the boil. (*Sound of carriage wheels offstage*)

ALL: Whoever can it be? Perhaps it's Sallie Moffat. Or Mr. Lawrence. (*Etc.*)

AMY (*Running to the window*): It's Aunt March!

JO: Christopher Columbus! Whatever have we done to deserve this? (*General consternation. The girls hurry round tidying the room.* BETH *hurriedly makes the tea.*)

MRS. MARCH: What can she want at this hour of the day? Put that chair tidy, Meg. Jo, do push your stage properties out of sight. You know how they irritate her. Make the hearth tidy, Beth, and get another cup. Come here, Amy, and let me re-tie that sash. (HANNAH's *face appears at the door. She is a red-faced, middle-aged servant with a practical, cheerful disposition.*)

HANNAH (*In a stage whisper*): It's your aunt! (*Then she steps back*) Please step this way, ma'am. (*She opens the door and stands behind it, announcing*) Miss March. (*Enter* AUNT MARCH. *She is an autocratic old lady.* HANNAH *retires, with a suspicion of a wink.* AUNT MARCH *stands, leaning on her cane, surveying the family.* MRS. MARCH *comes forward to greet her.*)

MRS. MARCH: I'm so glad you've dropped in. You're just in time for a cup of tea.

AUNT MARCH: Oh, I've not come for tea. Had mine long ago. And so would you if you hadn't spent all your day down at those stupid packing rooms. It's no place for a woman with a family. But there, it's no good talking to the mule-headed. (*Sharply*) How's March?

MRS. MARCH: We've heard from him today. I've just been reading the girls his letter. He's standing the hardships a great deal better than we expected.

AUNT MARCH: No business to be there at all. I told him so at the first. But March is a fool! He never would listen to common sense, any more than you. (MRS. MARCH *purses up her lips.*) He'll get pneumonia, that'll be the next thing. You mark my words. (*Points her cane at* MRS. MARCH) A man of his physique won't stand up to an Army winter. And black's expensive, and won't suit *you,* my lady. (*Points her cane at* MEG) Well, don't come to me. Remember, I told you so.

BETH (*Almost crying*): Oh, Marmee, does she mean Father's going to die?

MRS. MARCH (*Comforting her*): No, no, dear. Of course not. It's only Aunt's way. (*She looks across at* AUNT MARCH *imploringly, but the old lady ignores the look, and gazes round the room with disapproval.*)

MEG: Won't—won't you sit down, Aunt? (*There is an atmosphere of discomfort among the girls, who of course are still politely standing.* MEG *pulls forward the chair by the fire.*)

AUNT MARCH: Not by the fire. Brings out my rheumatism. Thank you, child. (*As* AMY *places a chair for her a little left of the table and arranges a cushion*) I see you've brought up one of them with some social promise. (*Seats herself, and the others do likewise, except* AMY, *who stands by her chair.* AUNT MARCH *pulls her curls playfully.*) She won't look so bad when she's a few years older. You must marry well. (*Looking at* AMY *critically*) You shall have the turquoise ring when you come out.

AMY (*Ecstatically*): Oh, Aunt! Not the *turquoise!*

AUNT MARCH (*Patting her hand*): There, there, child. Wait till you've grown a bit, and we'll see. (*In moving the chair,* AMY *has unwittingly disclosed one of* Jo's *riding boots which had been hastily pushed underneath it.*) What's *this? (She raises it on the end of her cane.*) Some tomfoolery of yours, I'll be bound, Josephine.

Jo: Oh, we're only getting up a pl—(*Stops and puts her hand over her mouth as* MRS. MARCH *signals to her*)

AUNT MARCH: Getting up a pl—, indeed! Some theatricals, I suppose. (*To* MRS. MARCH) I told you not to encourage her in that nonsense. It leads to no good!

MRS. MARCH (*With an effort not to show her irritation*): These are only harmless little home entertainments. I can't take the girls much to the theatre, as you know, and they must have some amusement.

AUNT MARCH: Oh, they get enough of that, by the way I see Josephine gallivanting with young Lawrence.

MRS. MARCH (*To* AMY): Pass Aunt a cup of tea, dear. (AMY *does so.*)

AUNT MARCH: Thank you, child. (*Bent on getting a rise out of* MRS. MARCH) A young tomboy, that's what she's becoming. She'll do some harum-scarum thing, and disgrace the family.

MRS. MARCH (*Quietly*): Well, we're only young once, and I thoroughly approve of Laurie as a companion to the girls. He's a bit wild at times, I own, but he's steady enough underneath.

AUNT MARCH: Oh, I dare say. The Lawrences have money. You've shown more sense there than I gave you credit for. It isn't the *boy* I object to, it's the tutor. And that brings me to the reason for my visit. (*Looks hard at* MEG) I've seen that young man come this way a great many more times than is good for him, *and* you!

MEG (*On the defensive*): Mr. Brooke is kindly helping me with my German.

AUNT MARCH: And teaching you a great many other things besides.

Mrs. March *and* Meg: Aunt!

Mrs. March: I must really beg you not to put such ideas into the girls' heads.

Aunt March: Oh, *I* haven't put them there. It's young Brooke, by the way she's blushing.

Meg (*In an agony of confusion and anger*): I'm *not* blushing, and I don't know what you mean. Mr. Brooke is only a friend.

Aunt March: Oh, I've heard of those friendships. They weren't allowed when *I* was a girl. (*To* Mrs. March) But you'll go your own way, and bring up your girls as you please, to marry penniless tutors and be nothing but a burden on the family. After your own troubles with March I should have thought you would have more sense.

Meg (*Tossing her head*): I shall marry whom I choose!

Aunt March: No doubt you will, and your mother will let you—the more fool she. But when Cooke's out of work and the cupboard's bare, don't come to me.

Meg: I certainly shall never do that, Aunt March.

Aunt March: Well, I'll remember that you've said it. This Looke hasn't any rich relations, has he?

Meg: No, but he has many warm friends.

Aunt March: You can't live on friends. Try it, and see how cool they'll grow. He hasn't any business?

Meg: No. Mr. Lawrence is going to help him.

Aunt March: That won't last long. James Lawrence is a crotchety old fellow, and not to be relied on. Young Looke probably thinks *you've* got rich relatives. Well, warn him not to look this way. I've a better use for my money than helping poverty-stricken teachers.

Meg (*With heat*): Mr. Brooke wouldn't dream of such a thing! He's honest and good and means to stand on his own feet. He wouldn't marry for money any more than

I would. He's above such meanness. And, anyway, I'd
far rather be the wife of a poor man, who loves me, than
have carriages and a mansion and no one to care for me
in it!

AUNT MARCH: Highty-tighty! Is that the way you take my
advice, miss? You'll be sorry for it, by and by, when
you've tried love in a cottage and found it a failure.

MEG (*Sharply*): It can't be worse than some people find
in big houses! (AUNT MARCH *puts on her glasses and
gives* MEG *a long look.*)

AUNT MARCH (*In a conciliatory tone*): Now, Meg, my dear,
be reasonable. I mean it kindly, and don't want you
to spoil your whole life by making a mistake at the
beginning. You ought to marry well, and help your
family; it's your duty to make a good match, and it
ought to be impressed upon you.

MEG: Father and Mother don't think so.

MRS. MARCH: Money is a needful and precious thing, and
when well used, a noble thing—but I never want my
girls to think it is the only prize to strive for. I'd rather
see them poor men's wives, or even happy old maids,
than *un*happy wives or unmaidenly girls, running about
to find husbands.

AUNT MARCH (*Turning to* MEG): It's easy to see that your
pa and ma, my dear, have no more worldly wisdom than
two babies.

MRS. MARCH *and* MEG: I'm glad of it!

AUNT MARCH: Well, I wash my hands of the whole affair!
You're a willful child, Meg, and you've lost more than
you know. (*Rising, and waving away the plate of muffins which* AMY *is offering*) No, I won't stop. I'm disappointed in you. If you mean to marry this Cooke, not
one penny of my money goes to you. Don't expect anything from *me*. Your Mr. *Rooke's* friends must take

care of you. I'm done with you forever! (*She exits in high dudgeon.* MRS. MARCH *follows her out, looking vexed.*)

MEG: Of all the interfering old ladies—!

JO (*In horror, to* MEG) : *Don't* say you've gone and fallen in love!

MEG: Well, and why ever shouldn't I?

JO (*Ruffling her hair*): Oh, it'll be dreadful!

AMY: I think it is a most interesting event, don't you, Beth?

BETH: Yes, very.

AMY: We can all be bridesmaids in pale blue with pink nosegays, and you can have a lovely wedding cake with doves in white icing on it.

JO: It'll be the end of everything. They'll go lovering round the house and we shall have to dodge. Meg will be absorbed, and no use to me any more. (MRS. MARCH *re-enters.*) And just when I'd planned for her to marry Laurie!

MRS. MARCH: Don't worry about the future, Jo. I think it can safely take care of itself.

JO: Well, I hate to see things going all criss-cross and snarled up, when a pull here, and a snip there, would straighten them up. I wish wearing flat irons on our heads would prevent us from growing up. (*All laugh, except* MEG, *who still looks embarrassed and annoyed. There is a knock, and* HANNAH *enters.*)

HANNAH: Oh ma'am, there're some little German beggar children at the door. Shall I send them packing?

MRS. MARCH: Send them packing! Hannah, it's Christmas time! I could never send anyone from my door at such a season. Bring them into the warmth.

HANNAH: Well, I never! In with the young ladies! There never was such a critter for giving away more than you've got.

BETH: Oh, please bring the little children in, Hannah. (*Exit* HANNAH)

BETH: I'll cut some more bread.

MRS. MARCH: That's right, Beth.

HANNAH (*Off*): Now wipe your feet on the mat and mind you behave in front of the young ladies. (*Enter* HANNAH *with the two Hummel girls. They are pathetically ragged and dirty, and look half starved*)

MRS. MARCH: Come along in, dears.

BETH (*Coming forward*) : Come to the fire, children. (*She leads them to it. They stretch out their hands to the blaze.*)

CHILDREN: *Das ist gute!*

MRS. MARCH: Poor things! They look as if they'd never seen a fire.

JO: Haven't you one at home? (CHILDREN *shake their heads.*)

BETH: They look so hungry. (CHILDREN *look hungrily at the full table.*) Come to the table and have some tea. (*The girls begin to feed them.*)

AMY: Have some muffins. (CHILDREN *devour these ravenously.*)

MRS. MARCH: Have you no food at home? (CHILDREN *shake their heads.*)

MRS. MARCH: No fire and no food! How many are there of you? (CHILDREN *look puzzled, then show seven fingers*)

JO: Seven of them!

MRS. MARCH: Have you a father and mother?

OLDER GIRL: *Mutter.* (*She cradles and rocks her arms*)

BETH: I know, she means they've a mother with a tiny baby. Oh, Marmee!

MRS. MARCH: And no fire or food! (*She looks at the well-spread table and the faces of the girls.*) Girls, I can't help thinking of another little baby who had no warm home on the first Christmas of all—only a draughty stable.

Don't you think, for His sake, we ought to do something for this one?

Jo: I think we're greedy, selfish pigs! Here we've been grumbling about our small troubles and thinking ourselves poor, and these people have nothing at all! Let's bundle everything together and take it to them.

BETH: Oh, do let's! (*They get busy;* MEG *superintends the packing of food in* MRS. MARCH's *shopping bag*)

MRS. MARCH: Hannah, get some wood. We must make them a fire.

HANNAH (*Exits, grumbling slightly, though good naturedly*): Well, if I ever come across the like!

MRS. MARCH (*As business proceeds*): That's right, Meg.

BETH: Here's some tea. (*She produces the teapot.*)

AMY: I'll carry the muffins.

Jo: Mind you don't eat any of them! (HANNAH *re-appears with wood.*)

BETH (*To* CHILDREN): Now you'll show us the way, won't you, dears?

CHILDREN: *Der Angel-Kinder!* (*They begin to sniff.*)

BETH (*To* CHILDREN): Oh, please don't cry. Everything is going to be all right.

Jo: Come on, everyone! Let's sing "Deck the Halls." It's such a cheerful carol. (*The girls begin to sing as they snatch bonnets and cloaks from pegs on the door or hall outside.* BETH *shares hers with* CHILDREN *and putting an arm around each, she leads off, the others following, carrying baskets or bags of food.* AMY *clutches the bag of muffins.* Jo *brings up the rear with a basket of wood.*)

HANNAH (*Standing with her hands on her hips, and watching them go out*): I've never seen the like! Giving away their food and leaving nothing for themselves! Christmas angels they are, and may the good Lord bless them!

THE END

PRODUCTION NOTES

CHRISTMAS SPIRIT

Characters: 4 male; 4 female.
Playing Time: 20 minutes.
Costumes: Modern dress. When Tom, Bob, Miss Pennypacker, Mrs. Gray and Mr. Griggs enter they wear coats, scarves, hats, etc. Mr. Gillum might wear horn-rimmed glasses.
Properties: Long wrapped package, scroll, certificate, knitting, papers, pencil.
Setting: The living room of the Gillum home. At right is a fireplace. Downstage right is a large sofa. At center is a table holding books and magazines. At left is a well-stocked bookcase. On either side of the table are comfortable chairs. A door at right leads to the rest of the house, one at upstage center to the outside. Near the fireplace is a decorated Christmas tree with a number of wrapped presents underneath. Other Christmas decorations may be placed around room.
Lighting: No special effects.

STAR OF BETHLEHEM

Characters: 9 male; 16 female; male and female extras to be children and angels. Betsy has role in pageant.
Playing Time: 35 minutes.
Costumes: Mrs. Carey wears the uniform of a hospital volunteer. Betsy, Enid, Alice and Mac wear white robes. Mary Sue and the other children in Scene 2 wear bathrobes over nightgowns or pajamas, and slippers. Mary Sue has her arm in a sling. Characters in the pageant wear white robes. Everyone else wears everyday modern dress. In Scene 1, Margo enters wearing a Santa Claus hat, beard and red jacket. In Scene 2, Rick is dressed as Santa Claus and carries bells and a sack.

Properties: Chair and desk lamp for Rick; four record books; book for the Narrator; cardboard suit box and compact for Margo; two chairs and a music stand for Jim; bag containing doll for Emily; the "Window of Heaven," a large wooden frame braced so that it can stand by itself and draped with curtains; music for Malcolm; chair for Mrs. Tillstrom; notebook and pencil for Reporter; table with banner (Jewel Tone Products), and glassware for Netta Noble; book for Mrs. Cranford; Christmas stocking for Donny. Note: The "Window of Heaven" is optional.
Setting: Scene 1: The stage of a high school auditorium using curtain backdrops. A table and chairs are down right, a desk and chair up left. A ladder is at one side. Scene 2: A room in the children's wing of a hospital. There is a table with a Christmas tablecloth, down right. Three chairs are by the table. Up left is a desk; a telephone and a small tree are on desk, and a chair is in back of it. There are small chairs for the children.
Lighting: Spotlights, as indicated in text.

TWAS THE NIGHT BEFORE CHRISTMAS

Characters: 3 male; 2 female.
Playing Time: 35 minutes.
Costumes: Modern everyday dress. Uniform, or house dress and apron for Ruby.
Properties: Wreath, two boxes of decorations, hammer and nails, cookies and small cakes, large package, large odd shaped bottle of cologne, small package, large flat package shaped like suitbox with scrapbook inside, another large flat package shaped like suitbox, small oblong box, several miscellaneous sized

packages including one large Christmas angel.

Setting: Typical modern American living room, almost decorated for Christmas. Upstage center, fireplace with mantel above it and mirror over mantel. Some empty socks hanging from mantel. In rear wall to right, a door leading into a small reception hall and front door. Now wall is blocked by stepladder, but you can walk around it. In center of left wall, another door leads to stairway and rest of house. against right wall stands a large old-fashioned desk with books, papers and telephone. There are also some Christmas packages piled on it. Upstage form desk, a worn but comfortable easy chair, and at rear left a large Christmas tree. Occasional chairs, tables and lamps around room.

Lighting: None required.

MERRY CHRISTMAS, CRAWFORDS!

Characters: 8 male; 7 female; male and female extras.

Playing Time: 35 minutes.

Costumes: Modern, everyday dress. When Father first appears, he wears indoor working clothes; before going to office party, he has changed into dress clothes, carrying hat and coat. Mother wears indoor clothes on first appearance, then puts on hat and coat before leaving for party. All visitors to crawfords wear outdoor winter clothes upon entrance. Expressman may wear uniform. Bill Coleman wears working clothes.

Properties: Pair of straight curtains, ladder, Christmas tree, string of lights, Christmas tree decorations, 2 cartons containing various tree decorations and Christmas cards, radio, telephone, bicycle bell for sound of telephone ringing; pins for Myra; Christmas tree angel for Father; carton of broken tree decorations for Mother; hats and coats for Mother and Father; several gaily wrapped packages for Mother, Father, and Bascolms; large carton with torn wrap-

pings containing a few smaller gaily wrapped parcels, pad, pencil, for Expressman; tool box for Bill Coleman; carton of tree decorations for Frances Saunders; bulging shopping bag for Mrs. Saunders; wrapped pie for Mrs. Coleman; candlesticks and candles for Jimmy Coleman.

Setting: The living room of the Crawfords' new home. In right wall is a window with straight curtains looking out onto street. Downstage right is exit to street; at left is exit leading to other rooms of house. Fireplace with mantel is at upstage center. Upstage right is a partially trimmed Christmas tree, with lights on it not yet lighted. Near the tree stands a ladder and two cartons of decorations. Upstage left is a radio, and near it, a small table with telephone. Other tables and chairs, etc., may be placed around stage.

Lighting: No special effects, except for Christmas tree lights which should go on, as indicated in the text.

THE CHRISTMAS REVEL

Characters: 8 male; 8 female; as many players as desired for Other Boys and Girls.

Playing Time: 35 minutes.

Costumes: Appropriate dress of the Elizabethan period. In Scene 2, Walter wears a small scabbard which contains a jeweled knife. In Scene 3, he and Katherine wear masks and peasant costumes. Titania also wears a mask. Sir Thomas is dressed as the Lord of Misrule.

Properties: Box containing gloves, fan, marionette, basket containing two bags of gold sovereigns, yule log, firebrand, three dolls.

Setting: Warwickshire, England. Scene 1 takes place in a village square, and may be played before the curtain if desired. Scenes 2 and 3 take place in the Great Hall at Charlecote. A fireplace with large mantel is up center. In Scene 2, Lady Joyce's fan is on a table. In Scene 3, benches are placed about the room, and there is a dais set beside the fireplace; at rise, Betsy and Nan's marionette is on the mantel. If desired, traditional mummers' pantomime or other appropriate Christmas program material may be added to the opening festivities of Scene 3.

Lighting: No special effects.

PUPPY LOVE

Characters: 3 male; 4 female.
Playing Time: 30 minutes.
Costumes: Modern dress.
Properties: Cards, wrapping paper, boxes, string, greens, small tree, a large stuffed toy dog, wrapped packages, red bow, tag, lights for tree, trays, plates of cakes, teacups, teapot.
Setting: The living room of the Bradley home. It is attractively and comfortably furnished with chairs, tables, bookcases, etc. Upstage center are two card tables. Downstage right, near a large armchair, is a small tea table.
Lighting: No special effects.

VISIONS OF SUGAR PLUMS

Characters: 3 male; 4 female.
Playing Time: 30 minutes.
Costumes: Modern everyday dress. Dena and Mr. Benson wear watches. Kim later puts on long old-fashioned nightdress and nightcap, and Mr. Benson puts on parts of a Santa Claus costume. Aunt Vinnie and Bruce wear coats when they first enter, and Aunt Vinnie carries a suitcase and a bag of knitting. All have coats when they leave.
Properties: Mistletoe, hammers, tacks, nails, pins, Christmas cards, pen and stamps, newspaper, small box and large carton, box containing Santa Claus suit, beard, and boots, box containing nightgown and nightcap.
Setting: The Benson living room. A lighted Christmas tree is down right. Beside it is a stepladder. At center is a sofa with

pillows, with a coffee table in front of it. On the table is a dress box containing Kim's costume. A desk and straight chair are at right. An easy chair and lamp are at left. Up left is a table which Eddie works on. The exit at left leads to rest of house, exit at right leads to hallway and outside.
Lighting: The lights on the tree are on during the play, and turned off as the family leaves.
Sound: Recording of carolers singing; doorbell.

CHRISTMAS COMES TO HAMELIN

Characters: 13 male; 13 female; male and female extras.
Playing Time: 20 minutes.
Costumes: Suggestion of medieval clothes. The men wear knickers, soft hats with plumes, and swords. The Mayor wears an elaborate cape. The Stranger is dressed simply and carries a staff. The Toyman wears a long apron. The women wear long, bright full dresses with shawls or capes. Some wear caps and aprons. The children are dressed very plainly: the boys in knickers; the girls in long dresses, or rain capes.
Properties: A large book, a ruler or pointer, oilcan.
Setting: All that is required for the first scene is a table, a sofa, a few easy chairs, and a fireplace. The scenes in the orphanage only require a few chairs or stools, perhaps some old toys, a blackboard or a globe. A large framed sampler, reading "God Bless Our Home," hangs on a wall.
Lighting: No special effects.

NO ROOM AT THE INN

Characters: 15 male; 1 female; extras.
Playing Time: 20 minutes.
Costumes: The players wear the traditional flowing garments of the Orient, not necessarily white. The Boy is dressed in a short tunic. Sandals are worn by all.

Properties: Pitchers, staffs for the shepherds, three coffers.

Setting: On two sides of the stage, rear and left, runs the wall of the courtyard. This is about six feet high and is broken by two arched gateways. One arch is at the center of the rear wall and leads to the stables. It has a wooden gate. The other arch is at the center of the left wall and is the entrance to the inn yard from the highway. It has no gate. On the right of the stage is the wall of the inn. There is a door in the center of the wall; to the right of the door, a bench; to the left, a small window. The stage is bare save for the bench and at the rear left a circular well-curb of stone wide enough to use as a seat. Above the wall sky is seen.

Lighting: Red overheads and footlights are used in Scene 1, with most of the light from the overheads concentrated at left or perhaps additional red spots shining from the left wings. For Scene 2 dark blue overheads and footlights are desirable. A white spot from offstage can be placed to shine directly over the stable to represent the star; or the desired effect can also be attained by hanging a silver star above the stable and using a white spot on it.

Note: This play can be combined effectively with a musical program by preceding and following it with the singing of carols. One verse of a carol could be sung also while the curtain is lowered to denote passage of time. Nothing longer should be introduced here as it would break the continuity of the play. Appropriate carols are "O Little Town of Bethlehem," "While Shepherds Watched Their Flocks," "Away in a Manger," "We Three Kings," "Silent Night," "All my Heart this Night Rejoices," "It Came Upon a Midnight Clear," "First Noel," "In Bethlehem 'neath Starlit Skies," "Adeste Fidelis."

Costumes: Dr. Fisher and Mr. and Mrs. Shearer wear modern, everyday dress; Nurse wears a uniform; Jessica wears a bathrobe and slippers. Father Christmas is dressed in an over-sized white laboratory coat which comes to his shoe tops, and his large pockets are filled with candy and fruit. He wears a hat covered with flowers and ribbons. The characters in the English episode wear rustic breeches, long stockings, and jackets. St. Sylvester is dressed in a robe and slippers, with a feed sack over his shoulder. Babouscka, the Wisemen, and the children of other lands wear traditional costumes.

Properties: Small table, wheelchair, boxes of Christmas tree ornaments, small Christmas tree, large Christmas tree, small box containing wooden angel, large yule log, small model of yule log, ropes, feedbag full of grain, gold ring, broom for Babouscka, jar of honey, silver lamp, two large gingerbread men, model of stable with figures of Jesus, Mary, and Joseph, birds' tree (pole with a sheaf of grain tied to it), wooden or cardboard bird, pinata (bag made of heavy paper, covered with tissue paper and tinsel), other Christmas tree ornaments.

Setting: The stage in front of the curtain represents a hospital corridor. On the center of the curtain hangs a sign reading: "Children's Ward: Quiet Please." There is a small table before curtain. For the Christmas in England episode, the stage is bare, with a large Christmas tree in the center and a yule log at stage left. For the Russian episode, the front of a hut with a door and a lighted window is added, at stage right.

Lighting: Either Christmas tree lights or a single blue spotlight on the tree can be used for the last scene.

AND CHRISTMAS IS ITS NAME

Characters: 16 male; 9 female.
Playing Time: 25 minutes.

SANTA CLAUS FOR PRESIDENT

Characters: 6 male; 1 female; 11 characters, either male or female.

Playing Time: 10 minutes.

Costumes: The Prologue and the elves should be dressed in red and green. Santa wears the traditional red and white costume. The reporters can wear suits; they should also wear hats with "Press" signs stuck in the brims. The foreign children might wear costumes suggesting the countries they represent.

Properties: Telegrams, pencil and paper, big red notebooks and large green pencils for reporters, banners with names of foreign countries, American flags.

Setting: Santa's workshop. This can be as elaborate or as simple as desired, and might contain a few tables, chairs, tools, wood, paper, toys, etc.

Lighting: No special effects.

PICCOLA

Characters: 2 male; 3 female.

Playing Time: 15 minutes.

Costumes: Snow wears a glittering white gown, and Wind wears tunic, high boots, winged helmet, and carries a whip. Others wear shabby clothes, and Piccola wears wooden shoes.

Properties: Artificial bird, fishnet, candles, kettle.

Setting: A fisherman's hut in Brittany. A fireplace is up center, and to one side of it is a window. Stools are at either side of the hearth, and a broom leans against the wall in one corner. An exit is at right. In Scene 1, there are two candles on the mantel. In Scene 2, mounds of snow (cotton batting) are piled around the room, and the stools are overturned.

Lighting: Red bulbs concealed in the fireplace may be used for the fire and turned on and off as required. In Scene 2, the sun shines in through the window.

Sound: Howling of wind, peeping and singing of bird, as indicated in text.

THE SANTA CLAUS TWINS

Characters: 9 male; 4 female; the Weigher and the Measurer may be male or female; male and female extras.

Playing Time: 10 minutes.

Costumes: Miss Jingle and some of the children wear everyday clothing. The costumes of the other characters may be as simple or as elaborate as desired (these characters might wear everyday clothing and carry props or wear hats, etc.). The Christmas Fairy should have a wand and a crown, the Toy Soldier a sword and gun. Ned and Fred wear identical Santa Claus costumes.

Properties: Scales, tape measure, telegram.

Setting: A bare stage with a decorated Christmas tree in one corner.

Lighting: No special effects.

MR. SCROOGE FINDS CHRISTMAS

Characters: 14 male; 4 female; as many male extras as desired, for carolers. (A number of parts may be doubled up.)

Playing Time: 30 minutes.

Costumes: Marley's Ghost is dressed in nineteenth-century clothes, with a long, heavy chain dragging from his waist to the floor. The Ghost of Christmas Past wears a white tunic, with a golden belt and bright crown on his head, and carries a bunch of holly. The Ghost of Christmas Present is dressed in a simple green mantle bordered with white fur, and a holly wreath on his head. The Ghost of Christmas Yet to Come is shrouded in a black garment from head to foot. Scrooge, Fred, the Cratchits, etc., wear nineteenth-century clothes. The Cratchits' clothing is meagre and threadbare; Bob wears a long white muffler.

Properties: Long, heavy chain; coal shovel; candle; ruler; books and papers; plates, cups, spoons, etc.; saucepan, lemons, two water tunblers, cup without handle; crutch; sewing basket; pieces of materials; Bible; teacup; large turkey wrapped in a bundle; coins; watch chain.

Setting: Scenes 1, 3, 5, and 7 are played before the curtain or in a spotlight on the darkened stage. Scene 2: The office of Scrooge and Marley. Near the door is a high bookkeeper's desk and stool. On the other side of the dimly lit room is Scrooge's desk. There is a grate on each side containing a small fire, and a coal-box on Scrooge's side of the room. Scene 4: The kitchen-dining room of the Cratchit house. It is simply furnished with a large table and chairs, cupboard, and grate with kettles over the fire. Scene 6: Same as Scene 4.

Lighting: A spotlight, if Scenes 1, 3, 5, 7 are played on a darkened stage.

THE BIRDS' CHRISTMAS CAROL

Characters: 8 male; 10 female; Narrator may be male or female; there can be any number of Carolers, both male and female.

Playing Time: 25 minutes.

Costumes: Everyday dress. The Carolers wear outdoor winter clothing. Carol wears a bathrobe and pajamas. The Nurse can wear a uniform. The Ruggles children are dressed as indicated in the text; the whole Ruggles family should have on rather elaborate, odd-looking clothing.

Properties: Letter; large paper bag of oranges, watch, dolls, various packages wrapped in Christmas paper for the Ruggles.

Setting: If desired, the entire play may be produced without using a curtain, or any of the scenes indicated in the text may be played before the curtain. If a curtain is used, the settings may be as simple or as elaborate as desired; however, it is suggested that a minimum of furniture be used so that the scenes may be changed quickly and easily. Scene 1: A chair for the grandmother, plus Christmas presents and perhaps a small decorated Christmas tree. Scene 2: A wheel chair, chaise-longue or bed for Carol, a chair for Uncle Jack. Carol should be covered with a blanket and propped up on pillows. (Uncle Jack might sit on the bed.) Scene 3: Seven chairs, a wood box and a coal hod (or any combination of chairs and boxes). Scene 4: A bed for Carol.

Lighting: No special effects.

CHRISTMAS EVERY DAY

Characters: 5 male; 4 female.

Playing Time: 25 minutes.

Costumes: Kindheart, Tinsel and Tassell wear appropriate fairy and elf costumes with Christmas decorations added. In Scenes 2 and 3, Abigail wears a nightgown, Robin wears pajamas, and Mr. and Mrs. Phillips wear dressing gowns. In Scenes 4 and 5, the Phillips family wears everyday clothes. Jenny and Jim wear everyday summer clothes.

Properties: Scene 1: letter in envelope. Scene 2: four stockings (one containing a jackknife; one, a fruitcake Santa; one, a wrapped potato; and one, wrapped lumps of coal). Scene 3: the same filled stockings; a blindfold for Abigail; wrapped Christmas presents for Mr. and Mrs. Phillips; letter. Scene 4: shopping list for Mrs. Phillips; bills for Mr. Phillips; newspaper pattern for Jenny; paper bag containing raisin "torpedoes" for Jim; two boxes of candy cane "fireworks" for Robin; doll and toy gun for Abigail; letter. Scene 5: Noisemaker for Robin.

Setting: The living room of Abigail's home, decorated for Christmas. There is a fireplace at center of the rear wall, with four stockings hanging from the mantelpiece. At left, French windows lead to a side porch. At right, an archway opens on the front hall. There is a divan left center, an easy chair and small table, right center. In Scene 4, the French windows are open to indicate summer.

Lighting: If possible, in Scene 1 the stage should be lit only by light coming through the French windows until the Elves turn on the lamps.

Sound: Offstage noises (bells ringing, whistles blowing, people cheering) at beginning of Scene 5.

LITTLE WOMEN

Characters: 9 female.

Playing Time: 30 minutes.

Costumes: All, except Hummels, wear the long full-skirted gowns of the period. All girls have long hair, but Jo and Meg wear theirs caught up in hair nets. Mrs. March wears a cloak and hat when she first enters, and all wear cloaks and bonnets when they exit at end. Hannah wears a plain dress and white apron, Aunt March wears fancy dress, cloak and bonnet. Hummel girls are dressed in ragged clothes.

Properties: Knitting, sewing materials, sketching materials, broom, slippers, coal scuttle, witch's hat, cloak, tablecloth, broad-brimmed hat, riding boots, salt and pepper shakers, poker, umbrella, three cups, tray, toasting forks, shopping bag, muffins, butter, bread, milk, dishes, wood, letter, teapot, cane, glasses for Aunt March.

Setting: The living room of the March home. There is a door left, leading to hall, and one right, leading to kitchen. There is a large window up center in front of which stands a sofa. A large fireplace is at right and a comfortable chair and stool in front of this, upstage right. There is a large table at center. Chintz-covered chairs at various positions complete the furnishings.

Lighting: No special effects.